# VOLUNTEER VACATIONS

## SIXTH EDITION

## Other Books by Bill McMillon

*The Archaeology Handbook*
*Best Hikes with Children: Around Sacramento*
*Best Hikes with Children: San Francisco's North Bay*
*Best Hikes with Children: San Francisco's South Bay*
*Birding Arizona*
*California's Underwater State Parks: A Divers' Guide*
*Camping with Kids in California*
*Country Roads of Florida*
*Fairs and Festivals of California, Hawaii, and Nevada*
*Great Outdoor Getaways to the Southwest*
*Nature Nearby*
*The Old Lodges and Hotels of Our National Parks*
*Paradise Family Guide to Florida*
*Seasonal Guide to Natural Year: Northern California*
*Wilderness U* (also from Chicago Review Press)

# VOLUNTEER VACATIONS

## SIXTH EDITION

*Short-Term Adventures
That Will Benefit
You and Others*

Bill McMillon

CHICAGO
REVIEW
PRESS

Library of Congress Cataloging-in-Publication Data

McMillon, Bill, 1942–
    Volunteer vacations : short-term adventures that will benefit you and others /
Bill McMillon. – 6th ed., rev.
        p.   cm.
    Includes bibliographical references and indexes.
    ISBN 1-55652-314-9 : $16.95
    1. Voluntarism—Directories.   2. Associations, institutions, etc.—Directories.
3. Vacations—Directories.   I. Title.
HN49.V64M35     1997
302'.14—dc20                                                          94-48174
                                                                        CIP

Sixth edition
Published by Chicago Review Press, Incorporated
814 N. Franklin Street
Chicago, Illinois 60610
ISBN 1-55652-314-9
Printed in the United States of America

5  4  3  2  1

*To volunteers everywhere—God bless you all,
and may you always have fun
while doing good work.*

# Contents

## Additional Resources  357

## Cross-Referenced Indexes  367

# Acknowledgments

Obviously, a guide such as this could never have been compiled without the cooperation and assistance of hundreds of organizations that accept short-term volunteers, and I deeply appreciate their willingness to share their needs with me. I would especially like to thank all the people behind the scenes at these organizations who took the time out from their heavy schedules to answer my questions and supply me with vignettes and photos. I would also like to thank all of the people at Chicago Review Press who have done an excellent job of designing, editing, and selling the previous editions of *Volunteer Vacations.*

In addition, I would like to thank the thousands of readers who have purchased the previous editions of the guide, and who have helped make it the premier guide for volunteers.

# Foreword

*Ed Asner*

It's been said that "man would rather spend himself for a cause than live idly in prosperity." I'm sure upon uttering that axiom in a group, you'd see everyone nodding wisely—agreeing that hard work for a cause is preferable to the good life unfulfilled. It's a noble thought during a philosophical discussion. When everyone's in accord on that point, pull out some airline tickets to Perryville, Arkansas, and ask who's willing to give up their Bermuda vacation in order to work with livestock. Any takers?

It's a hard sell. Public service is an antiquity in today's society. In the thirties the Civilian Conservation Corps instilled in the minds of young men and women the notion that national service is an obligation, indeed, a privilege: putting something back into the country in exchange for all the benefits derived from living in a free and democratic society. It was a wonderful setup and one that should have been perpetuated.

Since that time, however, our country's military bent has made national service an anathema—national service has come to mean the draft, the military, risk of life and limb on some foreign shore. Some states, to supplement low budget allocations, use public service as punishment for misdemeanors. In Oregon, for instance, DWI offenders can be seen picking up highway litter.

In short, the notion of a "volunteer vacation" sounds like a disciplinary measure akin to assigning extra household chores to a balky teenager.

A Mar de Jade volunteer constructs a wall for a home in Mexico. Photo courtesy of Mar de Jade.

Happily, there are people like Bill McMillon (along with the hundreds of people who have taken volunteer vacations) to set us straight; volunteering for a worthy cause can be fun, fulfilling, and an adventure you'll anticipate year after year. Maybe working with livestock isn't your thing, but there's plenty of variety: go on archaeological expeditions, assist with health care in remote villages, maintain trails in beautiful mountain climes, or build homes for the homeless. Some programs encourage you to bring the kids; some pay part of your expenses.

Best of all, you'll be helping people who need you. These days our local, state, and federal government budgets (and many government budgets around the world) have cut "people programs" in favor of big business and the military. More and more, our nation and our world must look to volunteers to fill the gaps that governments are unwilling or unable to fill—in health care, education, and programs for the disabled and underprivileged.

Read this book . . . try a volunteer vacation. The world will be a better place and so will you.

# Preface

It seems an age since I first began research on a book that became known as *Volunteer Vacations*. And it has been one full decade—a decade that has seen interest in volunteering reach epidemic proportions. Fortunately, organizations have gladly accepted the rush of people interested in short-term volunteering.

While there have been many articles written about why volunteering has caught on with the public, none has given as good a reason as famous psychiatrist Dr. Karl Menninger did in a speech a number of years ago.

When asked "What would you advise a person to do if that person felt a nervous breakdown coming on?" Dr. Menninger gave a unique response, one far from the expected "Consult a psychiatrist."

He replied, "Lock up your house, go across the railway tracks, find someone in need, and do something to help that person." His response hit a chord with me. It didn't matter what side of the track you lived on, you could help yourself by helping others.

What Dr. Menninger recommended for individuals could also apply to society at large, and I think that is why there has been a surge in volunteering. People have felt a societal breakdown approaching, and they have decided to help society by helping others.

This could mean traveling to far corners of the world to help in undeveloped nations or across town to help a particularly needy and deserving organization, but it seems without question to have helped those who have made the commitment required of volunteers.

From Chelsea Clinton, who volunteered with over seventy other young people for the Appalachian Service Project through their church, to the over eight hundred employees of Chevron who helped with an oak-restoration project in Yosemite National Park four weekends a year for three years, volunteers from all walks of life are helping themselves by helping others.

Each of the previous editions of *Volunteer Vacation* has been larger than the one before, and that is because the book has reflected the increasing interest in social service, with a general increase of both volunteers and the agencies that use them. This edition is only the second to hold fairly steady in the number of organizations listed, but that is not because there has been a decrease in volunteers. It is more because over the years there has been a fallout of some agencies that didn't have a good focus on how to utilize the vast pool of potential volunteers, and because many denominational religious organizations have begun restricting their recruiting efforts to their own members. The number of new environmentally oriented organizations is also much smaller than it has been in previous editions. New organizations continue to spring up around the world, however, and this is reflected in this edition as new organizations from such disparate locations as India and South America have been included to replace those that have ceased operation.

On another note, I constantly hear from both volunteers and organizations thanking me for the work I have put into this guide, but recently I have heard a complaint that actually indicates how successful the book has become. Many inquiries to the organizations appear to be more fanciful or exploratory than real. This may be because a student is writing a paper on volunteering or just wishes to take a trip to a specific spot. Whatever the reason for them, these casual inquiries cost the organizations time and money.

A volunteer liaison person for a British organization best expressed the complaint when he said, "I would think that most organizations appealing for volunteers have limited resources, limited funds, and many are charities, or similar nonprofit bodies. The cost, for example, of replying to an inquiry from the U.S.A. on behalf of our organization is in the region of £2.50 (postage and cost of brochure, etc.), and in addition the time taken by a volunteer to do the work, time which could be spent doing other work. I wonder if you could stress in your publication that non-genuine inquiries are costly, and can have a direct effect on what the organization is trying to achieve."

Other organizations have written to ask that all queries be accompanied by a self-addressed stamped envelope. For overseas organizations, enclose postal reply coupons.

Other than that I have had no complaints about the use of this book or the quality of volunteers who have participated in various volunteer efforts. A huge number of you do seem to be letting the organizations know where you heard about them. Thank you—for keeping *Volunteer Vacations* alive and well. May your volunteering be all and more than you expect.

A World Horizons International volunteer enjoys a card game with a local youth. Photo courtesy of World Horizons International.

We live in a society that has always depended on volunteers of different kinds—some who can give money, others who give time and a great many who will freely give their special skills, full-time or part-time. If you look closely you will see that almost anything that really matters to us, anything that embodies our deepest commitment to the way human life should be lived and cared for, depends on some form—more often many forms—of volunteerism.

Margaret Mead and Rhoda Metraux
*Aspects of the Present*

# Introduction

"What's a volunteer vacation?"

"One where you work for some organization on a special project."

"You mean really work? On your vacation?"

"Right."

"Who would want to do that?"

This conversation is often quoted as I promote this guide on radio and TV programs. Many interviewers really can't grasp the idea that tens of thousands of people take volunteer vacations each year.

Obviously, some people can't envision working on a vacation. Others, however, find doing so a refreshing change of pace.

If you are one of the latter or think you might be, and want to work on something other than projects around the house during your next vacation, this book can be your passport to vacation happiness. Nineteen-year-old Rory Camp used this passport when he volunteered for a summer at the Theodore Roosevelt National Park in North Dakota with the Student Conservation Association. Retired city manager Mel Davis used it to head from his home in northern California to a small, struggling village in Nicaragua, where he helped build a school and community center.

More and more people are volunteering to work for organizations that need help completing scientific, ecological, social service, and other types of projects that can't be handled by regular staff because of personnel or financial problems. These projects can be near home or in a foreign land. Distance matters less than the deep satisfaction that can be gained from doing worthwhile work.

# How to Select a Volunteer Project

There is no shortage of volunteer projects. Some are near home; others are across oceans. Some are helping to complete scientific investigations; others lead to social change. Some cost nothing but your travel expenses to the project site; others are more expensive than traditional guided tours. The one you select will depend upon your needs and abilities—physical, emotional, intellectual, and financial.

# What This Guide Tells You

This guide is divided into three sections. The first, Sponsoring Organizations, is an alphabetical listing of organizations that offer opportunities for volunteers. This directory includes the name, address, and phone number of each project; the project location, type, costs, and dates; how to apply; what work is done by volunteers; and what special skills may be required. In the case of telephone numbers for overseas organizations, the country codes have been omitted and what appears in the listing is the city code and phone number only. Consult your long-distance carrier for country codes and dialing instructions. Similarly, due to fluctuating currencies, foreign currencies in the Project Costs sections have not been converted to U.S. dollars. Check with your local bank or financial newspaper for current exchange rates.

When requesting information from the organizations listed, it is best to include a self-addressed, stamped envelope or international postal reply coupons. Many of the organizations in this book are nonprofit and run on tight budgets, and the cost of mailing information to prospective volunteers can add up. For this reason, also, it is often best to correspond with an organization only once you have really made a decision to volunteer, as it also costs the organizations time and money to respond to people who are merely curious. Your consideration will undoubtedly be greatly appreciated.

The second section is Volunteer Vignettes, containing personal stories from and about travelers who have taken a wide variety of volunteer vacations in the United States and abroad. Please note that the entries that appear in vignettes are marked with the symbol # in the Sponsoring Organizations section.

The third section provides cross-referenced indexes. Their purpose is to help you define the types of projects you are interested in and to help you locate the organizations that offer such projects. The indexes include project cost, length, location, season (spring, summer, fall, winter, or year-round), and project type (scientific, ecological, social action, and other special interests). To use the indexes, begin by defining your criteria for a volunteer vacation. The first step will probably be deciding what subject area interests you. You can then decide where you would like to pursue this subject, how much you want to spend on your trip, what time of year you want to go, and how long you want to be gone. Let's say you want to work on an archaeological dig in the United States for two weeks during the summer and keep costs other than travel to the project site to less than $500. You would first look in the project type index to find a list of organizations that have archaeological projects. You can then compare this list with the project location index to come up with a shorter list of organizations that offer digs in the United States.

Then compare this list against the project season, cost, and length indexes in turn to come up with your final list, which will give you a list of organizations that offer two-week archaeological dig projects during the summer in the United States for under $500.

You can now return to the first section of the book and read about the organizations on your list. Then you can contact the organizations that fit your needs and find out if they have vacancies on the projects that interest you.

## General Information

Although each project differs, the following are some general characteristics that you can expect most of them to have.

### Transportation

Almost all projects require volunteers to arrange and pay for their own transportation to the project site. The exception is the final leg to isolated sites; the sponsoring organization generally arranges this portion of the trip.

## Special requirements and skills

Although some projects have no requirements for volunteers other than an interest and a willingness to work, others have very specific requirements. Many of the Sierra Club and American Hiking Society projects, for example, require superb physical conditioning. Other expeditions may require special skills, such as scuba certification. No project allows unqualified volunteers to register, however, so there should be no on-site surprises for volunteers or project leaders.

## Food and housing

Many of the projects arrange for housing for all volunteers, along with some provision for meals. Both food and housing range from the bare minimum to semi-luxurious, and this is generally stated in the project brochure. On other projects volunteers are responsible for their own food and housing.

## What to bring

Again, each project is different, and each requires different types of clothing, equipment, and housekeeping gear. After you have been accepted for a project, you will receive a list of recommended articles. Follow this list closely, and contact your project leader if you have any questions. Not only your comfort but the comfort of the other volunteers may be involved.

Most volunteers like to bring a camera to record their trip, but the project leader should be contacted to see what special precautions should be taken with photographic equipment. Many of the projects are in isolated locations where climatic conditions can cause serious problems for cameras and lenses.

## Group interaction

These projects are carried out in groups, and while some groups are larger than others, volunteers on any project must be prepared to spend extended time in close contact with a group of strangers. This means dealing with unpleasant situations as well as enjoyable ones. While the project leaders interviewed for this guide emphasized that most projects have few problems within the groups, they said there were occasional conflicts that had to be worked out on the site.

La Sabranenque volunteers restore a medieval house in southern France. Photo courtesy of La Sabranenque.

## Tax Information

The media have emphasized the tax advantages of volunteer vacations, but not everyone qualifies for them. To deduct your expenses for a volunteer vacation, there are several conditions that must be met. The most important one is that the organization must be registered with the Internal Revenue Service as a tax-exempt, nonprofit corporation; and many of the organizations in this guide are. But there are exceptions, such as the Sierra Club and foreign organizations. The only way to ensure a tax write-off is to contact a knowledgeable tax accountant before registering for a trip.

## What This Guide Doesn't Tell You

It is difficult, if not impossible, for any guide that covers as broad a range of activities as this one does to comprehensively evaluate the organizations and how they run their projects. All of the organizations included here are reputable, and they have served thousands of volunteers over the years, but it would be impossible for all of those volunteers to have had only positive experiences. There are just too many variables.

The only way you can find out if a particular organization is one that you will feel comfortable with is to contact them directly, ask specific and pointed questions of the staff, and interview previous volunteers.

Even with these precautions there are no guarantees that your experience will be 100 percent trouble free, but the lack of guarantees is one of the positive aspects of volunteer vacations. People who want guarantees go on guided tours. Those who want adventure and a change of pace go on volunteer vacations.

## Other Sources of Information

Opportunities for volunteers are so numerous that it would be impossible to mention them all. The Additional Resources section at the end of the book can help those who want to take longer volunteer vacations or who prefer to go on adventure or learning vacations without work commitments. Also included are several periodicals that include information about volunteer, learning, and adventure vacations.

If you are interested in finding out more about volunteering, look around your hometown. Ask about subjects you are interested in, and see if any of your acquaintances have ever volunteered for some related project. Contact state or national organizations that are concerned and involved with your area of interest to see if they know of any local volunteer possibilities. More and more large companies are helping employees find volunteer positions in their communities. For instance, Wells Fargo, one of the largest banks in California, has an extensive program that encourages employees to volunteer in their hometowns and even offers sabbaticals so volunteers can spend extended periods of time on projects. These companies also regularly publish volunteer bulletins for employees listing volunteer opportunities. Universities are other possible sources for information on volunteering. For example, in 1988 the state of California passed AB 1820, the "Human Corps" bill, which requires all students enrolled at the twenty-nine campuses of the California State University system and the nine campuses of the University of California to provide at least thirty hours of community service each year. In response, each campus has developed a list of volunteer opportunities for its students.

Also, the federal government is encouraging volunteerism through the new national service program that President Clinton initiated, which targets college-aged youth. This program enrolled more volunteers within the first six months of its operation than the Peace Corps has enrolled in its existence. Lastly, hundreds of volunteer centers around the country often publish lists of current needs in the Help Wanted sections of their local papers.

Several of the organizations listed in this guide work extensively with state and national parks and with the U.S. Forest Service, and although some of their offices are also listed in the guide, there are always new projects that need volunteers but aren't listed anywhere. Many campgrounds offer free camping to their volunteer hosts, who assist other campers in return. Ministers often are given free camping privileges in exchange for performing services on Sunday. And some national forests offer free housing to people who are willing to be volunteer naturalists at isolated sites. Contact either the regional offices or national headquarters of these agencies to find out about unlisted volunteer opportunities.

Religious groups also offer many volunteer opportunities for social activists, and colleges and universities often offer summer courses that serve as vehicles for gaining research assistants. Colleges and universities also offer many travel courses through their extension programs. Service organizations are another possible source of information.

For those over fifty-five, an interesting program is Elderhostel, which is held on college and university campuses, using regular faculty, throughout the year. To find out more about this program, contact Elderhostel, listed in the resources section.

Remember, volunteer opportunities are unlimited. It is just a matter of finding a project that suits you. After all, it is your vacation.

# Sponsoring Organizations

🌍 = Organization that appears in the "Vignettes" section.

# Alaska State Parks

3601 C Street, Suite 1200
Anchorage, AK 99503-5921
(907) 269-8708; Fax (907) 269-8907

*Project location*: Parks throughout the state.

*Project type*: Park management and maintenance.

*Project costs*: Volunteers are responsible for transportation to and from Alaska. There is a small expense allowance for volunteers, but volunteers should have their own funds. Campground hosts provide their own trailer or RV to live in.

*Project dates*: Most positions are from May to September for varying periods of time. There are a few winter positions.

*How to apply*: Write to the Volunteer Coordinator at the above address for a catalog, which contains general information, specific positions, and an application.

*Work done by volunteers*: Campground hosts, natural history interpreters, ranger assistants, park caretakers, park researchers, trail crews, and archaeological assistants.

*Special skills or requirements*: Varies with position. Some require excellent physical health; others require some college education in natural resource management. All require knowledge, skill, and experience in the outdoors. Good communication skills are preferred.

*Commentary*: Alaska State Parks began its volunteer program in 1983, when severe budget cuts forced the division to seek creative economic strategies. Since then hundreds of people have generously donated their time and energies to the continued preservation and management of Alaska's State Parks. Park volunteers do not replace paid staff; they supplement existing staff and provide programs to the public that would not otherwise be available.

# American Friends Service Committee
1501 Cherry Street
Philadelphia, PA 19102-1479
(215) 241-7295

*Project location*: Primarily Mexico and Cuba, but occasionally other Latin American countries.

*Project type*: There is no set pattern to these projects. Past projects have included construction of schools, clinics, roads, and houses, as well as reforestation, gardening, and health programs.

*Project costs*: Participants pay $900 for orientation, insurance, food, and lodging at the project site. Volunteers are responsible for transportation to the project site.

*Project dates*: Most projects run for six weeks from the end of June to mid-August.

*How to apply*: Send a letter of interest to American Friends Service Committee, Summer Community Service in Latin America, at the above address.

*Work done by volunteers*: All volunteers share both the labor on the project itself and in the normal living activities, such as cooking, cleaning, and weekly shopping. All actively participate in the normal life of the village where they are living.

*Special skills or requirements*: Applicants should be between 18 and 26 years old and speak good Spanish, since it is the project language at all times. Familiarity with construction, gardening, and arts and crafts are all useful, as is previous group experience.

*Commentary*: AFSC is a Quaker organization. This service project is done in conjunction with a Mexican service organization. Each summer fifty volunteers are chosen to work in different villages in Mexico and are divided into teams of two leaders and fifteen volunteers. Half of the volunteers are from Latin America; the other half are from the U.S.

# American Hiking Society

PO Box 20160
Washington, DC 20041-2160
(301) 565-6704

*Project location*: AHS has projects throughout the continental U.S., primarily in remote locations.

*Project type*: Trail building, trail maintenance, and similar work for the National Park Service, National Forest Service, or state park systems.

*Project costs*: Volunteers pay a $40 registration fee upon acceptance and must furnish their own camping gear, equipment, and transportation to the project site. AHS arranges for the final leg of trip to remote sites. Insurance is provided while participants are working. Cooperating agencies supply hard hats, tools, and food. AHS sometimes finds donors for food.

*Project dates*: Projects usually last two weeks in June, July, and August with occasional projects in May and September. Previous projects in Florida were held in January.

*How to apply*: Send a self-addressed, stamped, letter-sized envelope and a request for an application and a list of projects to AHS at the above address. Many of these projects fill quickly, so send your request as early as possible.

*Work done by volunteers*: Hard manual labor in rugged, remote locations, many at high altitudes.

*Special skills or requirements*: Applicants must be experienced backpackers who can easily hike five to ten miles a day and live for a two-week stretch in the outdoors. Applicants under 18 must have permission of their parents; those under 16 must be accompanied by an adult.

*Commentary*: The AHS Volunteer Vacation program began in 1979 with thirty volunteers working at two Forest Service sites. It now has over three hundred volunteers each year; about one-third are returnees from previous years. Since many sites are in remote and rugged areas, volunteers can expect to explore some of the most outstanding wilderness in the U.S., sharing this experience with ten to twelve other volunteers. National Park or Forest Service personnel supervise most of the sites.

*Sample projects*: In the past volunteers have helped maintain three cabins on Hassleborg Lake in Admiralty Island National Monument, Alaska, which included general maintenance and cutting firewood for each cabin. Other volunteers have worked on a new section of the Ozark Trail in the Buffalo National River park, Arkansas. Still others have helped with exotic plant control in Haleakala National Park, Hawaii, which included hiking ten miles to the base camp.

# American Mexican Medical Foundation (AMMEX)

2305 El Indio Highway, Suite 463
Eagle Pass, TX 78852
(210) 773-2568

*Project location*: Remote villages in the state of Durango, Mexico.

*Project type*: Health and community development.

*Project costs*: $275 for a two-week project covers on-site lodging, groceries, laundry, and transportation between Eagle Pass, Texas, and the project site. Occasionally volunteers can stay on beyond the two-week project for $130 per week.

*Project dates*: Usually in February, May, August, and December.

*How to apply*: Send a self-addressed, stamped, letter-sized envelope to the Project Director at the above address for more information and application forms.

*Work done by volunteers*: According to their qualifications and desires, volunteers assist in a variety of tasks on a one-to-one basis or in a community setting. Each volunteer is asked to have "one special goal" that they will carry out on their own. All volunteers are responsible for their share of regular housekeeping chores at the site or with their host family.

*Special skills or requirements*: Volunteers must have basic conversational Spanish, and AMMEX always welcomes volunteers with special medical or construction skills. The minimum age is 18, and a birth certificate or passport is needed with application.

*Commentary*: AMMEX began in 1969 as Roger and Eva Belisle started making mercy trips into remote and isolated areas of Mexico. After a time they began taking friends with them as volunteers. From this, AMMEX was formed as a nonprofit organization devoted to helping the residents of the state of Durango. While interest in the project has grown over the years, the bulk of the work and funding that keeps AMMEX going comes from the Belisles, and this specialized organization is very much in need of continued and expanded support.

# American Rivers

801 Pennsylvania Avenue SE, Suite 400
Washington, DC 20003
(202) 547-6900

*Project location*: Phoenix, Arizona; Seattle, Washington; and Washington, D.C.

*Project type*: Research, clerical, legal work, correspondence with members, database maintenance, and word processing.

*Project costs*: Participants are responsible for all their living costs.

*Project dates*: Year-round, although summer positions are the most popular.

*How to apply*: Send a résumé, cover letter, writing sample, and two letters of reference to Kirsten Artman at the above address.

*Work done by volunteers*: Depends on assignment. Interns focus on a single project during their time in Washington, and every effort is made to match their interests with the needs of the organization.

*Special skills or requirements*: An intense interest in saving America's rivers and the environment in general, plus basic office skills. Knowledge of legal, political, and environmental issues is helpful.

*Commentary*: American Rivers is the nation's principal river-saving organization. It is the only nonprofit charitable group devoted exclusively to preserving the nation's outstanding rivers and their landscapes. Highlights of its five-year plan include an expanded mission to protect and restore America's river systems, a commitment to a long-term watershed protection and restoration strategy, an expanded set of program areas, a continued focus on the protection of outstanding river segments, a greater commitment to research and public education, a commitment to grassroots assistance, and a plan to build a more secure membership base.

# Amigos de las Americas

5618 Star Lane
Houston, TX 77057
(800) 231-7796 or (713) 782-5290

*Project location*: Throughout Latin America.

*Project type*: Wide variety of public health projects.

*Project costs*: $2,600 to $3,080 covers training materials, transportation from Houston to the host country, and field supplies. Volunteers are responsible for transportation to and from Houston. The host country provides food and housing.

*Project dates*: Projects run for four, six, or eight weeks during mid-June to mid-August.

*How to apply*: Contact Amigos de las Americas at the above address for local chapter locations or information about their correspondent training program for volunteers. There is a March 1 application deadline.

*Work done by volunteers*: Wide variety of public health projects, from helping plan and dig public latrines, to canoeing through tropical rain forests to inoculate people against yellow fever, to distributing medical supplies in local settlements. All projects are done under the supervision of a route leader who lives in the host country and is experienced with volunteers.

*Special skills or requirements*: Volunteers must speak at least minimal Spanish, be at least 16 years old, and have completed the Amigos training program. Although the majority of volunteers are high school and college students, there is no upper age limit.

*Commentary*: Amigos began in 1965 as a religious organization but has since dropped all association with any church or religion. It has maintained its benevolent spirit, however, and has placed over ten thousand volunteers in thirteen Latin American countries in the past twenty years. Most of these have been youths who have been given responsibilities far beyond those normally accorded them in the U.S. Consequently, volunteers return home with an appreciation of and a sensitivity to others that far surpasses their peers'.

*Sample projects*: Amigos has conducted projects in Costa Rica, the Dominican Republic, Ecuador, Mexico, and Paraguay that have taught dental hygiene, developed community sanitation, and provided immunizations, vision screening, and animal health services.

# Amizade, Limited

1334 Dartmouth Lane
Deerfield, IL 60015
(847) 945-9402; Fax (847) 945-5676

*Project location*: Santarem, Brazil.

*Project types*: Community service projects.

*Project costs*: $2,600 includes round-trip fare from Miami and room and board while in Brazil.

*Project dates*: Two-week trips in June, July, and August.

*How to apply*: Send to above for current application and brochure.

*Work done by volunteers*: Participants work side by side with Brazilian volunteers building public facilities, restoring forests, tutoring health care workers, and working with at-risk youth.

*Special skills or requirements*: No special skills except a desire to help others.

*Commentary*: This program was started by Donald Weiss, who became aware of the abject poverty of Santarem during a visit. Dr. Weiss, when discussing the purpose of Amizade, quotes Ghandi, "Consciously or unconsciously, every one of us does render some service or other. If we cultivate the habit of doing this service deliberately, our desire for service will steadily grow stronger, and it will make not only for our own happiness, but that of the world at large."

# Andover Foundation for Archaeological Research

PO Box 83
Andover, MA 01810
(508) 470-0840

*Project location*: Cochabamba, Bolivia; Kichpanha and Street George Key, Belize; Nuku Hiva Island, Marquesas Islands, Polynesia; Nanchang, China; and the southwestern U.S.

*Project type*: Cave excavations, early Mayan village specialization, underwater archaeology of Little Spanish Armada, and early pottery surveys.

*Project costs*: Between $1,200 and $2,540 for two weeks. Underwater and projects in China are more expensive.

*Project dates*: Throughout the year.

*How to apply*: Write or call the office listed above.

*Work done by volunteers*: Regular field and lab work at an archaeological excavation. Most volunteers work as partners with a field school student.

*Special skills or requirements*: No special skills are required, but an interest in archaeology is expected.

*Commentary*: The Andover Foundation for Archaeological Research was founded in 1984 by Dr. Richard (Scotty) MacNeish to provide opportunities for both students and interested amateurs to become involved in archaeological expeditions.

*Sample projects*: Previous volunteers have excavated unlooted rock shelters of the Archaic period (up to 6000 B.C.) in Fort Bliss, New Mexico. Volunteers have also served on the site of a Mayan village that was occupied between 250 B.C. and A.D. 250 in Kichpanha, Belize.

## APARE (Association pour la Participation et l'Action Regionale)
41, cours Jean Jaures
84000 Avignon, France
(90) 85-51-15

*Project location*: Throughout Europe.

*Project type*: Work camps that are part of European Heritage Campuses.

*Project costs*: $100 plus travel expenses.

*Project dates*: July and August.

*How to apply*: Write to the above address for the seasonal program and application.

*Work done by volunteers*: Restoration and conservation of buildings, excavation work, and writing and editing booklets.

*Special skills or requirements*: Strong interest in or study of cultural history.

*Commentary*: The European Heritage Campuses allow volunteers to contribute to restoring and reinstating elements of the urban or rural heritage as part of a European cultural policy.

# Appalachian Mountain Club
Volunteer Trail Opportunities
PO Box 298
Gorham, NH 03581
(603) 466-2721; Fax (603) 466-2822

*Project location*: National parks and forests in Idaho, Montana, the Northeast, and Wyoming.

*Project type*: Trail building and maintenance, many in remote locations.

*Project costs*: Projects range from $35 to $230. Volunteers are responsible for travel to project sites and all personal gear and camping equipment. Food, cooking and eating equipment, and first aid supplies are furnished by AMC.

*Project dates*: From June through September volunteers can participate in weekend, weeklong, and ten- to twelve-day service projects. Five weeklong volunteer projects are sponsored in Maine, Massachusetts, New Hampshire, and Pennsylvania.

*How to apply*: Write to the AMC Trails Program at the above address for an application and a program booklet.

*Work done by volunteers*: Strenuous, physical manual labor building trails.

*Special skills or requirements*: Volunteers should be in good physical condition and have an enthusiastic willingness to work. Some backpacking experience is helpful, as is previous experience in trail building. Training in the use of tools and maintenance techniques is given at each project site. Minimum age is 16; 18 for service trips. Most volunteers are between 20 and 40, but the range is from 16 to over 65.

*Commentary*: AMC is the nation's oldest (founded in 1876) and largest (more than sixty thousand members) nonprofit conservation and recreation organization. It has eleven chapters in the Northeast and maintains more than twelve hundred miles of trail, including 350 miles of the Appalachian Trail. The Trails Program is an extension of their regular activities, and anyone may apply for participation.

*Sample projects*: Past projects include work in Chugach National Forest, Alaska, and the Selway-Bitterroot Wilderness Area in Idaho. Previous volunteers have worked on new trails in Acadia National Park and Baxter State Park, Maine; Wyoming; England; and Iceland; as well as weekly base camps with day and overnight projects in the Berkshires and White Mountains in New England.

# Appalachian Trail Conference

PO Box 807
Harpers Ferry, WV 25425
(304) 535-6331

*Project location*: Volunteer trail crews operate along the length of the Appalachian National Scenic Trail from North Carolina to Maine.

*Project type*: Land management projects and the design, construction, and rehabilitation of trails.

*Project costs*: Volunteers are responsible for transportation to base camps. Once there, ATC and agency partners provide lodging, food, transportation, tools, and safety equipment.

*Project dates*: The Virginia-based Konnarock crew, the Maine-based FORCE crew, and the Wermont-based Long Trail Patrol operate during the summer; the mid-Atlantic crew works during the cooler fall months. Crew members may volunteer for a week to a full season, but the Maine crew requires a two-week commitment.

*How to apply*: Send for an application from the ATC Volunteer Crew at the above address.

*Work done by volunteers*: Work includes new trail construction, rock work, log work, shelter construction, and other physically demanding tasks. Trail crews of six to eight volunteers work under the supervision of a skilled leader. Most of the crews work Thursday to Monday, with a Tuesday and Wednesday weekend in base camp.

*Special skills or requirements*: Volunteers must be 18 years old; retirees are welcome. Good health, cooperation, and enthusiasm are more important than previous experience. Base camps provide rustic accommodations; volunteers also camp in tents in the field.

*Commentary*: The Appalachian Trail is the longest continuously marked footpath in the world and America's first national scenic trail. It follows the crest of the Appalachian Mountains for more than 2,100 miles along mountain crests, and through farm valleys and rugged high country. The ATC is a private, nonprofit, educational organization that coordinates public and private efforts to maintain and protect the Appalachian Trail. ATC crews are cosponsored by the U.S. Forest Service and the National Park Services. ATC member clubs are assigned a section of the Appalachian Trail to maintain, and clubs are helped by the volunteer crews.

# Arizona State Parks

800 W. Washington Street, Suite 415
Phoenix, AZ 85007
(602) 255-4174

*Project location*: Throughout Arizona.

*Project type*: Campground, interpretive, and visitor services hosts.

*Project costs*: Volunteers are responsible for travel and living costs.

*Project dates*: Year-round for varying lengths of stay. Campground hosts usually stay at least four weeks.

*How to apply*: Write to the Volunteer Coordinator at the above address for a list of parks and an application.

*Work done by volunteers*: Campground hosts greet campers, assist with registration, give information about the park, and perform light park cleanup. Interpretive hosts conduct research and give visitors special information about natural or historical aspects of the park. Visitor services hosts provide park managers with assistance as needed.

*Special skills or requirements*: Most positions require only a desire to volunteer.

*Commentary*: Most state and national parks depend upon volunteers to keep their parks presentable and interesting to visitors.

# Artimas Cloud Forest Preserve

PO Box 937
San Pedro de Montes de Dea 2050 Costa Rica
Tel/Fax 253-72-43

*Project location*: Talamanca Mountains of Costa Rica.

*Project types*: Maintain the forest preserve.

*Project costs*: $150 per week for room and board.

*Project dates*: Projects are four to eight weeks long, beginning the first of each month.

*How to apply*: Send for an application and information.

*Work done by volunteers*: Volunteers maintain the existing trails in the preserve and construct new trails. They also plant trees, work in the preserve garden, and some teach English to the locals.

*Special skills or requirements*: A willingness to work hard within a group of strangers.

# Ashram Community Service Project

23/25 Grantham Road
Sparkbrook, Birmingham B11 1LU United Kingdom
(0121) 773-7061

*Project location*: Sparkbrook in inner-city Birmingham, one of the poorest areas in the United Kingdom with a large Pakistani and Muslim population and very high unemployment.

*Project type*: The project runs two work camps a year, but welcomes volunteers year-round to help in the range of social action and community development projects that are run here.

*Project costs*: $110 per week.

*Project dates*: Year-round.

*How to apply*: Write for an application at the above address.

*Work done by volunteers*: Mostly practical, such as organic gardening, maintenance, driving, cooking, organizing social events, supervising children, and animal husbandry.

*Special skills or requirements*: Must speak English reasonably well, have a commitment to social justice and antiracism, and be more than 20 years old and adaptable.

*Commentary*: Accommodations are with members of the residential community who have adapted their lifestyles to fit in with local culture. Volunteers share in the daily chores and social activities of the community. Ashram Community Service Project is a multipurpose social action center, with a range of different projects, including bilingual training for the unemployed, legal advice, land reclamation, animal keeping, a credit union, and a home security project.

# Association for All Speech Impaired Children
347 Central Markets
London EC1A 9NH United Kingdom
(0171) 236-3632 or (0171) 236-6487

*Project location*: Various, including Holland, Ilkley (Yorkshire, England), and Northamptonshire (England).

*Project type*: Social service and youth work.

*Project costs*: Travel cost to the project site.

*Project dates*: One week in July or August.

*How to apply*: Contact the office listed above in January or February for a summer schedule.

*Work done by volunteers*: During "Activity Weeks" volunteers befriend and care for children with communication disorders.

*Special skills or requirements*: An interest in helping the disabled and some experience in a camp or outdoor setting.

*Commentary*: AFASIC represents children and young people with difficulties using speech or language. The disabilities range in severity from an inability to articulate speech to a failure to understand the basic elements of language. In many cases these disabilities are not associated with physical or intellectual impairments.

*Sample projects*: Volunteers and disabled campers go canoeing, climbing, pony trekking, swimming, sailing, walking, cave exploring, or they work with music or arts and crafts.

# Association pour la Défense et l'Étude Canton de Levroux

Sophie Krausz
CNRS/ADEL
2, rue Traversière
36 110 Levroux, France

*Project location*: Chantier de Levroux.

*Project type*: Archaeological excavation and restoration.

*Project costs*: Fr 100 covers registration and insurance. Participants are responsible for transportation to the site and room and board.

*Project dates*: One-, two-, and four-week sessions from early June to late August.

*How to apply*: Write to Sophie Krausz at the above address for information and an application. Don't expect English translations of brochures and applications; they will send their regular French forms.

*Work done by volunteers*: Manual labor on excavations and restorations.

*Special skills or requirements*: Must be 18 years old and speak some French.

*Commentary*: This is one of several French projects that uses volunteers to restore medieval sites.

# Australian Trust for Conservation Volunteers

PO Box 423
Ballarat, Victoria 3353 Australia
(053) 331-483; Fax (053) 332-290
E-mail: atcv@peg.apc.org
Web site: http://www.peg.apc.org/~atcv/atcv.html

*Project location*: Throughout Australia.

*Project type*: Conservation projects.

*Project costs*: Projects and costs vary, so send for current information.

*Project dates*: Weekend and weeklong projects are year-round.

*How to apply*: Write to the above address for information and an application.

*Work done by volunteers*: Intensive conservation work that generally involves heavy physical labor.

*Special skills or requirements*: Strong interest in conservation work and a desire to meet new people.

*Commentary*: The ATCV is a nonprofit, nonpolitical, hands-on conservation organization that works throughout Australia and is dedicated to practical conservation. Members consider themselves "doers" rather than "talkers."

# Bala Lake Railway

The Station, Llanuwchllyn
Bala, Gwynedd LL23 7DD United Kingdom
Tel/Fax (01678) 540 666

*Project location*: Along a narrow-gauge railway in Wales.

*Project type*: Railway restoration and operation.

*Project costs*: Volunteers are responsible for room, board, and transportation.

*Project dates*: The railway operates between Easter and October, and volunteers are needed during the entire season. Some volunteers are accepted off-season by prior arrangement.

*How to apply*: Send a letter to the Manager at the above address.

*Work done by volunteers*: All aspects of running and operating a small railway.

*Special skills or requirements*: Basic knowledge of trains is a plus, but there are plenty of basic maintenance and restoration chores available for those who have no prior experience.

*Commentary*: This is one of several steam railroads in Wales that are operated by active volunteer groups.

# 🌏 Bardou Restoration Project

Bardou
34390 Olargues, France
(67) 97-72-43

*Project location*: In the hamlet of Bardou, located in the regional park of Haut Languedoc in the southern Cévennes Mountains, 90 kilometers west of Montpellier.

*Project type*: Restoration and maintenance of sixteenth-century, stone peasant houses and the surroundings, plus shepherding.

*Project costs*: Transportaion to site and $50 to $60 per week for food.

*Project dates*: The minimum stay is one month within the period between September 1 and December 1, or March 1 and June 30.

*How to apply*: Send a letter in English giving your full name, age, experience, educational level, and cultural interests to the above address.

*Work done by volunteers*: Assisting builders with painting, forest clearance, and mountain path maintenance; and tending sheep and dogs.

*Special skills or requirements*: Neither specific skills nor French are required; however, a good cultural education and background are appreciated.

*Commentary*: Bardou is a meeting place for world travelers and nature lovers. Short-term visitors and study groups staying a minimum of one week will be charged Fr 45 nightly per person for accommodations.

*Sample projects*: In the spring, restoration of houses takes place. Building and lambing are scheduled for fall.

# Belizean Department of Archaeology

Social Science Department
Collin Community College
2800 E. Spring Creek Parkway
Plano, TX 75074
(214) 881-5800; Fax (214) 881-5700

*Project location*: Small Mayan fishing village in Belize.

*Project type*: Archaeological excavations.

*Project costs*: Travel expenses to and from Belize, plus $50 per day.

*Project dates*:December through January and May through June.

*How to apply*: Contact Dr. J. Jefferson MacKinnon, Collin Community College, for a current schedule and an application form.

*Work done by volunteers*: General excavation work.

*Special skills or requirements*: No experience is necessary, but volunteers should be physically strong enough to excavate in the field.

*Commentary*: This continuing project of the community college is done in cooperation with the Belizean Department of Archaeology. Dr. MacKinnon received a kidney transplant in early 1996; inquire as to when projects will start again.

# Bermuda Biological Station for Research, Incorporated
Ferry Reach GE 01 Bermuda
(441) 297-1880; Fax (441) 297-8143

*Project location*: In and around Bermuda.

*Project type*: Both educational and volunteer opportunities are available at this marine research center.

*Project costs*: Programs vary. For more information, contact BBSR for information about specific programs.

*Project dates*: Year-round.

*How to apply*: Write to the above address for information and an application.

*Work done by volunteers*: Volunteers help in several areas at the center, working as clerical staff in the education office, leading school groups on tours, and helping develop educational material. They also help in the library, as staff assistants, and in the preparation for Marine Science Day held in June on even years. On the scientific side they help as divers on some projects and do nontechnical work on other investigations.

*Special skills or requirements*: Strong interest in marine science. Diving certification is required for those who wish to dive as research assistants.

*Commentary*: BBSR was established in 1903 and in the past decade has become one of the foremost marine science research centers in the world. Volunteers are exposed to the work of some of the premier marine scientists in the world as they help at the station.

# Breakaway

6026 Station B
Nashville, TN 37235
(615) 343-0385; Fax (615) 343-3255
E-mail: BRAKAWAY@ctrvax.vanderbilt.edu

*Project location*: Throughout the U.S. and Latin America.

*Project type*: Alternative college break activities.

*Project costs*: Vary with project and location. Travel is the largest cost.

*Project dates*: The length of the projects varies from a weekend to ten days, and projects are scheduled during traditonal college break times.

*How to apply*: Contact your local campus representative or the headquarters above for information.

*Work done by volunteers*: Community involvement of varous types, some of which involve intensive physical activity.

*Special skills or requirements*: An open mind and a willingness to work hard. At present only college or high school students are accepted.

*Commentary*: Breakaway was begun as a student-run community service organization that focused on promoting social consciousness and community involvement among university students. The projects provide a soul-searching alternative to conventional spring breaks. Although Breakaway began on the Vanderbilt campus it has spread to 40 formal associate chapters and association with 353 universities.

# Bristol Industrial Museum

Princes Wharf, City Docks
Bristol BS1 4RN United Kingdom
(0117) 925 1470; Fax (0117) 929 7318

*Project location*: At and near the museum.

*Project type*: Restoration and operation of museum exhibits, most of which are steam-powered.

*Project costs*: Volunteers are responsible for all travel and living costs.

*Project dates*: Most weekends throughout the year.

*How to apply*: Write to Andy King at the above address.

*Work done by volunteers*: Volunteers work as crew for an operating railway and a working steamship. They also do restoration work on trains and ships.

*Special skills or requirements*: A vague knowledge of engineering principles is useful, but not necessary.

*Commentary*: This is a small museum with a minimal budget that can use all the volunteers it can get.

*Sample projects*: In the past, volunteers have served on crews on the Bristol Harbour Railway, a dockside railway run by steam locomotives, or on the steam tug *Mayflower*, an 1861 steam-powered tug that now carries passengers. Volunteers have also helped maintain an 1878, 35-ton steam crane and have served as crews on a 1934 fire-fighting vessel.

# ◉ British Trust for Conservation Volunteers

36 Saint Mary's Street
Wallingford, Oxfordshire OX10 0EU United Kingdom

*Project location*: United Kingdom, Europe, and Asia.

*Project type*: Practical conservation.

*Project costs*: $60 to $100 per week.

*Project dates*: Year-round.

*How to apply*: Write to the above address for brochures.

*Work done by volunteers*: Practical conservation work.

*Special skills or requirements*: An interest in conservation and the physical ability to complete difficult projects.

*Commentary*: BTCV aims to harness people's energies and talents to protect and improve the environment by practical action. More than sixty thousand volunteers participate in BTCV projects each year. One ongoing project in need of volunteers is the Animal Habitat Project on the Isle of Wight, United Kingdom.

## BUSCA (Brigade Universitariua de Servicios Comunitarios para la Autogestion)
Edificio Montana Pelada Departmento 004
Rimanada de Volcanes Villa Panamericana
C.P. 04700 Mexico D.F.
Tel/Fax (665) 40-70

*Project location*: Throughout Mexico.

*Project type*: Community development work.

*Project costs*: Minimum of $400 for food, accommodations, and travel within Mexico.

*Project dates*: Mid-June through mid-August.

*How to apply*: Contact BUSCA after March.

*Work done by volunteers*: Work with the indigenous population on a variety of community development projects. Most of the work is manual labor.

*Special skills or requirements*: Must have basic knowledge of Spanish and an interest in working in a cross-cultural setting.

# California Department of Parks and Recreation
PO Box 942896
1416 9th Street
Sacramento, CA 94296-0001
(916) 653-6995

*Project location*: Sixty-seven campgrounds in state parks around California.

*Project type*: Campground hosts and interpreters.

*Project costs*: Volunteers furnish their own trailers, campers, or mobile homes. Campsites are free.

*Project dates*: Year-round. Hosts must commit to a minimum of thirty days and work two to five hours per day. Interpreters should make individual arrangements.

*How to apply*: Write to one of the regional offices listed below and specify whether you are interested in a campground host or an interpreter position.

*Work done by volunteers*: General campground host duties and specialized interpreter duties, such as living history, environmental studies, and natural science programs.

*Special skills or requirements*: Volunteers must be at least 18 years old.

*Commentary*: The regional offices are as follows.

**American River**
7806 Folsom-Auburn Road
Folsom, CA 95630-1797
(916) 988-0205

**Angeles**
1925 Las Virgenes Road
Calabasas, CA 91302
(818) 880-0350

**Bay Area**
250 Executive Park Boulevard
Suite 4900
San Francisco, CA 94134
(415) 330-6300

**Calaveras**
PO Box 151
Columbia, CA 95310
(209) 532-0150

**Channel Coast**
1933 Cliff Drive, Suite 27
Santa Barbara, CA 93109
(805) 899-1400

**Colorado Desert**
200 Palm Canyon Drive
Borrego Springs, CA 92004
(619) 767-5311

**Four Rivers**
31426 Gonzaga Road
Gustine, CA 95322-9737
(209) 826-1196

**Gold Rush**
101 J Street
Sacramento, CA 95814
(916) 445-7373

**Hollister Hills**
7800 Cienega Road
Hollister, CA 95023
(408) 637-8186

**Hungry Valley**
PO Box 1360
Lebec, CA 93243-1360
(805) 248-7007

**Los Lagos**
17801 Lake Perris Drive
Perris, CA 92571
(909) 657-0676

**Marin**
1455A E. Francisco Boulevard
San Rafael, CA 94901
(415) 456-1286

**Monterey**
2211 Garden Road
Monterey, CA 93940
(408) 649-2836

**North Coast Redwoods**
600A W. Clark Street
Eureka, CA 95501
(707) 445-6547

**Northern Buttes**
400 Glen Drive
Oroville, CA 95966-9222
(916) 538-2200

**Oceano Dunes**
576 Camino Mercado
Arroyo Grande, CA 93420
(805) 473-7230

**Ocotillo Wells**
PO Box 360
Borrego Springs, CA 92004
(619) 767-5391

**Orange Coast**
3030 Avenida del Presidente
San Clemente, CA 92672
(714) 492-0802

**Russian River/Mendocino**
PO Box 123
Duncan Mills, CA 95430
(707) 865-2391

**San Joaquin**
PO Box 205
Friant, CA 93626
(209) 822-2332

**San Luis Obispo**
3220 S. Higuera Street, Suite 311
San Luis Obispo, CA 93401
(805) 549-3312

**San Simeon**
750 Hearst Castle Road
San Simeon, CA 93401
(805) 927-2020

**Santa Cruz**
600 Ocean Street
Santa Cruz, CA 95060
(408) 429-2850

**Sierra**
PO Box 266
Tahoma, CA 96142
(916) 525-7232

**Silverado**
20 E. Spain Street
Sonoma, CA 95476
(707) 938-1519

**Twin Cities**
17999 Tesla Road
Livermore, CA 94550
(510) 447-0426

# California Institute for Peruvian Studies

45 Quakie Way
Bailey, CO 80421
(303) 838-1215

*Project location*: South coast of Peru.

*Project type*: Archaeological field work, including surveys, ceramic and textile analysis, and preservation.

*Project costs*: Approximately $800 per week.

*Project dates*: Excavations are held in March, June, July, and August, with participants invited to work for two to six weeks.

*How to apply*: Write or call Sandy Asmussen at above address or phone for an application and brochure.

*Work done by volunteers*: Participants perform difficult, routine, tiring archaeological field work under the supervision of qualified professionals.

*Special skills or requirements*: Ability to adapt to living in a remote region of a Third World country while performing hard work. While no experience is needed, a willingness to work hard under adverse conditions is.

*Commentary*: The objective of CIPS is to contribute to a more thorough understanding of Peru's prehistory. CIPS is currently preserving archaeological ruins, building a museum, and searching for new ruins along the south coast of Peru.

# Cape Tribulation Tropical Research Station

PMB 5
Cape Tribulation
Queensland 4873 Australia
(70) 980-063; Fax by arrangement (The station relies on solar power and cannot leave the fax on. Call and ask them to switch on the fax machine before sending a fax.)
Email: Hugh.Spencer@jcu.edu.au
Web sites:
http://www.ece.jcu.edu.au/ece/misc/capetrib/capetrib.html
http://www.ece.jcu.au/ece/misc/capetrib/rescue.html

*Project location*: Cape Tribulation on the Coral Sea coast of Queensland, Australia, about 100 kilometers north of Cairns. The area has a variety of habitats from coastal reefs to tropical rain forest.

*Project type*: Ecology of flying foxes (fruit bats) and their relatives; productivity and pollination of cluster fig trees; development of techniques for assisted regeneration of rain forests; development of radiotracking technology; development of appropriate technology for the wet tropics; rainforest conservation; plus a wide variety of projects by researchers from outside the station.

*Project costs*: Participants pay $100 per week for food and modest accommodations. Transportation to and from Cape Tribulation is at the volunteer's expense, although every reasonable attempt will be made to find free transport.

*Project dates*: Year-round; whether a specific project is available depends on the weather and the idiosyncrasies of plants, animals, and funding authorities. The normal stay is two weeks, but extensions are available at the discretion of the director.

*How to apply*: Send a letter of interest to the Director of the Field Station at the above address, and include a résumé and statement of your particular interests. If there is no response after a month, contact again. This is a small organization, and responses get lost in the workload.

*Work done by volunteers*: Volunteers assist research activities, ranging from radiotracking blossom bats and monitoring fig populations to constructing station buildings and working on rain forest regeneration. All volunteers are expected to actively participate in the household activities of the station.

*Special skills or requirements*: Volunteers can be of any age, but are preferably more than 20 years old. They should have an open and flexible attitude and not have preconceived notions about their role at the station. They should be willing to actively contribute, even to the most mundane activity. The facilities are spartan.

*Commentary*: Cape Tribulation Tropical Research Station is a research organization specializing in researching lowland tropical ecosystems. It is nonaffiliated and is funded by the AUSTROP Foundation.

# Caretta Research Project

Savannah Science Museum
4405 Paulsen Street
Savannah, GA 31405
(912) 355-6705; Fax (912) 355-0182

*Project location*: Wassaw Island, one of the barrier islands off the Georgia coast.

*Project type*: Scientific research of the loggerhead sea turtle population.

*Project costs*: $425 per week.

*Project dates*: May to September.

*How to apply*: Write to the Project Research Director at the above address.

*Work done by volunteers*: Tagging adult turtles, recording data, monitoring nests, and working with hatchlings.

*Special skills or requirements*: Volunteers must be physically able to work at night.

*Commentary*: Days are free for individual activities. Volunteers have come from all fifty states and numerous foreign countries in the twenty years of the project's existence. The project has an unusually high percentage of returning participants.

# Caribbean Conservation Corporation

4424 N.W. 13th Street, Suite A-1
Gainesville, FL 32609
(352) 373-6441 or (800) 678-7853; Fax (352) 375-2449
E-mail: ccc@atlantic.net

*Project location*: Tortuguero, Costa Rica.

*Project type*: Marine turtle and migrant and resident bird research.

*Project costs*: $1,500 to $2,000 for eight- to fifteen-day expeditions, with all groups leaving from Miami.

*Project dates*: March through October for turtle projects and year-round for birds, with emphasis on fall and spring migrations.

*How to apply*: Write or call for an application.

*Work done by volunteers*: Assisting researchers with sea turtle tagging operations, as well as taking measurements and observing nesting habits. Assist bird researchers by making observations along transects and within specific habitats.

*Special skills or requirements*: Good physical condition, ability to work with others, and ability to maintain a sense of humor in spite of occasional inclement weather. Must be 18 years of age or older.

*Commentary*: This organization was formed in 1959 to support the work of the late Archie Carr, one of the world's foremost sea turtle authorities. Since then it has blended applied research and conservation projects in efforts to reverse the worldwide decline of sea turtles. It has recently begun bird research.

# Caribbean Volunteer Expeditions

PO Box 388
Corning, NY 14830
(607) 962-7846

*Project location*: The Caribbean, including the Bahamas, the British Virgin Islands, Trinidad, St. Lucia, Nevis, Antigua, Tobago, Barbados, Guyana, Honduras, and the U.S. Virgin Islands.

*Project type*: Surveys of sites such as sugar plantations, measured drawings and photography of buildings, and building inventories.

*Project costs*: $200 to $700 plus airfare.

*Project dates*: One- to two-week projects year-round.

*How to apply*: Write to the above address.

*Work done by volunteers*: Measurements of buildings, survey work, photography of buildings, and drafting.

*Special skills or requirements*: None.

*Commentary*: Accommodations are rental houses, hotels, or camping.

Volunteers with Caribbean Volunteer Expeditions measure an old courthouse in St. Johns, Antigua. Photo courtesy of Caribbean Volunteer Expeditions.

# Casa de los Amigos

Ignaciao Mariscal 132
06030 Mexico D.F.
(5) 705-0521 or (5) 705-0646; Fax (5) 705-0771
E-mail: amigos@laneta.apc.org

*Project location*: Mexico City, Momostenango, and Guatemala.

*Project type*: One- to two-week service and learning seminars and six-month internships of full-time work with communities in need.

*Project costs*: Seminars are $35 per day, and internships have a $50 placement fee and a $25 per month administrative fee.

*Project dates*: Both seminars and internships are held year-round.

*How to apply*: Contact Service and Education Project at the above address.

*Work done by volunteers*: Variety of social service work with children, adult literacy, AIDS patients, and an indigenous artisans' co-op.

*Special skills or requirements*: Very good Spanish and a commitment to service.

*Commentary*: Cultural sensitivity and overall maturity, with developed goals, are sought in volunteers.

# Casa de Proyecto Libertad, Incorporated

113 N. 1st Street
Harlingen, TX 78550
(210) 425-9552; Fax (210) 425-8249

*Project location*: South Texas along the Texas-Mexico border.

*Project type*: Direct legal services to immigrants and refugees mainly from Central America. Advocacy on behalf of the immigrant and refugee community in the U.S.

*Project costs*: Participants are responsible for all transportation, room, and board. Occasionally stipends are available.

*Project dates*: Year-round.

*How to apply*: Send a résumé and cover letter to the above address.

*Work done by volunteers*: Client interviews, case documentation, and education and advocacy work.

*Special skills or requirements*: Volunteers should be bilingual in English and Spanish and able to work in a multicultural setting. Computer skills are helpful.

*Commentary*: Volunteers are asked to make a six-month commitment, but occasionally shorter commitments are accepted.

*Sample projects*: Other than legal and educational projects, there are often fund-raising projects which appeal to special groups for money.

# CEDAM International

Fox Road
Croton-on-Hudson, NY 10520
(914) 271-5365

*Project location*: Worldwide.

*Project type*: Preservation and archaeological expeditions, especially marine archaeology.

*Project costs*: $1,000 to $4,500, plus transportation to and from the site.

*Project dates*: Generally between May and August for one to two weeks, but some expeditions are year-round.

*How to apply*: Write to the above address for complete registration information.

*Work done by volunteers*: Volunteers—divers and nondivers—participate in marine research projects and help scientists with research activities.

*Special skills or requirements*: CEDAM prefers volunteers who are certified divers, but others are accepted as needed. Volunteers receive basic, on-site training for their project.

*Commentary*: CEDAM (Conservation, Education, Diving, Archaeology, and Museums) is one of the premier marine research organizations that uses volunteers extensively.

# Central American Institute of Prehistoric and Traditional Cultures of Belize

PO Box 59
San Ignacio, Cayo District, Belize
(92) 3110; Fax (92) 3136
E-mail: evas@btl.net.attn:Central American Institute

*Project location*: A 150-acre tropical forest in the Maya mountains of the Cayo District in Belize.

*Project type*: Volunteers participate on projects in anthropology, archaeology, and ethnobotany.

*Project costs*: $750 per week for room and board, field trips, and study programs. This fee does not cover transportation to Belize.

*Project dates*: Project dates vary, but learning programs are generally held between January and March and July and September, for one to nine weeks.

*How to apply*: Write to the above address for information on programs. Be sure to indicate your field of interest in your letter.

*Work done by volunteers*: Participants attend programs where they study natural healing and shamanistic practices and work on field projects in anthropology, archaeology, and ethnobotany.

*Special skills or requirements*: A background in cultural studies or health sciences is useful but not required. All participants must be at least 18 and in good health.

*Commentary*: The institute promotes the preservation of ancient and traditional culture through scientific research, archaeological investigations, preservation, ethnobotanical studies, and educational programs. Participants can receive academic credit for programs.

# e for Alternative Technology

Pantperthog
Machynlleth, Powys SY20 9AZ United Kingdom
(01654) 702 400; Fax (01654) 702 782
E-mail: cat@gn.apc.org

*Project location*: A former slate quarry in the hills of central Wales.

*Project type*: The Centre is a working demonstration of alternative technology, renewable energy, and organic growing.

*Project costs*: About $10 per day, plus travel expenses.

*Project dates*: The Short-Term Volunteer Programme runs on specified weeks from March to August.

*How to apply*: Write or call the office listed above for full details and a booking form.

*Work done by volunteers*: Gardening, course facilities preparation, site maintenance, landscaping, plus whatever jobs are most urgent at the time.

*Special skills or requirements*: None.

*Commentary*: Volunteers come for one or two consecutive weeks, as available. Demand is high—the program was completely booked for 1996 by early spring—so book early. There are no facilities for young children.

# Centro de Estudios de Español

Pop Wuj
Apartado Postal 68
Quetzaltenango, Guatemala
61-82-86
or
PO Box 43685-9685
Washington, DC 20010-9685
(415) 868-1786

*Project location*: Guatemala.

*Project type*: Community development programs and language study.

*Project costs*: $100 to $115 per week.

*Project dates*: Year-round, for one-week sessions.

*How to apply*: Contact the Washington office for application information.

*Work done by volunteers*: This is primarily a language study program, but each student has the opportunity to practice Spanish by working with locals on community service projects.

*Special skills or requirements*: None but an interest in learning Spanish and meeting local people.

# Golodrinas Cloudforest Conservation

e Isabel la Catolica 1559
Quito, Ecuador
(2) 226602; Fax (2) 502640

*Project location*: Either the reserve on the western slopes of the Andes in northern Ecuador or the agroforestry center in the village of Guallupe in the Mira Valley.

*Project type*: Forest conservation and demonstration of agroforestry.

*Project costs*: From $155 to $180 per month.

*Project dates*: Year-round for a minimum of one month at level 1 involvement, which requires only basic Spanish and no experience. Level 2 involvement requires some experience or training, advanced Spanish, and a three-month commitment.

*How to apply*: Contact the above office for more information. Golondrinas requires three months' notice before arrival.

*Work done by volunteers*: Assist scientists with investigations or work in the tree nursery planting trees and doing general maintenance.

*Special skills or requirements*: Volunteers should have at least basic Spanish, and people with some experience in gardening are preferred. Ability to work hard and live in somewhat primitive conditions is required.

*Commentary*: Fundacion Golondrinas is a nongovernmental, private organization aiming to protect twenty-five hundred hectares of highland forest on the western slopes of the Andes in Ecuador. The project was established in the early 1990s and is seeking to preserve this area with its exceptionally rich biodiversity and endemic plants and animals. As of 1996 the project has purchased eighteen hundred hectares of the forest.

# Chantier de Jeunes

Provence Côte d'Azur
La Ferme Giaume
7, avenue Pierre de Coubertin
06150 Cannes la Bocca, France
47-89-69; Fax 48-12-01

*Project location*: Sainte Marguerite in Annes, France, and various locations in Belgium.

*Project type*: Work camps.

*Project costs*: About $200 per week.

*Project dates*: All holidays in winter and summer.

*How to apply*: For special information, send a letter in French with a self-addressed, stamped envelope.

*Work done by volunteers*: Building, environmental protection, and preserving historical monuments. Volunteers work in groups of fourteen for fifteen days. Work lasts for five hours in the morning; pariticipants are free for the afternoon and night.

*Special skills or requirements*: Participants must be 14 to 18 years old and speak at least minimal French.

*Commentary*: CJPCA is over twenty-five years old and offers youth an international living experience.

# Chantiers d'Études Medievales

4, rue du Tonnelet Rouge
67000 Strasbourg, France
(88) 37-17-20

*Project location*: Châteaux d'Ottrott.

*Project type*: Restoration of medieval sites and monuments, plus archaeological digs.

*Project costs*: Fr 450 to Fr 550 covers insurance, meals, and accommodations. Volunteers are responsible for transportation to sites.

*Project dates*: July 1 to late August, with fifteen-day sessions.

*How to apply*: Write to the above address for an application and more information.

*Work done by volunteers*: Mostly manual labor, including excavation. There is an opportunity for volunteers to participate in the study of finds made during digs. Volunteers work in teams of twenty or thirty for six hours per day, five days a week.

*Special skills or requirements*: Volunteers who aren't French must be at least 16 years old and should speak at least minimal French.

*Commentary*: For the past fifteen years, three hundred to five hundred volunteers each year from more than twenty countries have participated. While accommodations are modest, they are sufficient and offer participants an opportunity to experience a true camaraderie with other volunteers.

# Charleston Museum
360 Meeting Street
Charleston, SC 29403
(803) 722-2996

*Project location*: In and around Charleston.

*Project type*: Archaeological excavations on urban homesites and rural plantations.

*Project costs*: Participants are responsible for their transportation to Charleston, plus room and board.

*Project dates*: Lab work is year-round, but excavation schedules are often unknown until one to two months before a project begins. Most projects last one to three weeks.

*How to apply*: Write to Martha Zierdon, Curator of Historical Archaeology, for an application and more information.

*Work done by volunteers*: Volunteers work both in the field (digging, screening, and measuring) and in the lab (washing and processing artifacts).

*Special skills or requirements*: Participants should be in good physical health and able to withstand hard physical labor, heat, and insects.

*Sample projects*: Recently, volunteers have helped excavate Georgian townhouses. The museum also has an ongoing excavation at a plantation site on Dill Wildlife Refuge.

# Cholsey and Wallingford Railway
Hithercroft Road
PO Box 16
Wallingford, Oxfordshire OX10 ONF United Kingdom
(01491) 835 067 (weekends only)

*Project location*: Along two and one-half miles of track running from Cholsey to Wallingford in England.

*Project type*: Railway restoration and maintenance.

*Project costs*: Volunteers are responsible for their room, board, and transportation.

*Project dates*: Weekends year-round.

*How to apply*: Write to the above address for information.

*Work done by volunteers*: General railway restoration and maintenance.

*Special skills or requirements*: None but the ability to do heavy work.

# Christian Medical/Dental Society—Medical Group Missions

PO Box 5
Bristol, TN 37621-0005
(423) 844-1000; Fax (423) 844-1005
E-mail: 75364.331@compuserve.com

*Project location*: Central America, China, the Dominican Republic, Eastern Europe, Ecuador, Jamaica, Mexico, Philippines, and Vietnam.

*Project type*: Medical or dental.

*Project costs*: Per person for projects in the following countries: Honduras, Mexico, and Nicaragua, $475; the Dominican Republic and Guatemala, $500; Ecuador and Jamaica, $550; Africa, Asia, and Europe, $700. Volunteers pay airfare.

*Project dates*: Year-round, for two or three weeks.

*How to apply*: Write to the above address for an application and a list of projects.

*Work done by volunteers*: All work is medically oriented. Physicians perform their specialties and are generally supported by two nurses. About one-third of the volunteers are nonmedical personnel who act as support workers for the medical volunteers.

*Special skills or requirements*: Medical training is required for nurses, dentists, and physicians; but nonmedical volunteers need only a desire to help others.

*Commentary*: There are great contrasts between the various projects. In some countries the living conditions and medical facilities are very primitive, while others, such as Mexico and Jamaica, offer semi-luxurious accommodations(dorms or small cottages for families). This is one of the few medical volunteer organizations that welcome entire families; however, they do prefer older children (age 12 and up).

# A Christian Ministry in the National Parks

222½ E. 49th Street
New York, NY 10017
(212) 758-3450

*Project location*: Volunteers serve in sixty-five national parks and recreation areas across the country.

*Project type*: Ministerial services for employees and visitors of the parks.

*Project costs*: Volunteers pay for their transportation to and from the parks but are provided room, board, and wages from a secular employer.

*Project dates*: From June 1 to Labor Day.

*How to apply*: Write to the above address for an application and more information.

*Work done by volunteers*: Lead worship services and Bible studies, direct choirs, and pursue other ministerial duties.

*Special skills or requirements*: A commitment to the Christian faith, creativity, maturity, and the ability to work with Christians of all denominations. Volunteers should be lay leaders with special skills in music, Bible study, recreation, drama, or Christian education.

*Commentary*: This program is for singles and married couples who are more than 20 years old and who wish to spend a full summer working in a national park and ministering to the religious needs of others.

# Christian Movement for Peace

United Reformed Church
Pott Street
Bethnal Green
London E2 0EF United Kingdom
(0171) 729-7985

*Project location*: Primarily in Europe, but also Africa, India, the Middle East, and North and South America.

*Project type*: Work camps.

*Project costs*: Volunteers pay a registration fee to their home organization and must arrange their own transportation.

*Project dates*: Mostly in the summer.

*How to apply*: In the U.S., apply to Volunteers for Peace, 43 Tiffany Road, Belmont, VT 05730. In Canada, apply to Chantiers Jeunesse, C.P. 1000, succ. M, Montreal, Quebec, HIV 3R2.

*Work done by volunteers*: Work on the camp as well as daily chores such as cooking and cleaning.

*Special skills or requirements*: Must be at least 18 years old. Some knowledge of the local language is always useful, but not necessary.

*Commentary*: Volunteers should apply to the Christian Movement for Peace branches in their own country; if there isn't one, they should apply to their national work camp organization.

# Club du Vieux Manoir

10, rue de la Cossonnerie
75001 Paris, France
16-45-08-80-40

*Project location*: There are three permanent sites at Guise, Argy, and Pontpoint, and twelve to fifteen other sites throughout France.

*Project type*: Restoration of ancient monuments and sites.

*Project costs*: Fr 80 for membership and insurance for one year, plus Fr 65 per day for room and board. Participants are responsible for supplying transportation to and from the site and their personal sleeping, eating, and toilet gear. Summer accommodations are in tents, which often have very rustic facilities.

*Project dates*: There are no set dates for the three permanent sites, but all other sites operate during the summer months only. Volunteers must stay a minimum of fifteen days, with new sessions beginning on the second and sixteenth of each month.

*How to apply*: Write to the Secretary at the above address for an application and a brochure.

*Work done by volunteers*: Normal manual labor of a restoration project. Volunteers are required to accept the demands of project supervisors, or they will be asked to leave.

*Special skills or requirements*: Excellent health and a willingness to do hard physical labor are primary requirements. The club is open to everyone over the age of 14 from all nations, with no maximum age limit. Groups organized in advance are welcome.

*Commentary*: As the club's brochure states, these projects aren't "something to while away spare hours." The projects are aimed not at the consumer but at the enthusiastic volunteer who wants to do something worthwhile.

# Colonial Williamsburg Foundation

Department of Archaeological Research
PO Box 1776
Williamsburg, VA 23187
(804) 220-7330; Fax (804) 220-7990

*Project location*: The restored area of Williamsburg, Virginia, the eighteenth-century capital of the Virginia colony.

*Project type*: Archaeological field and laboratory work.

*Project costs*: Volunteers are responsible for transportation, room, and board. Out-of-state participants in the Field School of the College of William and Mary pay approximately $2,700, plus room and board for a five-week session. In addition, participants in Learning Weeks in Archaeology program pay room and board, plus $350 tuition for a one-week session and $550 for two weeks.

*Project dates*: Some projects continue almost year-round (weather permitting). Projects affiliated with field schools are during the summer.

*How to apply*: Send a query letter to the above address.

*Work done by volunteers*: Tasks related to daily excavation (troweling, recording, and screening soil) and laboratory processing of artifacts (washing and numbering).

*Special skills or requirements*: Field volunteers must have some archaeological background, as well as the physical ability to perform excavation tasks. No experience or special skills are required for laboratory positions. A commitment of at least three days is required of all volunteers.

*Commentary*: There are three different programs offered through the foundation. The first is the Field School of the College of William and Mary. Participants in this program must register through the college for at least one five-week session. They do not need a background in archaeology and will receive six semester units of credit for the session. The second program is Learning Weeks in Archaeology, where participants enroll in one- or two-week sessions and are introduced to the goals and methods of the research program at Williamsburg. The third is for individual volunteers who have some background in archaeology. Participants in this program help with the excavation and laboratory work under minimal supervision and can choose the time and length of their stay, provided it coincides with an active project and the commitment is for at least three days.

# 🌐 Colorado Trail Foundation

548 Pine Song Trail
Golden, CO 80401
(303) 526-0809

*Project location*: Colorado national forests.

*Project type*: Trail building and maintenance on the Colorado Trail.

*Project costs*: $25 registration fee. The foundation sets up base camps for volunteers and provides food. Volunteers provide their own sleeping bags, tents, and personal items.

*Project dates*: June, July, and August, with both weekend and weeklong projects.

*How to apply*: Write to the above address for a summer trail crew schedule.

*Work done by volunteers*: Trail building and maintenance and trail signing.

*Special skills or requirements*: Volunteers should be in good health and willing to work. The foundation provides experienced leaders and tools.

*Commentary*: The Colorado Trail is a 470-mile trail stretching from Denver to Durango. It was built (and continues to be improved) largely by a massive volunteer effort.

# Commission on Religion in Appalachia

111 Crutcher Pike
Richmond, KY 40475-8606
Tel/Fax (606) 623-0429

*Project location*: Ninety work camps in the Appalachian states of Alabama, Georgia, Kentucky, Maryland, North Carolina, Ohio, Pennsylvania, South Carolina, Tennessee, Virginia, and West Virginia.

*Project type*: Work camp groups perform tasks that include home repair and small farm development.

*Project costs*: Varies with each project, but materials and meals cost generally $100 to $200 per person per week.

*Project dates*: Year-round.

*How to apply*: Apply to John MacLean, Coordinator of Volunteers, at the above address. If you wish to organize a group, list the number of people in the group, their ages, and preferred dates.

*Work done by volunteers*: Carpentry, plumbing, painting, weatherproofing, and other general home repair projects.

*Special skills or requirements*: CORA prefers to have one or two skilled craftspeople with experience in home repair in each group, and one adult for every five youths.

*Commentary*: CORA only accepts groups of eight to thirty people for work camps. Volunteers are usually adult and youth church groups or college groups. All groups should apply by January for spring or summer assignments.

*Sample projects*: In the past, volunteer groups have built a shed for, cleaned, and painted a house in Harlan, Kentucky. A church youth group insulated and paneled a two-room home in London, Kentucky. In Neon, Kentucky, other church groups built five new homes for low income families. A college group dug a new water line, hauled wood, and cleared a garden in Street Paul, Virginia.

# Commission on Voluntary Service and Action

PO Box 117
New York, NY 10009

*Project location*: New York.

*Project type*: Publishing a book on volunteer opportunities.

*Project costs*: Volunteers are responsible for travel, room, and board.

*Project dates*: Year-round.

*How to apply*: Write to the Internship Coordinator at the above address.

*Work done by volunteers*: Writing, editing, correspondence, and administration.

*Special skills or requirements*: None.

*Commentary*: CVSA is the publisher of *Invest Yourself: The Catalogue of Volunteer Opportunities*, a book detailing more than forty thousand volunteer opportunities through two hundred service organizations. CVSA offers a limited number of volunteer internships to defray project costs.

# Committee for the Health Rights in Central America

347 Dolores Street, Suite 210
San Francisco, CA 94110
(415) 431-7760

*Project location*: El Salvador and Nicaragua.

*Project type*: Health colloquium and medical teaching exchange.

*Project costs*: $1,300 to $1,400.

*Project dates*: Usually ten days in the fall.

*How to apply*: Write to the above address for registration information.

*Work done by volunteers*: Medical teaching exchange in hospitals in Nicaragua and El Salvador, as well as attendance at the colloquium.

*Special skills or requirements*: Volunteers should be health care workers, health professionals, or others interested in community health projects.

*Commentary*: A task force of participants investigates particular issues each year in the delivery of health care in the country visited.

# Community Service Volunteers

c/o Worldwide Internships and Service Education
303 South Craig Street
Pittsburgh, PA 15213
(412) 681-8120; Fax (412) 681-8187
E-mail: wise@unix.cis.pitt.edu
or
237 Pentonville Road
London N1 9NJ United Kingdom
(0171) 278-6601

*Project location*: Throughout the United Kingdom.

*Project type*: Volunteers work alongside professionals in caring for people with disabilities, children in care facilities, the homeless, and elderly people.

*Project costs*: About $1,425 for the summer program, plus travel to and from the United Kingdom.

*Project dates*: Year-round.

*How to apply*: Write to the above address. All applicants must attend an information and interview session in the U.S. or London. Sessions are held six times a year in London, and twice a year in the U.S. Sessions in the U.S. are held in Pittsburgh and Spokane, Washington.

*Work done by volunteers*: Face-to-face work with those in need in both group and individual situations.

*Special skills or requirements*: No experience or special skills needed, except the ability to speak and understand English.

*Commentary*: CSV operates a nonrejection policy for volunteers. The organization feels that anyone who wishes to volunteer has something to offer. CSV volunteers must be able to work full-time for between four and twelve months.

# Companheiros Construtores
Rua Pedro Monteiro, 3-1
3000 Coimbra, Portugal

*Project location*: Throughout Portugal.

*Project type*: Home construction and repair, plus a few social service projects.

*Project costs*: Transportation to and from the project, plus spending money, room, and board.

*Project dates*: Short-term projects are for two to three weeks during the summer months.

*How to apply*: Write to Manuel Rocha at the above address for information.

*Work done by volunteers*: Hard manual labor on projects for the poor of Portugal.

*Special skills or requirements*: Willingness to work. Construction skills are desirable. Some social service projects need specialized skills such as physical therapy.

*Commentary*: This is a small organization that does most of its work in Portugal, with occasional projects in other European countries. Few Americans have worked as volunteers, but they are welcome. Companheiros Construtores also seeks financial support for its program.

*Sample projects*: A recent project involved building a small home for a family from Angola who had been evicted from the shed they were living in.

# Connecticut State Parks Division

79 Elm Street
Hartford, CT 06106-5127
(860) 424-3200

*Project location*: Campgrounds in various state parks and forests.

*Project type*: Campground hosts.

*Project costs*: Volunteers are responsible for trasnportation, room, and board.

*Project dates*: Memorial Day weekend through Labor Day weekend.

*How to apply*: Write to the above address for an application and a job description.

*Work done by volunteers*: Volunteers must be available for a minimum of four weeks and will serve as the live-in hosts of a campground. Their primary responsibility is to assist campers by answering questions and explaining campground regulations. Light maintenance work may also be performed. Volunteers are expected to work weekends and holidays, but different hours can be arranged with individual park managers.

*Special skills or requirements*: Volunteers must be neat, courteous, willing to meet the public, and they must possess a knowledge of state park programs and regulations.

*Commentary*: This is one type of volunteer work in which volunteers are encouraged to bring their families.

# Cooperation Project

International Ecological Camp
PO Box 52
Bratsk-18
Irkutsk Region 665718 Russia
or
Foundation for Ecological Cooperation
PO Box 13844
2501 EV
The Hague, The Netherlands

*Project location*: Eastern Siberia.

*Project type*: International work camps and educational expeditions.

*Project costs*: $330 and up.

*Project dates*: Year-round, but most of the projects are in the summer.

*How to apply*: Write for an application and a brochure.

*Work done by volunteers*: Unskilled and skilled carpentry and renovation, outdoor work, and teaching.

*Special skills or requirements*: Applicants must be over 18 years old. Russian language is helpful but not necessary.

*Commentary*: The Cooperation Project has brought people from different countries together since 1989 to promote multicultural perspectives on ecological and social issues.

*Sample projects*: Previous volunteers have worked in a historical open-air museum and gone on a bike expedition to Lake Baikal.

# Corrymeela Community

5 Drumaroan Road
Ballycastle, County Antrim BT54 6QU United Kingdom
(012657) 62626; Fax (012657) 62770

*Project location*: Ballycastle, County Antrim, in Northern Ireland.

*Project type*: Working with families in the village, and helping with kitchen work, housekeeping and reception, arts and crafts, recreation, and worship.

*Project costs*: Room and board are provided, but volunteers must pay for their own transportation to Northern Ireland. Donations to the program are also accepted.

*Project dates*: From one to two weeks in July and August.

*How to apply*: Write for information in late February, and an application will be sent to you in March. Selections are made in May.

*Work done by volunteers*: Changes by project type, but an emphasis is always placed on relationships between volunteers and families.

*Special skills or requirements*: Applicants should be more than 18 years old, speak good English, and have a genuine interest in being with people.

*Commentary*: Corrymeela is a Christian community whose members are dispersed around Northern Ireland and the rest of the United Kingdom, and throughout the Republic of Ireland. The center is a resource to the community, and a lot of work is done with families and youth. More than one hundred volunteers are recruited over the summer, twenty per week, half from Ireland and half from overseas.

# Costa Rica National Park Service Volunteer Program

Apartado 10104-1000
Avenida 6 y 8, C. 25
San Jose, Costa Rica
33-45-33; Fax 23-69-63

*Project location*: National parks of Costa Rica.

*Project type*: Maintenance and environmental education to help protect national parks.

*Project costs*: Participants must pay for their transportation to the site and their food (about $4 per day).

*Project dates*: Year-round. A minimum of three weeks is required of volunteers, but volunteers can spend this time at more than one park. Volunteers are used at Tortuguero, Cabo Blanco, Poas, Braulio Carrillo, Irazú, Guayabo, and Tapanti.

*How to apply*: Write a letter to the above address with the dates you are available. Include a brief personal history stating what knowledge or skills you have that may be useful to the park service.

*Work done by volunteers*: Volunteers have constructed trails, provided tourist information, gathered garbage, cooked, fought forest fires, weeded, and much more.

*Special skills or requirements*: No special skills are required, but artistic skills and the ability to do manual labor are helpful.

*Commentary*: It is important that volunteers be able to work in a tropical climate and in challenging conditions. When you apply you may suggest the park or type of climate in which you want to work. The park service will attempt to comply with your requests. Specific information on the work location and conditions will be provided in the service's reply to your application.

# Council on International Educational Exchange
205 E. 42nd Street
New York, NY 10017
(212) 661-1414

*Project location*: Eastern and Western Europe, North Africa, Thailand, Central America, South America, and North America.

*Project type*: Conservation, construction, archaeology, historical renovation, and work with children.

*Project costs*: $195 application fee, plus transportation, insurance, and spending money.

*Project dates*: From late June to early September.

*How to apply*: Write to CIEE at the above address for an application and a directory of projects. Projects fill up fast, so apply early.

*Work done by volunteers*: Manual labor, social work, playground supervision, painting, digging, planting and weeding, and visiting disabled people.

*Special skills or requirements*: Volunteers must desire to work hard in a multicultural setting and have a sense of adventure. Most projects require that participants be at least 18 years old.

*Commentary*: CIEE is one of the major work camp organizers in the U.S. The organization also offers many other programs for travel and study abroad.

*Sample projects*: In recent years, volunteers have been involved in forest conservation in Czechoslovakia and the U.S., care of the elderly in West Germany, construction of a water trench in Turkey, renovation of historic sites in France, and archaeological digs in Spain. In County Cork, Ireland, teams continued to excavate the castle of Edmund Spenser, celebrated author of *The Faerie Queene*, recording findings and using chemical sampling to detect buried features.

# Croatian International Youth Corps

3405 Southcreek Road, Unit 13
Mississauga, Ontario L4X 2X6 Canada
(905) 602-6608; Fax (905) 602-5432

*Project location*: Croatia.

*Project type*: Summer work camps.

*Project costs*: About $100.

*Project dates*: Mid-July to early August for three weeks.

*How to apply*: Contact above.

*Work done by volunteers*: Help rebuild damaged parts of Dubrovnik and Ravno.

*Special skills or requirements*: Volunteers must be between 18 and 30 years old and able to do hard work.

*Commentary*: This project needs to fill two work camps each summer.

# Cross-Cultural Solutions

PO Box 625
Ophir, CO 81426
(970) 728-5551; Fax (970) 728-4577
E-mail: CCSmailbox@aol.com
Web site: http://emol.org/emol/projectindia

*Project location*: New Delhi, India.

*Project type*: Medical, educational, and arts and recreational community development.

*Project costs*: $1,650

*Project dates*: Year-round for varying lengths of time, from three weeks to six months.

*How to apply*: Call or write to the above address for information.

*Work done by volunteers*: Teaching and serving at the community-based project. All volunteers have a three-day, intensive orientation before the project starts.

*Special skills or requirements*: No skills or experience are required. Volunteers must be over 18.

# Cross-Lines Cooperative Council

736 Shawnee Avenue
Kansas City, KS 66105
(913) 281-3388; Fax (913) 281-2344

*Project location*: Kansas City, Kansas, usually the Armourdale district.

*Project type*: Home repair for persons living in poverty, usually elderly and/or disabled persons.

*Project costs*: None.

*Project dates*: April through October, for one to five working days.

*How to apply*: Contact the Work Group Coordinator at the above address.

*Work done by volunteers*: General home repair, from replacing broken windows and reroofing to rebuilding foundations.

*Special skills or requirements*: General home repair skills are preferred but not necessary.

*Commentary*: Cross-Lines will match appropriate projects to a group's skill level, size, average age, and length of time available.

# Crow Canyon Archaeological Center

23390 County Road K
Cortez, CO 81321
(970) 565-8975 or (800) 422-8975; Fax (970) 565-4859
Web site: http://www.swcolo.org/crowcanyon

*Project location*: Southwestern Colorado near Mesa Verde National Park.

*Project type*: Archaeology excavation and cultural workshops.

*Project costs*: Adults, $795 per week; high school and college students, $525 per week; and high school students in the field schools, $2,450 for four weeks.

*Project dates*: End of May through the end of September.

*How to apply*: Write to the above address or call Lynn Baca at the 800 number, extension 130.

*Work done by volunteers*: Excavation and lab analysis.

*Special skills or requirements*: No special skills are needed, but excavation requires manual labor.

*Commentary*: Participants will make a significant contribution to archaeological research.

# Cultural Heritage Council
PO Box 808
Middletown, CA 95461
(707) 987-9157

*Project location*: Clear Lake Basin in northern California.

*Project type*: Archaeological excavation.

*Project costs*: Volunteers are responsible for transportation to and from the site and tuition fees. Tuition varies from year to year, depending on donations received by the council.

*Project dates*: Generally for one week throughout July and August.

*How to apply*: Send a résumé to the above address. The deadline for the July program is May 1.

*Work done by volunteers*: Archaeological site preparation, grid layout, excavation, and lab work.

*Special skills or requirements*: Volunteers not enrolled in a field school course offered by the council must have at least two seasons of archaeological field and/or lab work.

*Commentary*: The Cultural Heritage Council offers field school courses in field and lab methods for high school and college students, as well as adults. An introductory course in archaeology is also offered for junior and senior high school students. This program has been conducted since 1983, and the study of a ten thousand-year-old Pomo Indian village has resulted in a collection of more than four thousand artifacts that have been excavated and cataloged.

# Dean Forest Railway Society
Norchard
Lydney, Gloucestershire GL15 4ET United Kingdom
(01594) 413423

*Project location*: Lydney to Parkeno in western England.

*Project type*: Restoration of four miles of railway line and running of steam trains on weekends from May through September.

*Project costs*: Annual membership in the society is £6. Volunteers may apply for a weekly rate of £1.

*Project dates*: Restoration work is year-round, and trains run only during the summer.

*How to apply*: Write to the Volunteer Coordinator at the above address for an application and more information.

*Work done by volunteers*: All work involved in the operation of the railway is done by members of the society who want to volunteer.

*Special skills or requirements*: The responsible jobs of running the trains require training and testing, but there are many maintenance, painting, and other manual labor jobs that require minimal on-the-job training.

*Commentary*: A limited number of beds in railway coaches are available for volunteers; volunteers should bring sleeping bags. Although there are no cooking facilities, there are numerous eating places a mile away in Lydney. The Forest of Dean is an ancient ironstone and coal mining area of considerable interest to industrial archaeologists. It now has beautiful deciduous and pine forests full of wildlife.

*Sample projects*: Painting a railway coach inside and out, building a dry stone wall, and assisting in a shop or restaurant are all examples of volunteer work on this project.

# Dental Health International

847 S. Milledge Avenue
Athens, GA 30605
(706) 546-1715

*Project location*: Bhutan, Cambodia, Cameroon, Cook Islands, Morocco, and Nigeria.

*Project type*: Creating rural dental clinics by installing American-made dental equipment donated by U.S. dentists.

*Project costs*: Airfare and transportation to and from the work site.

*Project dates*: Year-round.

*How to apply*: Telephone DHI between 7:00 P.M. and 10:00 P.M. EST Sunday through Thursday.

*Work done by volunteers*: Collecting and installing dental units, assisted by the host country plumber and/or electrician, and teaching medical specialties.

*Special skills or requirements*: All volunteers must have been in upper 50 percent of their graduating class, be an ADA member, and have excellent physical health.

*Commentary*: Dental students and dental hygienists are also asked to apply, but applicants must realize that this is back-breaking work in an inhospitable environment. Dr. Barry Simmons, founder and president of DHI, has often screened more than twelve hundred patients in one day, while giving some type of treatment to more than one hundred.

# Department d'Histoire Université
Avenue O. Messiaen
72000 Le Mans, France

*Project location*: Champagne (near Épernay), France.

*Project type*: Archaeological excavation.

*Project costs*: Volunteers must pay for their travel.

*Project dates*: From July through August for three weeks minimum.

*How to apply*: Send a letter and résumé to A. Renoux at the above address.

*Work done by volunteers*: Volunteers dig on the excavation during the day and participate in normal activities, including cooking and housekeeping, in the evening.

*Special skills or requirements*: Volunteers must be at least 18 years old, speak French or English, and be in good health.

*Commentary*: Fifteen to twenty-five volunteers work on the site each year. Many of them come from Europe.

# Derbyshire International Youth Camp

Derbyshire County Council, Education Department
Derby Youth House
Mill Street
Derby DE1 1DY United Kingdom
(01332) 345 538

*Project location*: Derbyshire, England.

*Project type*: Conservation projects on county parks, renovating community centers, and assisting with summer playground projects.

*Project costs*: Vary each year; contact the above address for current costs.

*Project dates*: Four weeks, between mid-July and mid-August.

*How to apply*: Contact the office listed above for an application before May 1.

*Work done by volunteers*: Volunteers help in a variety of ways, including constructing pathways from the city center to the county parks, working on summer play programs for children, and developing conservation areas. All volunteers share the work and have a choice of projects to work on.

*Special skills or requirements*: Applicants should be between 16 and 25 years old and have an interest in environmental conservation and community work.

*Commentary*: The youth camp houses fifty young people each week and aims to contribute to the environment and local communities. A variety of recreational activities is also available.

# Dyfed Wildlife Trust
7 Market Street
Haverfordwest, Dyfed SA61 1NF United Kingdom
(01437) 765 462

*Project location*: Skomer Island, Wales.

*Project type*: Assistant wardening.

*Project costs*: No cost to participants except transportation to the project site.

*Project dates*: March to October each year.

*How to apply*: Write to Mrs. Glennerster, Islands Booking Officer, at the above address. Reservations are normally taken in September and October for the next year, so apply early.

*Work done by volunteers*: Projects include practical maintenance, meeting day visitors off boats, supervising footpaths to make sure visitors do not stray from them, bird counts, and recording.

*Special skills or requirements*: None, except a general interest in natural history and a willingness to work. Volunteers must be at least 16 years old; there's no upper age limit.

*Commentary*: Skomer Island is a nature reserve that is internationally famous for its seabird colonies, especially the estimated 160,000 pairs of Manx shearwaters—the largest colony in the world.

# Earthwatch

680 Mount Auburn Street
PO Box 403N
Watertown, MA 02272
(800) 776-0188
Internet: info@earthwatch.org

*Project location*: Worldwide.

*Project type*: One hundred and fifty-five research expeditions in twenty-four fields of study, including art and archaeology, public health, marine mammology, ornithology, wildlife management, and ecology.

*Project costs*: Contributions, which are generally tax deductible, range from $700 to $2,400 for the average two-week project. These fees support the research and cover food and lodging expenses. Transportation to and from site is additional but is also generally tax deductible.

*Project dates*: Year-round; teams work from ten days to three weeks.

*How to apply*: Call, write, or E-mail for information.

*Work done by volunteers*: Varies according to project. Activities include photographing, excavating, interviewing, monitoring, mapping, and more.

*Special skills or requirements*: Most expeditions require no special skills, only a willingness to work and learn. When special skills are needed (for example, scuba or photography), they are noted in the organization magazine and expedition briefing. Volunteers who have special skills, such as surveying, birding experience, and nursing training, are always welcome.

*Commentary*: Earthwatch is a nonprofit membership organization with over sixty-five thousand members worldwide. Membership is $25 per year. Members receive a bimonthly magazine that includes in-depth articles on leading science issues of the day as well as descriptions of current Earthwatch projects that members can join. Founded in 1972, Earthwatch offers the public unique opportunities to work side by side with renowned scientists and scholars on a wide range of field research projects. Earthwatch receives more than one thousand proposals each year from researchers in need of funds and assistance. In 1994, 165 projects were selected for support; 4,000 people of all ages and backgrounds participated in these expeditions.

*Sample projects:* Recently, Earchwatch volunteers examined the effects of rain forest destruction in Los Tuxtlas Biological Preserve, Vera Cruz, Mexico, and looked for fossil evidence of what killed the dinosaurs in Montana. Other previous volunteers measured, tagged, and examined leatherback turtles in the U.S. Virgin Islands and rescued thousands of turtle eggs from erosion. Still other volunteers worked with the one hundred-plus resident dolphins in Sarasota Bay, Florida, netting, marking, and noting dolphins for age, sex, paternity, and social interaction.

# Eco-Escuela de Español

Conservation International
1015 18th Street NW, Suite 1000
Washington, DC 20036
(202) 973-2264; Fax (202) 887-5188
E-mail: m.sister@conservation.org

*Project location*: Guatemala.

*Project type*: Spanish language instruction, environmental education, and community development work.

*Project costs*: $110 per week, including room and board.

*Project dates*: Year-round. Classes begin each Monday.

*How to apply*: Write or call the office above for more information.

*Work done by volunteers*: Volunteers combine intensive language instruction with work in conservation and community development projects.

*Special skills or requirements*: None but an interest in learning Spanish and the culture of Guatemala.

# Ecumenical Work Camps

Australian Council of Churches
PO Box C199, Clarence Street Post Office
Sydney 2000 Australia

*Project location*: Central Australia and New South Wales.

*Project type*: Work camps.

*Project costs*: About $100 for two weeks.

*Project dates*: Late December and early January each year.

*How to apply*: Write to the above address for more information.

*Work done by volunteers*: Construction and maintenance work. Training and tools are provided.

*Special skills or requirements*: No special experience, but volunteers must have the ability to work hard under supervision.

# Ein Gedi Archaeological Expedition

26 HaPardess HaRishon Street
Rishon Le Zion 75209 Israel
Fax (3) 9501667

*Project location*: On the western shores of the Dead Sea.

*Project type*: Archaeological excavation.

*Project costs*: Between $200 and $375 per five-day week, including room and board.

*Project dates*: The season lasts for six weeks from late December to the end of January, and volunteers must commit to at least one week. Two weeks are recommended.

*How to apply*: Write to the above address for a current brochure and application.

*Work done by volunteers*: Standard excavation work in excellent conditions on an archaeology site. Winter months are pleasant near the Dead Sea, and the site is at an oasis.

# Enfants et Amis de Beauchastel

Rue de la Breche
07800 Beauchastel, France
(75) 62-05-42

*Project location*: Medieval village of Beauchastel, France.

*Project type*: Masonry and restoration work to rebuild the old village.

*Project costs*: Approximately $70.

*Project dates*: The first two weeks of August.

*How to apply*: Write to Marie-Jeanne Grandclere at the above address for information.

*Work done by volunteers*: Masonry, carpentry, roof repair, and pavement building.

*Special skills or requirements*: Must speak at least a bit of French and be at least 18 years old.

*Commentary*: This association is devoted to restoring the medieval village of Beauchastel, which has deteriorated over time.

*Sample projects*: Previous volunteers have built an open-air theater, a museum of local culture, a rural cottage, and a path by the river.

# Europe Conservation Italy
Via Giusti 5
20154 Milano Italy
2-33-103344; Fax 2-33-104068

*Project location*: Waters of Lussino, Italy.

*Project type*: Dolphin research.

*Project costs*: L 650,000 to L 800,000, plus about L 13,000 per day for housekeeping and food.

*Project dates*: Ten-day projects from April through October.

*How to apply*: Write or call the office above for application forms.

*Work done by volunteers*: Help scientists on an inflatable craft and at the base collect and catalog information.

*Special skills or requirements*: Ability to swim and an interest in dolphins.

# Farm Hands–City Hands

Green Chimneys, Putnam Lake Road
Brewster, NY 10509
(914) 279-2995, ext. 202

*Project location*: A large number of farms in the Northeast.

*Project type*: Farm work.

*Project costs*: Vary with each project.

*Project dates*: "Farm Days" are held throughout the year, and placements for extended stays are based on applicants' and farmers' needs.

*How to apply*: Send a self-addressed, stamped envelope to the above address.

*Work done by volunteers*: Everything from making maple syrup and planting flowers to making wine and cheese.

*Special skills or requirements*: Most special skills are taught by the farmers, but you need to be in excellent health and able and willing to work long, hard days.

*Commentary*: This program was created to involve and educate city dwellers about farms and farmers. Most of the placements are on farms that operate for profit, although most of these are small and specialized. Many volunteers who are interested in organic farms and produce are placed on such farms. One nonprofit farm that accepts volunteers is the Green Chimney Farm School, a private residential school that focuses on farming.

# Fellowship of Reconciliation Task Force on Latin America and the Caribbean

995 Market Street, Suite 801
San Francisco, CA 94103
(415) 495-6334

*Project location*: Latin America.

*Project type*: Volunteers work with grassroots peace and justice groups in Central American and South American countries.

*Project costs*: Costs vary depending on destination. Volunteers pay travel fees and living costs.

*Project dates*: One group per summer; volunteer placements are scheduled separately.

*How to apply*: Request an application from the office listed above for a specific program or country of interest.

*Work done by volunteers*: Volunteer placements vary; the work includes translation work with children and computer aid.

*Special skills or requirements*: Commitment to nonviolence and doing follow-up work. Some placements require other skills; all require Spanish language.

# Ffestiniog Railway Company

Harbour Station
Porthmadog, Gwynedd LL49 9NF United Kingdom
(01766) 512 340

*Project location*: The mountains of Snowdonia in Wales.

*Project type*: Wide variety of work projects on a working steam railway.

*Project costs*: Volunteers are responsible for transportation to the project, room, and board. There are several self-catering hostels nearby with reasonable accommodations.

*Project dates*: Year-round.

*How to apply*: Write to the Volunteer Resource Manager at the above address for an application and a brochure listing the types of volunteer opportunities available.

*Work done by volunteers*: Every aspect of railroading is open for volunteers, although some positions, such as locomotive operator, require that the volunteer spend considerable time gaining experience.

*Special skills or requirements*: Previous experience working on a railroad is always desirable, but a willingness to learn is all that is required.

*Commentary*: The history of the Ffestiniog Railway goes back to 1836. The railroad reached its peak in the last decades of the nineteenth century and faced a general decline until its closing in 1946. In the early fifties, a group led by Alan Pegler reopened the line as a nonprofit organization operated with the assistance of a voluntary society. Part of the line reopened in 1955, with other parts opening periodically until the line was completed in 1982. Today it is the busiest independent railway in Britain. It is also run by the oldest railway company in the world; it was originally incorporated in 1836 by an Act of Parliament and requires a new act to abandon the railway. Since such an act was never passed, the original company still exists. Some of the steam locomotives and coaches currently in use are more than one hundred years old.

# Flemish Youth Federation for the Study and Conservation of Nature
Bervoetstraat 33
Antwerpen B-2000 Belgium
(3) 231-26-04; Fax (3) 233-64-99

*Project location*: Belgium and Holland.

*Project type*: Nature study and conservation.

*Project costs*: $100 to $200 per camp.

*Project dates*: Mostly in July and August for one or two weeks.

*How to apply*: Write to the above address for information and an application, or contact one of the work camp organizations in the U.S., such as Volunteers for Peace, Incorporated (see Index).

*Work done by volunteers*: General physical labor connected with conservation efforts.

*Special skills or requirements*: Participants must be between the ages of 14 and 25 and interested in conservation work.

# Florida Department of Natural Resources

Division of Recreation and Parks
3900 Commonwealth Boulevard
Tallahassee, FL 32399
(904) 488-8243

*Project location*: State parks throughout Florida.

*Project type*: Campground hosts and general volunteer duties.

*Project costs*: None.

*Project dates*: Vary.

*How to apply*: Contact the above address for names of individual parks and park managers, and apply directly to the park managers.

*Work done by volunteers*: The primary work is as a campground host, assisting campers in park campgrounds, monitoring activities in the campground, and helping to maintain campground facilities.

*Special skills or requirements*: Clean appearance and the ability to work with people.

*Commentary*: Campground hosts volunteer for six to twelve weeks, and volunteers must be available in the campground for three hours each day and four nights each week.

# Florida Trail Association

PO Box 13708
Gainesville, FL 32604
(352) 378-8823 or (800) 343-1882; Fax (352) 378-4550

*Project location*: Throughout Florida.

*Project type*: Trail maintenance, development, and footbridge building.

*Project costs*: Minimal, mainly travel to work sites.

*Project dates*: Year-round.

*How to apply*: Membership in FTA ensures notification of work schedule.

*Work done by volunteers*: Trail-building and maintenance activities.

*Special skills or requirements*: None, but volunteers should be in good physical shape and willing to do manual labor.

*Commentary*: Most participants are FTA members, and membership is open to anyone.

Florida Trail Association members mark trail blazes along a Florida trail. Photo courtesy of the Florida Trail Association.

# Focus, Incorporated

Department of Ophthalmology
Loyola University Medical Center
2160 S. 1st Avenue
Maywood, IL 60153
(708) 216-9598; Fax (708) 216-3557

*Project location*: Nigeria.

*Project type*: Ophthalmology, medical and surgical.

*Project costs*: Volunteers responsible for all transportation to Lagos (about $1,800). Room and board are furnished at the site.

*Project dates*: Year-round, for three to four weeks.

*How to apply*: Write to the above address for an application and information.

*Work done by volunteers*: Eye surgery.

*Special skills or requirements*: Must be certified ophthalmologists.

*Commentary*: Most assignments are staffing a clinic in Abak, Cross River State, Nigeria.

# Food First

Institute for Food and Development Policy
398 60th Street
Oakland, CA 94618
(510) 654-4400

*Project location*: At the home office in San Francisco.

*Project type*: Varies.

*Project costs*: Volunteers are responsible for their travel and living costs.

*Project dates*: Year-round, for varying lengths of time.

*How to apply*: Contact Marilyn Borchardt at the office listed above.

*Work done by volunteers*: Volunteers update Food First publications, enter information into the data base, organize the Environmental Film Festival, and perform clerical work in various departments. Specific volunteer openings are always changing.

*Special skills or requirements*: Volunteers should be responsible, self-motivated, organized, and independent. Computer skills are desirable.

*Commentary*: Food First promotes Third World development that is participatory, equitable, and sustainable.

# Foundation for International Education

121 Cascade Court
River Falls, WI 54022
(715) 425-1774; Fax (715) 425-5101

*Project location*: Worldwide, but mostly in English-speaking countries.

*Project type*: Working as an elementary or secondary teacher or social service worker, alongside a counterpart.

*Project costs*: $495, plus accommodations and travel expenses.

*Project dates*: Mostly during summer months but occasionally during the winter, for three weeks.

*How to apply*: Write to Dr. Ross Korsgaard at the above address for more information.

*Work done by volunteers*: Assist counterparts with their usual duties.

*Special skills or requirements*: Should be an experienced, credentialed teacher or social service worker.

*Commentary*: Accommodations are generally quite inexpensive, as volunteers normally stay in the homes of counterparts. Retired persons are welcome to participate. Graduate credit is available.

*Sample projects*: Volunteers have served in England, Scotland, Ireland, New Zealand, India, and Australia since this program was begun in 1972.

# Four Corners School of Outdoor Education

PO Box 1029
Monticello, UT 84535
(800) 525-4456 or (801) 587-2156; Fax (801) 587-2193
E-mail: fcs@igc.apc.org

*Project location*: Arizona, Colorado, New Mexico, and Utah.

*Project type*: Educational and research programs on the natural and human history of the Colorado plateau region.

*Project costs*: Projects vary from $525 to $1,795.

*Project dates*: Between January and November.

*How to apply*: Write to the above address for a brochure and an application.

*Work done by volunteers*: Archaeological documentation, surveying, digging, and endangered species documentation.

*Special skills or requirements*: No special skills, just an interest in the subject matter.

*Commentary*: This program has many educational classes that involve volunteers in a number of archaeology and natural history projects. Volunteers are expected to contribute to research costs, which may be tax deductible. College credit is also available.

*Sample projects*: In the past years, projects have included an archaeological documentation project of Anasazi rock art along the shores of Lake Powell; archaeological excavations near Dolores, Colorado; and an ongoing peregrine falcon survey of river canyons.

# Friends of the Cumbres and Toltec Scenic Railroad

5732 Osuna Road NE
Albuquerque, NM 87109
(505) 880-1311; Fax (505) 881-2444
Web site:
http://ourworld.compuserve.com/homepages/drichter/focts.htm

*Project location*: Southern Colorado and northern New Mexico.

*Project type*: Projects include stabilization, preservation, and restoration of freight cars, work cars, and bunk cars.

*Project costs*: Volunteers are responsible for room and board while they are on site.

*Project dates*: Between early summer and late fall.

*How to apply*: All volunteers must be members of Friends, and members are notified of work sessions through their newsletter. To become a member, send for an information packet at the above address.

*Work done by volunteers*: Maintenance of the railway and trains.

*Special skills or requirements*: General maintenance and mechanical skills are always welcome, but the desire to work on a steam railroad is all you need. Volunteers should be in reasonably good health and able to work at high altitudes.

*Commentary*: This railroad is owned jointly by the states of New Mexico and Colorado and operated for them by Kyle Railways of San Francisco. The railway and its depots are registered national historic sites.

# Frontier
Society for Environmental Exploration
Studio 210
Thames House
566 Cable Street
London E1 9HB United Kingdom
(0171) 790-4424

*Project location*: Tanzania and Uganda, and potentially Argentina, Burkina Faso, and Vietnam.

*Project type*: Biological inventory and survey of natural habitats. Development of sustainable use of natural habitats.

*Project costs*: About $5,000 for ten weeks.

*Project dates*: Four projects yearly.

*How to apply*: Send a stamped, self-addressed envelope to the above address.

*Work done by volunteers*: Science data collection and construction plus all the day-to-day field camp maintenance activities.

*Special skills or requirements*: English-speaking volunteers between 17 and 30 years old with good attitudes are given priority, but science, construction, engineering, geographic map reading, and other outdoor and survival and/or first aid skills are also useful.

*Commentary*: All projects are developed and operated in conjunction with a parallel research institution, government department, or university in the host country.

# Frontiers Foundation—Operation Beaver

2615 Danforth Avenue, Suite 203
Toronto, Ontario M4C 1L6 Canada
(416) 690-3930; Fax (416) 690-3934

*Project location*: Northwest Territories, Quebec, Alberta, and Ontario.

*Project type*: In Canada most projects have been either building or renovating homes and community centers, although recently there have been some projects in cold-weather agriculture. These all involve joint community and volunteer efforts. Volunteers are also used in the national and regional offices. There are some short-term overseas positions when one of the overseas projects has special needs that aren't available locally, such as graphics, medical, or engineering skills.

*Project costs*: Varies by project.

*Project dates*: Recreation and building projects continue year-round with three-month minimum commitments. The project length varies according to the needs of both the foundation and the volunteer.

*How to apply*: Write to the above address for an information brochure and an application.

*Work done by volunteers*: A wide variety of construction and recreation work, plus some office and clerical tasks.

*Special skills or requirements*: Willingness to work hard in a cross-cultural setting. It helps to have previous construction experience, but it isn't required.

*Commentary*: Operation Beaver was begun in 1964 as an ecumenical work camp by the Canadian Council of Churches, and the Frontiers Foundation assumed responsibility for the program in 1968. In its first 29 years, 2,687 volunteers from 70 countries and 17 North American Indian Nations helped build or renovate over 1,748 homes, 30 community training centers, 3 greenhouses, and a cold-climate agriculture station.

# Fudan Museum Foundation

1522 Schoolhouse Road
Amber, PA 19002
Tel/Fax (215) 699-6448

*Project location*: Xian (Shaanxi), China.

*Project type*: Archaeology fieldwork.

*Project costs*: $4,100.

*Project dates*: Generally six weeks in July and August.

*How to apply*: Send a letter of interest to Dr. Alfonz Lengyel at above address.

*Work done by volunteers*: Excavation work connected with archaeology classes.

*Special skills or requirements*: All workers must sign up for a course in fieldwork (either credit or noncredit). Those who have not registered for a course can only observe.

*Commentary*: The program is accredited by the Shaanxi Province Education Commission (Department of Education) in Xian, China. It is cosponsored by Xian Tiastong University and the Archaeological Institute of Shaanxi Province of China.

# Genesis II Cloudforest Preserve

Apartado 655
Cartago 7.050 Costa Rica

*Project location*: Talamanca Mountains of central Costa Rica.

*Project type*: Trail construction and maintenance, reforestation project management, and cataloging of flora and fauna.

*Project costs*: $150 per week, plus transportation to and from the site.

*Project dates*: Month-long projects, year-round.

*How to apply*: Write to the above address.

*Work done by volunteers*: In addition to trail and reforestation work, projects include T-shirt design, landscaping, pictorial property mapping, cookbook design and scribing, water tank construction, and nursery construction. Projects may also include light housework and gardening.

*Special skills or requirements*: Participants must be at least 21 years old, and a strong environmental and/or conservation background is preferred.

*Commentary*: Genesis II is a private reserve owned and operated by two Canadians. It is a preserve for the endangered resplendent quetzal and has a unique reforestation project in operation.

# Global Children's Organization
1541 S. Beretania Street
Honolulu, HI 96826
(808) 538-1910; Fax (808) 545-2823

*Project location*: An island in the Adriatic near Dubrovnik.

*Project type*: Summer camp counselors.

*Project costs*: Must provide transportation to Croatia and sponsor at least two children at $480 per child.

*Project dates*: During July and August for three weeks.

*How to apply*: Write or call the office listed above for more information.

*Work done by volunteers*: Work as summer camp counselors for refugee children from Bosnia and Croatia.

*Special skills or requirements*: An interest in children and empathy with displaced children from a war zone.

*Commentary*: This group needs sponsors and counselors for more than three hundred youth each summer.

## Citizens Network

nglehart Avenue
Ju. raul, MN 55104
(612) 644-0960 or (800) 644-9292; Fax (612) 644-0960
E-mail: gcn@mtn.org

*Project location*: Belize, Guatemala, Kenya, the Yucatan, and New Mexico.

*Project type*: Community development and cultural immersion programs.

*Project costs*: Between $400 and $1,300, plus transportation to the site. Most trip-related expenses are tax deductible. Limited partial scholarships are available.

*Project dates*: Year-round for one, two, or three weeks.

*How to apply*: Contact the office listed above for more information and a current project schedule.

*Work done by volunteers*: Participants live with local families while working on community development projects, such as building health clinics, installing potable water systems, and developing materials for day-care centers.

Global Citizens Network volunteers work alongside local workers on a community project. Photo courtesy of Global Citizens Network.

*Special skills or requirements*: Volunteers only need a willingness to experience and accept a new culture.

*Commentary*: This organization was formed in 1992 and its philosophy is, "The peoples of the world are the one people, enriched by individual differences, united by the common bond of humanity. The diversity of the Global Community is its greatest gift."

# Global Routes

5554 Broadway
Oakland, CA 94618
(510) 665-0321

*Project location*: Ecuador, Kenya, and Thailand.

*Project type*: Teaching and sports instruction.

*Project costs*: $3,200 to $3,400.

*Project dates*: Summer months.

*How to apply*: Contact the office listed above for more information.

*Work done by volunteers*: Teach, coach sports, and design and execute a small development project.

*Special skills or requirements*: Teaching, coaching, or construction experience helpful. The Ecuador program requires the ability to speak Spanish.

# 🌍 Global Service Corps

300 Broadway, Suite 28
San Francisco, CA 94133-3312
(415) 788-3666, ext. 128; Fax (415) 788-7324
E-mail: gsc@igc.apc.org
Web site: http://www.earthisland.org/ei/gsc/gschome.html

*Project location*: Costa Rica, Kenya, Guatemala, and Thailand.

*Project type*: Short- and long-term service projects that actively contribute to sustainable international development and provide participants with a broader global perspective.

*Project costs*: Short-term projects are between $1,400 and $1,700, plus airfare. A portion of the cost goes to the ongoing support of these projects in the form of small grants. Long-term costs include a $500 placement charge and a monthly fee of $250 to $400. All costs associated with the projects, inlcuding airfare, are normally tax deductible.

*Project dates*: Two- and three-week projects and long-term placements available year-round.

*How to apply*: Contact the above office for an application and more information.

*Work done by volunteers*: Assisting communities involved in becoming both self-sustainable and ecologically sound in rain forest regions of Costa Rica; initiating garden plots or training community members in preventative health care in Kenya; providing community service work and English language instruction in Thailand; training community members in sustainable agriculture in Guatemala.

*Special skills or requirements*: The desire and flexibility to live and work in a developing country, plus good health. Participants will be given in-country orientation and training specific to each project.

*Commentary*: Global Service Corps is a project of the Earth Island Institute, an umbrella organization that works to develop projects for the conservation, preservation, and restoration of the global environment. Global Service Corps is committed to fostering global awareness by providing volunteers with international grassroots exposure to global issues, particularly sustainable development activities. Volunteers are welcome at both the project sites and the home office to assist in GSC's international and environmental goals.

# 🌐 Global Volunteers

375 E. Little Canada Road
St. Paul, MN 55117
(612) 482-1074 or (800) 487-1074

*Project location*: Costa Rica, China, Italy, Greece, Turkey, Ecuador, Indonesia, Jamaica, Mexico, Poland, Russia, Spain, Tanzania, Vietnam, the Mississippi Delta, and along the Rio Grande in Texas.

*Project type*: Business consulting, construction, painting, planting, public health, home repair and building, and teaching.

*Project costs*: Vary from $350 to $2,150, plus airfare. All costs are tax deductible.

*Project dates*: There are more than one hundred one-, two-, and three-week projects year-round.

*How to apply*: Contact the above office for an application.

*Work done by volunteers*: Tutoring local schoolchildren, teaching conversational English, painting and constructing homes and public buildings, dentistry, nursing, or laying pipe for water systems—all in cooperation with local villagers.

*Special skills or requirements*: No special work skills required, but a willingness to share, learn, and work alongside others is expected.

*Commentary*: Volunteers from all ages, professions, and backgrounds join together in teams on these projects to live in rural villages or in communities in emerging democracies by invitation to help raise the standard of living. Predeparture orientation materials are provided by Global Volunteers.

# Great Georges Project
(The Blackie) Great George Street
Liverpool L1 5EW United Kingdom
(0151) 709-5109; Fax (0151) 709-4822

*Project location*: Liverpool, England.

*Project type*: Art activities.

*Project costs*: £17.50 per week.

*Project dates*: Year-round, one-month minimum commitment.

*How to apply*: Contact the office listed above for information.

*Work done by volunteers*: Volunteers work in the community in cooking, office administration, working with young people, and arts activities.

*Special skills or requirements*: Interest in the arts and young people, and providing art activities to the public.

# Great Western Society Limited
Didcot Railway Centre
Didcot, Oxfordshire OX11 7NJ United Kingdom
(01235) 817 200

*Project location*: Didcot, England.

*Project type*: Railway restoration and maintenance.

*Project costs*: Approximately £5 per day for food.

*Project dates*: The first week of August each year. Other times are available by appointment.

*How to apply*: Write to the above address for an application and more information.

*Work done by volunteers*: Restoration and maintenance work on locomotives and all other aspects of a railway museum.

*Special skills or requirements*: None but the willingness to work.

*Commentary*: All of the work on projects of the Didcot Restoration and Preservation Committee of the Great Western Society is done by volunteers. Accommodations on-site are limited, but local hotel guest houses can be provided. Volunteers are required to become members to cover their insurance while working.

# Greenpeace, U.S.A.

1436 U Street NW
Washington, DC 20009
(202) 462-1177

*Project location*: Home office in Washington, DC.

*Project type*: Light clerical work.

*Project costs*: Volunteers pay all transportation and living costs.

*Project dates*: Year-round.

*How to apply*: Write to the above address for information.

*Work done by volunteers*: Light clerical work, such as stuffing envelopes, copying, and answering and posting mail.

*Special skills or requirements*: Commitment to the Greenpeace cause.

*Commentary*: While the excitement and headlines about the Greenpeace movement come out of the confrontations the organization has with their targeted opponents, nothing could take place without the volunteers who help raise money and get the word out on what Greenpeace is doing.

# ᵒuth Activities Service

ddesi, 44/6
‿₄₂0 Kizilay, Ankara, Turkey
312-433-22-00 or 312-433-46-21; Fax 312-433-22-27

*Project location*: Aliaga, Avanos, Bornova, Foga, Gozne, Marvaris, Mugla, Silifke, Silivri, and Urla.

*Project type*: Laying out parks and gardens, and environmental arrangements and restoration.

*Project costs*: A registration fee of $150 covers food, accommodations, and excursions during the camp period.

*Project dates*: During July and August, for two weeks.

*How to apply*: Send a letter with a photo and résumé to the above address, and include an international postal reply coupon. Applications must be submitted by the end of May.

*Work done by volunteers*: All volunteers share in the labor on the project, which lasts five hours a day, and participate in the normal life of the town where they live.

*Special skills or requirements*: Applicants should be between 18 and 26 years old and speak English. No other special skill is needed.

*Commentary*: GSM is a nongovernmental youth organization in service since 1985.

# Gurukula Botanical Sanctuary
Alattil PO
North Wynad, Kerala 67044 India

*Project location*: The western Ghat Mountains of India in the rainforest belt.

*Project type*: Conservation, horticulture, research in native plant species, reforestation, sustainable agriculture, and education.

*Project costs*: $10 per day.

*Project dates*: Open throughout the year, but prefer volunteers between October and April, depending upon ongoing projects. Volunteers determine their length of stay.

*How to apply*: Send a letter of personal interests to above address for further information and an application.

*Work done by volunteers*: Various maintenance duties, kitchen and garden chores, and building tasks.

*Special skills or requirements*: Volunteers should be in good health and cooperative. Willingness to learn is crucial, and an appreciation of local cutlure is necessary for a mutually beneficial interaction.

*Commentary*: The Sanctuary welcomes individuals who are concerned with nature conservation. It is possible to work on research projects in rainforest ecology, horticulture, and plant and animal biology. The sanctuary borders a large tract of rainforest, and it is possible to explore the valleys and ridges in the vicinity. The people who work here are almost all local, and the contribution from visitors and volunteers goes toward supporting the work of the sanctuary. This is not a place for general tourists, but individuals concerned with issues regarding the sanctuary are welcome.

# Habitat for Humanity
Habitat and Church Streets
Americus, GA 31709
(912) 924-6935

*Project location*: Throughout the U.S. and in thirty countries around the world.

*Project type*: House building projects.

*Project costs*: Volunteers are responsible for all transportation, room, board, and insurance costs. On overseas work camps, all participants must contribute an amount equal to the cost of one new house, which averages between $1,000 and $3,000. For a group of ten volunteers, that means a cost of $100 to $300 for each participant. In the U.S., work camp costs per participant vary.

*Project dates*: U.S. projects generally run one to two weeks during the summer, and overseas projects run year-round for about two weeks.

*How to apply*: For an application and information packet describing current projects, call or write to the Global Village Work Team Coordinator at the above address.

*Work done by volunteers*: General construction.

*Special skills or requirements*: At least one member of each overseas group should speak the language of the host country, and all participants should be at least 18 years old.

*Commentary*: Habitat is an ecumenical Christian housing ministry that helps build bridges between people as they help those in need build their own houses through "sweat equity."

# 🌐 Health Volunteers Overseas

c/o Washington Station
PO Box 65157
Washington, DC 20035-5157
(202) 296-0928; Fax (202) 296-8018
E-mail: hvo@aol.com

*Project location*: Africa, Asia, the Caribbean, Central America, and South America.

*Project type*: Anesthesia, dentistry, nurse anesthesia, internal medicine, oral surgery, orthopedics, pediatrics, and physical therapy.

*Project costs*: Average expenses for a one-month assignment are $2,500 for transportation, housing, and living costs.

*Project dates*: Year-round, usually for one month.

*How to apply*: Contact Kate Skillman, Program Coordinator, at the office listed above for more information and a membership application.

*Work done by volunteers*: Provide medical training and education to medical personnel in developing countries.

*Special skills or requirements*: All volunteers must have medical training.

*Commentary*: HVO is a private nonprofit organization committed to improving health care in developing countries through training and education. HVO currently solicits trained medical volunteers to participate in programs in the following specialties: anesthesia, dentistry, general surgery, internal medicine, oral and maxillofacial surgery, orthopedics, pediatrics, and physical therapy.

# Heifer Project International

International Livestock Center
Route 2
Perryville, AR 72126
(501) 889-5124

*Project location*: Most volunteer positions are at the International Livestock Center forty miles west of Little Rock, Arkansas. There are a few positions in project areas around the world and at the regional offices of Heifer Project International.

*Project type*: Both individual volunteers and work camp participants do general ranch work. Some office work is available occasionally for those who can't do the more strenuous ranch work.

*Project costs*: No registration fee, except for work camps, which have a $500 fee per group. Individual volunteers who stay for a month or longer receive a small stipend twice a month. Room and board are provided. Volunteers are responsible for preparing their own breakfasts, suppers, and weekend meals, while noon meals are prepared for the whole group. Completely furnished volunteer housing is available. Work camp volunteers live together in an open-air bunk barn with foam mattresses on wood platforms.

*Project dates*: Work camps last one week during the summer months. Other volunteers have no standard length of stay, although most stay six to eight weeks. Summer staffing for work camp groups is done with volunteers from late May to late August.

*How to apply*: Write to the Volunteer Coordinator at the above address for a brochure and an application. Specify whether you are interested as an individual or wish to organize a work camp group.

*Work done by volunteers*: General ranch work. Work camp groups may spend all week on one project or may do a variety of jobs. Other volunteers are given some choice of work according to the needs of the ranch.

*Special skills or requirements*: No ranch or farming skills are necessary, although they are helpful for volunteers who want to work as staff for the work camps. Work camp volunteers should be in ninth grade or above for youth camps, and 19 years old or above for adult camps. The minimum age is 18 for general volunteers.

*Commentary:* Heifer Project International works around the world on projects that help low-income farmers from impoverished areas develop livestock herds, including cattle, donkeys, sheep, goats, pigs, ducks, rabbits, chickens, and honeybees by supplying breeding stock and technical know-how. The International Livestock Center is a 1,225-acre ranch where much of this livestock is held for shipping. There is also a commercial livestock operation at the ranch that helps support the interdenominational activities of HPI. Much of the money raised each year for the support of HPI comes from thousands of Sunday school classes across the U.S. where young people donate nickels, dimes, and quarters for projects.

# Heritage Trails Fund

5301 Pine Hollow Road
Concord, CA 95421
(510) 672-5072; Fax (510) 943-7431

*Project location*: Northern California.

*Project type*: Trail building and maintenance.

*Project costs*: Transportation to and from work sites.

*Project dates*: Various times during the year, mostly for weekend work crews.

*How to apply*: Write to the above address for a schedule of current work projects.

*Work done by volunteers*: Trail maintenance and building.

*Special skills or requirements*: Volunteers should have an interest in trails and be in good physical condition.

*Commentary*: Heritage Trails works on a variety of trails in northern California, with particular emphasis on those in the San Francisco Bay area.

# Heron Island Research Station

Great Barrier Reef
Via Gladstone
Queensland 4680 Australia
(079) 781-399

*Project location*: Heron Island, Great Barrier Reef.

*Project type*: Marine science and environmental research.

*Project costs*: Participants are responsible for their transportation to the project site and for their food.

*Project dates*: Year-round.

*How to apply*: Send a letter to the above address.

*Work done by volunteers*: There is no set pattern to the projects; they may include clerical or computer work, station beautification, or scientific research, such as monitoring effects of coral bleaching. All volunteers work four hours per day on the projects.

*Special skills or requirements*: Background in marine science is useful but not mandatory.

*Commentary*: Heron Island Research Station is one of the principal coral reef research centers in the world and plays an important role in the tropical marine sciences.

*Sample projects*: Helping out in the station library, appending environmental data on the computer, assisting with environmental monitoring, monitoring the annual coral spawning event, and island cleanup and recycling projects are all examples of work that has been done by previous volunteers.

# Human Service Alliance

3983 Old Greensboro Road
Winston-Salem, NC 27101
(910) 761-8745; Fax (910) 722-7822

*Project location*: Winston-Salem, North Carolina.

*Project type*: Direct care of individuals with terminal illnesses, dispute resolution, respite care for families with a developmentally disabled child, and work with individuals who are experiencing chronic pain. In addition to providing valuable service to others, there are many opportunities for learning hands-on skills.

*Project costs*: Volunteers who commit to a specific period of time of service receive room and board at no charge. Volunteers are responsible for their travel expenses and spending money.

*Project dates*: Year-round.

*How to apply*: Send a letter describing your background to the above address.

*Work done by volunteers*: Every aspect of the center's operation is staffed by volunteers, and everyone contributes in a number of ways. In addition to direct care of clients, there are opportunities for gardening, grounds maintenance, carpentry, general upkeep of the facilities, cooking, housekeeping, and answering the telephone.

*Special skills or requirements*: No prior special training is needed; any training required will be provided.

*Commentary*: Based on the idea that ordinary human beings can do extraordinary things when they work together as a group in service of others, HSA is a nonprofit organization comprised completely of volunteers providing all services at no charge. Approximately 250 people from every walk of life volunteer at the center. Many come from across the U.S. and around the world.

# Illinois Department of Conservation
524 S. 2nd Street, Room 400
Springfield, IL 62701-1787
(217) 785-9416

*Project location*: Throughout the state in parks, conservation areas, forests, and recreational areas.

*Project type*: Volunteers serve as campground hosts, park interpreters and park technicians, and assist the department field biologists in the departments of wildlife, forestry, national heritage sites, and fisheries.

*Project costs*: Volunteers are responsible for all travel and living expenses.

*Project dates*: Year-round, for varying lengths of time.

*How to apply*: Write to the Illinois Department of Conservation Land Management at the above address for information and an application.

*Work done by volunteers*: Campground hosts serve at a state park campground for a minimum of four weeks, working approximately thirty-five hours per week, helping other campers check in and providing them with information about the park. Park interpreters lead educational programs, workshops, hikes, and other activities that enhance visitors' experiences at the parks. They also conduct some research on the natural vegetation, wildlife, and geology. Park technicians help with the maintenance of the parks, including construction, renovation, and general maintenance.

*Special skills or requirements*: An interest in parks, a willingness to learn on the job, and the ability to follow through are all necessary skills. Campground hosts must be 21 or older.

# Indiana Division of State Parks

402 W. Washington Street, Room W298
Indianapolis, IN 46204
(317) 232-4124

*Project location*: State parks throughout Indiana.

*Project type*: Landscaping and grounds and trail maintenance.

*Project costs*: Participants pay camping and entrance fees to the parks.

*Project dates*: Year-round.

*How to apply*: Contact the office listed above for a list of parks currently requesting volunteers, and contact the parks directly.

*Work done by volunteers*: Maintenance, gardening, hosting the campground, and working in nature centers.

*Special skills or requirements*: Projects are based on the skills of the volunteers, and volunteers are selected for projects by park managers.

*Commentary*: Projects will be developed according to the length of stay. Camping in parks is limited to fourteen days, and projects as short as two days can be arranged.

# Insight Nepal

PO Box 6760
Kathmandu, Nepal
(1) 418 964; Fax (1) 416 144

*Project location*: Kathmandu and Pokhara.

*Project type*: Language and cross-cultural experiences through various activities.

*Project costs*: $20 application and $600 program fee.

*Project dates*: For three to four weeks in February, April, and August.

*How to apply*: Send for an application form.

*Work done by volunteers*: Participants will teach English or other subjects at primary to high school levels. Placements can be arranged for those who wish to work in community development.

*Special skills or requirements*: Volunteers should be flexible, physically fit, and willing to immerse themselves in another culture.

An Insight Nepal volunteer learns to make a Nepali dish during her homestay with a local family. Photo courtesy of Insight Nepal.

# Institute for Central American Development Studies

Apartado 3 (2070) Sabanilla
San Jose, Costa Rica
(506) 225-0508; Fax (506) 234-1337
or
Department 826
PO Box 025216
Miami, FL 33102-5216
E-mail: icadscr@expresso.co.cr

*Project location*: Throughout Costa Rica and Nicaragua.

*Project type*: Internships in social action projects, plus a Spanish language program.

*Project costs*: $6,500 for a full semester and $4,900 for the summer semester, including full academic credit for those who wish it. Spanish language programs are four weeks long and cost about $1,200.

*Project dates*: Coincide with college semester dates.

*How to apply*: Write to the above address for information.

*Work done by volunteers*: Agricultural, health, journalism, environmental, and women's studies projects are just a few of the intern positions available.

*Special skills or requirements*: Basic communication skills in Spanish.

*Commentary*: ICADS offers about thirty structured internships each year and creates special ones for those who have specific interests or needs. There is a rigorous academic component to the internships in addition to the field practicum.

# International Camp Counselor Program

71 W. 23rd Street, Suite 1904
New York, NY 10010
(212) 727-8800, ext. 119

*Project location*: More than twenty-five countries around the world.

*Project type*: Camp counselors.

*Project costs*: $100 application fee plus all transportation costs. All camps provide room, board, and insurance, and some also provide a small stipend and domestic transportation to the camp. The French camps require a weeklong course at additional cost.

*Project dates*: Between June and August, except for those in the Southern Hemisphere, which are between December and February. Most require volunteers to stay for the season, although some require only a two-week commitment.

*How to apply*: Write to the above address for an application and brochure. The application deadline for Northern Hemisphere camps is January 1; for the Southern Hemisphere, October 1.

*Work done by volunteers*: All positions are for camp counselors, although there is some variety in the types of programs offered by the different camps.

*Special skills or requirements*: Most of the camps have an age requirement of 20 to 30 years old. Some camps don't require volunteers to speak the native language, but the organization says it does help them to understand the culture better. Some camps require language fluency; French and Tunisian camps require that applicants complete the French version of the application. Applicants should also have experience working with youth in programs such as scouts, recreational projects, church activities, and schools.

*Commentary*: This program is operated by the YMCA and is the counterpart of the inbound International Camp Counselor Program that the YMCA has operated since the 1950s, which gives young people from around the world an opportunity to come to the U.S. to work in camp programs. The abroad program began in the mid-sixties so that American youth could have the same opportunity in other countries.

*Sample projects*: Past volunteer positions include a private camp with an emphasis on sports in Colombia, a camp in Hong Kong teaching swimming, singing, handicrafts, and games (this position paid $30 a week), a nonprofit day camp in Nepal, and various locations throughout Hungary.

# International Center for Gibbon Studies

PO Box 800249
Santa Clarita, CA 91380
(805) 296-2737; Fax (805) 296-1237
E-mail: pjdahle@aol.com

*Project location*: Saugus, California, which is approximately an hour north of Los Angeles International Airport.

*Project type*: Captive breeding of several species of rare gibbons and behavioral research.

*Project costs*: Volunteers are responsible for travel and food, and insurance is required. Housing is provided.

*Project dates*: One month minimum, but there is no maximum limit. There is a shortage of volunteers from September through April.

*How to apply*: Request a volunteer application and send a résumé and two letters of recommendation to the above address.

*Work done by volunteers*: Depending on the volunteer's skills, work includes feeding and care of captive gibbons, data entry, light maintenance work, observation, library research, and word processing.

*Special skills or requirements*: A love for animals is required. Word processing, library research, and maintenance skills are preferred. Ova and parasite and stool cultures, CBC and blood panels, and tuberculosis tests are necessary for admission to the facility.

*Commentary*: ICGS is a nonprofit organization and the only facility in the world devoted exclusively to the study, preservation, and propagation of gibbons by establishing secure captive gene pools in case attempts to preserve species or subspecies in the wild fail. It has the second largest collection of gibbons in North America, including six of the nine extant species. The comfort and well-being of these primates is the center's primary concern. They are housed in spacious enclosures, ranging from thirty to sixty feet in length and from twelve to twenty feet in height.

# Internationale Begegnung in Gemeinschaftsdiensten e.V.

Schlosserstrabe 28, 70180
Stuttgart, Germany
0-711-649-11-28; Fax 0-711-640-98-67

*Project location*: Throughout Germany and occasionally in Switzerland and Italy.

*Project type*: Work camps.

*Project costs*: There is a minimal application fee; food and accommodations are provided.

*Project dates*: From late June to late September for two to four weeks

*How to apply*: Write to the above address for current programs and an application form, and include two international reply coupons.

*Work done by volunteers*: Reconstruction, renovation, working with children and handicapped people, and other work depending upon the individual project.

*Special skills or requirements*: Volunteers should be open, tolerant, willing to work, and eager to enjoy an international setting.

# International Exchange Center

2 Republic Square
Riga LV–1010 Latvia
3717-027 216; Fax 3717-830 257
E-mail: iec@iec.vernet.lv

*Project location*: Latvia, Lithuania, Russia, and Ukraine.

*Project type*: Camp counselors in former USSR summer camps.

*Project costs*: Application fee of $50 plus travel and medical insurance.

*Project dates*: June, July, and August for one to three months.

*How to apply*: Send an inquiry to the above address.

*Work done by volunteers*: Supervising and teaching camp activities to local children.

*Special skills or requirements*: Knowledge of local languages, experience in working with children, and a proficiency in camp activities are desired.

*Commentary*: Camps in the region are generally much less structured than in the U.S., and counselors must take more initiative than in similar camps in the U.S. Also, the standard of living in most of the above countries is far below what Americans are used to, so counselors must be prepared for more hardships than what they would find in comparable work settings in the U.S.

# International Families

RR2 Box 81
Lincolnville, ME 04849
(207) 338-5165

*Project location*: Throughout the Russian republic.

*Project type*: Social action.

*Project costs*: 1994 costs were $975 for each participant.

*Project dates*: June or July.

*How to apply*: Write to the above address.

*Work done by volunteers*: Volunteers help in orphanages in whatever ways are needed, including spending time with orphanage children and creating recreational experiences.

*Special skills or requirements*: Two years minimum of college Russian and interest and experience in working with children.

*Commentary*: International Families is a nonprofit service agency formed to help children living in Russian orphanages. It provides professional and staffing assistance to the orphanages; sends material support in the form of needed supplies, clothing, and teaching equipment; and provides adoptive homes with American families for Russian children who are legally available for adoption.

# International Fourth World Movement
7600 Willow Hill Drive
Landover, MD 20785
(301) 336-9489; Fax (301) 336-0092
E-mail: 4thworld@his.com

*Project location*: Work camps in France and internships based in the Washington, DC, area.

*Project type*: Two-week summer work camps and three-month internships for those exploring long-term commitments to fighting poverty.

*Project costs*: Food and travel.

*Project dates*: Internships are held during September and February. Three work camps of two weeks each are held during the summer.

*How to apply*: For more information and an application, send a stamped, self-addressed envelope to the above address. Include a letter with your comments and personal observations about extreme poverty.

*Work done by volunteers*: Interns' work is determined by their skills and the national office's current needs. Volunteers in work camps do manual labor and office work at the movement's centers. They also view videos and participate in discussions about the effects of poverty.

*Special skills or requirements*: A willingness to learn from the poorest families around the world.

*Commentary*: The Fourth World Movement is an international human rights movement working closely with the extremely poor families in the industrialized and developing nations. Practical projects support families' efforts toward independence and provide them with the means of self-representation within their own communities and on a broader political level.

*Sample projects*: Volunteers set up street libraries with books, computers, and art materials. The movement's long-term volunteers seek out the poorest children in urban shelters, welfare hotels, and isolated mountain villages.

# Interplast, Incorporated
300 B Pioneer Way
Mountain View, CA 94041
(415) 962-0123

*Project location*: Bangladesh, Brazil, China, the Dominican Republic, Ecuador, Honduras, Myanmar, Nepal, Nicaragua, Peru, Thailand, Vietnam, Chile, Peru, Mongolia, the Philippines, and El Salvador.

*Project type*: Providing reconstructive surgery in underdeveloped countries.

*Project costs*: Vary by project.

*Project dates*: Year-round, for two weeks.

*How to apply*: Write to the Professional Services Coordinator at the above address for an application and more information.

*Work done by volunteers*: Medical work in reconstructive surgery.

*Special skills or requirements*: All volunteers must be plastic surgeons, anesthesiologists, pediatricians, or registered nurses (operating and recovery room).

*Commentary*: This nonprofit volunteer organization sends medical teams to developing nations to provide free surgeries, primarily for children who have been born with deformities or have been burned or received other crippling injuries, where there are neither the skills nor the funding for this type of care.

# Involvement Volunteers of Australia
PO Box 218
Port Melbourne, Victoria 3207 Australia
Tel/Fax (3) 646-5504

*Project location*: Australia, Bangladesh, California, Estonia, Fiji, Finland, Germany, Greece, Hawaii, India, Italy, New Zealand, Papua New Guinea, and Thailand.

*Project type*: Ecologically sustainable development programs that involve revegetation, planting, and maintenance.

*Project costs*: Involvement Volunteers' 1995 program cost $400 Aus., plus travel to the work sites. Room and board can range from free to $120 Aus. per week, depending on the project.

*Project dates*: Year-round.

*How to apply*: Send for an application, information sheets, and the latest newsletter to the above address; or to Involvement Volunteers of Deutschland, Post Fach 110024, W-3400 Gottingen, Germany. Include return postage or two international postal reply coupons.

*Work done by volunteers*: Generally manual labor, including restoration of historic parks and gardens; national park conservation and maintenance; environment and conservation research; farm and bird observatory operations; and special medical clinics, disaster prevention, and institutes for disadvantaged adults and children.

*Special skills or requirements*: Skills are not necessary but are appreciated and will be directly or indirectly utilized on a project whenever possible. All volunteers must understand spoken English for safety. Involvement Volunteers communicate only in English.

*Commentary*: Involvement Volunteers is set up to enable people to travel and participate in volunteer activities for the benefit of the natural environment and social support of communities. Volunteers may be placed on projects on an individual basis or in groups. The groups have up to twelve volunteers from different countries.

# Israel Antiquities Authority

Rockefeller Museum Building
PO Box 586
Jerusalem 91004 Israel
(2) 560-2607; Fax (2) 560-2628
E-mail: harriet@israntique.org.il

*Project location*: Throughout Israel.

*Project type*: Archaeological excavations.

*Project costs*: Varies by project, but volunteers usually must pay for room and board.

*Project dates*: Mostly for two weeks or more in late spring and summer.

*How to apply*: Send for a booklet of opportunities at above address.

*Work done by volunteers*: Normal excavation work of digging, shoveling, hauling, and cleaning.

*Special skills or requirements*: Good physical condition and ability to work long hours in very hot weather.

# Jewish National Fund—Canadian and American Active Retirees in Israel

JNF Missions
42 E. 69th Street
New York, NY 10021
(212) 879-9300, ext. 283; Fax (212) 517-3293
or
1980 Sherbrooke Street W, Suite 500
Montreal, Quebec H3H 1E8 Canada
(514) 934-0313; Fax (514) 934-0382

*Project location*: Eliat, Galilee, Jerusalem, Tel Aviv, and Nahariya.

*Project type*: Community and forestry work.

*Project costs*: About $4,000, including airfare, three kosher meals per day, hotels, tax and tips, tour guide, insurance, and incidental expenses.

*Project dates*: Late December or early January through late March.

*How to apply*: Call the Canadian or U.S. office for information.

*Work done by volunteers*: Work in schools, retirement homes, nurseries, libraries, hospitals, and JNF forests.

*Special skills or requirements*: None, except good health, an enthusiastic personality, and a willingness to participate in all activities.

*Commentary*: The number of participants in this program more than doubled in the first ten years after its inception. Many participants have returned over and over because of their love for the country. Volunteers get a complete tour of Israel by professional tour guides, work together as a family, attend seminars in archaeology and ecology, and visit museums and cultural events.

# Joint Assistance Centre

PO Box 14481
Santa Rosa, CA 95402-6481
(707) 573-1740; Fax (707) 528-8917
E-mail: jacusa@aol.com

*Project location*: Rural locations around India.

*Project type*: Short-term work camps in community welfare, education, rural health, agriculture, and youth development; long-term projects lasting three months or more working with children and women and in education and community development.

*Project costs*: Volunteers are responsible for transportation to the project site, insurance costs, a $50 registration fee, and a monthly contribution of approximately $125. There is a $100 fee for long-term placements. No visitors to India may receive any remuneration for work or study, and volunteers who do work must make a contribution to their sponsor organization and apply for a tourist visa only.

*Project dates*: A schedule of work camp dates is included in the information packet. Long-term projects are arranged on an individual basis.

*How to apply*: Write to the above address for more information and an application.

*Work done by volunteers*: Construction work, agriculture, office work, public education, and various social service activities.

*Special skills or requirements*: No special skills are needed. Volunteers must be flexible to adapt to living in a different culture, often in difficult conditions. All volunteers must be over 18 years old.

*Commentary*: JAC is a voluntary, nongovernmental organization that attempts to improve the disaster preparedness of the people of India. In the work camps there are stringent rules concerning living conditions and activities. Only vegetarian food is served; no smoking, drugs, or alcohol are allowed; and living quarters are primitive. JAC is also involved in alternative, nontraditional medicine and offers volunteers homeopathy and solar therapy, although volunteers may consult other doctors for any illness they have while in a camp.

# Kansas Archeology Training Program Field School

Kansas State Historical Society
6425 S.W. 6th Avenue
Topeka, KS 66615-1099
(913) 272-8681, ext. 268; Fax (913) 272-8682

*Project location*: Throughout Kansas.

*Project type*: Archaeological excavations of prehistoric and historic sites.

*Project costs*: Participants must join the Kansas Anthropological Association ($22 per year for individuals, $25 per year for families) and pay for all transportation, room, and board. Motels and camping are always available near the project sites.

*Project dates*: First two weeks of June each year.

*How to apply*: Send a letter of interest to the above address.

*Work done by volunteers*: Archaeological excavation and laboratory work, specialized processing of artifacts, and formal class instruction.

*Special skills or requirements*: Volunteers must be at least 10 years old; those between the ages of 10 and 14 must work with a sponsoring adult.

*Commentary*: The Kansas Archaeology Training Program is a cooperative effort of the Kansas State Historical Society and the Kansas Anthropological Association. It began in 1975 and offers volunteers the opportunity to participate in the scientific excavation of archaeological sites. The program is structured as an educational experience in which participants may be involved in a wide range of excavation and laboratory functions.

# Kenya Voluntary Development Association

PO Box 48902
Nairobi 25379 Kenya

*Project location*: Rural areas of Kenya.

*Project type*: Community development projects.

*Project costs*: About $260.

*Project dates*: Two-week projects held in March or April, July or August, and November or December each year.

*How to apply*: Write to the Director at the above address at least four months in advance of the start of your project of choice.

*Work done by volunteers*: Volunteers work with members of the local communities under the supervision of local experts and instructors. Projects include helping to construct dams, bridges, health centers, homes for teachers, and similar public development projects.

*Special skills or requirements*: No special skills are required, except ability to live in a new culture.

*Commentary*: KVDA is an indigenously inspired and oriented organization that each year offers youth and adults from Africa and overseas opportunities to serve in Kenya's rural and/or needy areas during their free time and holidays.

# 🌐 Kibbutz Program Center

110 E. 59th Street, 4th Floor
New York, NY 10022
(800) 247-7852; Fax (212) 318-6134
E-mail: kibbutzdsk@aol.com

*Project location:*Various kibbutzim throughout Israel.

*Project type*: The center sponsors programs that range from learning Jewish heritage and studying drama or politics to archaeological excavations or simply working on a kibbutz.

*Project costs*: Range from $110 for work programs to over $1,600 for study programs.

*Project dates*: Projects range from two to six months in length throughout the year.

*How to apply*: Contact the office above for current information about the many programs offered.

*Work done by volunteers*: This varies greatly by program. It is best to obtain information about the various programs and then ask about the specific work each requires.

*Special skills or requirements*: Different programs have different requirements, but generally you must be between 18 and 35 years of age.

Kibbutzim volunteers have fun along with performing hard work. Photo courtesy of Kibbutz Program Center.

# Koinonia Partners

1324 Highway 49 S
Americus, GA 31709
(912) 924-0391; Fax (912) 924-6504

*Project location*: Seven miles from Americus, Georgia.

*Project type*: An ecumenical Christian organization offering a work-study program for full-time volunteers exploring Christian discipleship and racial conciliation.

*Project costs*: None. Participants receive a stipend of $50 per month and food allowance of $25 per week. Housing, noon meals, and laundry facilities are also provided.

*Project dates*: Sessions are one month in January, three months February through May, two months June and July, and three months September through December. Yearlong internships are available in some ministries.

*How to apply*: Write to the Volunteer Coordinator for program information and an application.

*Work done by volunteers*: Organic gardening, farming, housing maintenance, mail-order shipping, computer and office work, youth work, child development center work, and library work. Workday is from 8:00 A.M. to 5:00 P.M., with one hour for lunch. Volunteers participate in three study sessions per week, one in the evening and the other two during work hours.

*Special skills or requirements*: Volunteers must be at least 18 years old. Families are welcome; parents must work at least part time.

*Commentary*: Although volunteers need not be Christians, the study sessions will include Bible study, as well as various worship and fellowship opportunities. Koinonia was started by two families as an experiment in Christian living in 1942. They had two goals: to live in the community and bear Christian witness, and to help local farmers improve their techniques. Over the years, goals and ministers have changed and evolved, but the beacon of Christian witness has been constant. Koinonia currently has a strong emphasis on racial conciliation, particularly in supporting African American leadership, and in local community development. In addition to the volunteer program, Koinonia welcomes visitors for up to two weeks; they are encouraged to participate in community life and work while there.

# Land and Culture Organization

138 E. 39th Street
New York, NY 10016
(212) 697-5822

*Project location*: Armenia, Iran, and Syria.

*Project type*: Architectural preservation, land cultivation, and community development.

*Project costs*: Vary by project; contact LCO for current costs.

*Project dates*: Generally in July and August for four, six, or eight weeks.

*How to apply*: Contact the office listed above.

*Work done by volunteers*: Manual labor.

*Special skills or requirements*: An interest in Armenian culture and a willingness to work.

*Commentary*: LCO is an organization for ethnic Armenians who have an interest in their ancestral sites in Iran, Syria, and Armenia. Most volunteers are of Armenian descent, but others are welcome to join the summer campaigns.

# La Sabranenque Restoration Projects

Saint Victor la Coste
30290 Laudun, France
(66) 50-05-05 or
c/o Jacqueline C. Simon
217 High Park Boulevard
Buffalo, NY 14226
(716) 836-8698

*Project location*: Several sites in southern France in Saint Victor la Coste,
near Avignon. There are three sites in Italy—one in Gnallo, a small
hamlet in northern Italy; one in Settefonti, near Bologna in central
Italy; and one in Altamura in the south.

*Project type*: Restoration of simple monuments, small structures, villages,
and sites that are typical of the traditional regional architecture, such
as medieval chapels, old village buildings, and other structures that
are property of villages and nonprofit organizations.

*Project costs*: $960 for a three-week project, half in France and half in
Italy; $535 for a two-week project in France.

La Sabranenque volunteers work on the restoration of a Romanesque chapel
in southern France. Photo courtesy of La Sabranenque.

La Sabranenque volunteers reconstruct a vaulted stairway at a castle in southern France. Photo courtesy of La Sabranenque.

*Project dates*: Two and three weeks in June, July, and August.

*How to apply*: Write to one of the above addresses for more information and an application.

*Work done by volunteers*: Volunteers participate directly in restoration projects, learn building skills on the job, and become part of an international team. Specific projects depend on the volunteer's time of arrival, since all projects are ongoing.

*Special skills or requirements*: No previous experience is necessary; very few volunteers have any previous building experience. The project organizers speak French, English, and Italian.

*Commentary*: Projects offer participants the opportunity to enter into the life of Mediterranean villages while taking an active part in practical, cooperative, and creative projects. Volunteers live in houses in Saint Victor la Coste and at Italian sites.

*Sample projects*: During summer of 1995, volunteers restored a small house at the medieval site of Allegre, twenty-five miles from Saint Victor la Coste. Its walls were consolidated, doorways, windows, and chimney were rebuilt, and an entire new roof was placed on the structure. At the same time, a section of the old village path was restored.

# Lesotho Workcamps Association

PO Box 6
Maseru 100 Lesotho
09266-314862

*Project location*: Various villages throughout Lesotho.

*Project type*: Work camps.

*Project costs*: Volunteers pay a $75 registration fee and their travel expenses to Lesotho, in southern Africa.

*Project dates*: December through January and June through July, for three weeks.

*How to apply*: The association accepts volunteers who are willing to come to Lesotho and pay their own travel expenses. They must apply beforehand, however, and confirm before leaving for Lesotho. Write to the above address, enclosing two international postal reply coupons, or apply through one of the partner organizations in the U.S.: Council on International Educational Exchange, Service Civil International, or Volunteers for Peace (see Index).

*Work done by volunteers*: Primarily construction, with some forestation and soil conservation projects. Twenty volunteers work with local residents on each project, and they build classrooms, dig pit latrines, improve water supplies, and plant forests.

*Special skills or requirements*: No special skills required, only the willingness to do manual work for two to three weeks during any one month.

# Lisle Fellowship, Incorporated
433 W. Sterns Road
Temperance, MI 48182
(313) 847-7126

*Project location*: Bali, India, Ohio, and South Dakota.

*Project type*: Lisle has attempted to integrate human relations in multicultural groups with field experience in its projects. One project, which has been held in Toledo, Ohio, since 1987, is a one-week Elderhostel program.

*Project costs*: Costs vary tremendously by project but are kept to a minimum.

*Project dates*: All projects are in the summer and vary in length. The India project is for six weeks; the Bali and South Dakota projects are for three weeks.

*How to apply*: Write to the above address for information and an application.

*Work done by volunteers*: Volunteers take part in cultural discussions, work side by side with local residents on subsistence projects, and share the effects of these experiences with one another.

*Special skills or requirements*: Participants are generally over 18, and the normal age range is from 18 to 75. All applicants are asked to consider the special demands of the Lisle format, which requires the ability to live in a cooperative, group-living situation with a consensual decision-making process, with the added responsibility of doing so in a multicultural group.

*Commentary*: The Lisle Fellowship is different from many organizations in this guide. While productive work is one goal of the fellowship, it is only a minor one. Lisle is more concerned with improving the quality of life and improving the chance for peace by giving volunteers an "opportunity to explore the moral and ethical dimensions of social interaction and world issues." For this reason potential volunteers should be aware of the philosophical demands placed on all participants.

# Little Children of the World, Incorporated
361 County Road 475
Etowah, TN 37331
Tel/Fax (423) 263-2303

*Project location*: Dumaguete City, Philippines, about 450 miles south of Manila.

*Project type*: Social services for children who are victims of poverty.

*Project costs*: Volunteers are responsible for transportation and food. Housing is provided.

*Project dates*: Volunteers may negotiate their preferred dates and length of stay.

*How to apply*: Write to LCW for information and application.

*Work done by volunteers*: Work includes teaching children on a non-formal basis, tutoring math or English, or working in a community-based health clinic assisting doctors or paramedics.

*Commentary*: The LCW program is not residential. Rather it is a community-based, holistic program that focuses on the needs of families and children. It is also participatory, training recipients to manage as much of the program as possible. All volunteers work alongside Filipino counterparts.

# Loch Arthur Community
Stable Cottage
Beeswing
Dumfries DG2 8JQ United Kingdom
(01387) 760 687

*Project location*: Located in the country, six miles from the town of Dumfries, Scotland.

*Project type*: Working and living in a community with adults who have mental handicaps.

*Project costs*: No cost except travel. The community provides board, lodging, and pocket money.

*Project dates*: Year-round, from one month to one year or more.

*How to apply*: Write to Lana Chanarin at the above address, sending your age, interests, previous work experience, and dates available.

*Work done by volunteers*: Gardening, housework, farming, weaving, cheese making, baking, helping in the houses and with care of people, and participating in all aspects of community life.

*Special skills or requirements*: No special skills are necessary, only willingness to work and openness to the community way of life.

*Commentary*: Life in the community is demanding—there are no set hours, and volunteers must be willing to participate in all aspects of life. Work is based on the ideas of Rudolf Steiner, and the group celebrates festivals throughout the year. The community prefers to have volunteers join them for from six months to one year but will accept shorter periods in the summer months.

# Los Medicos Voladores—The Flying Doctors

140 Magneson Terrace
Los Gatos, CA 95632
(800) 585-4LMV

*Project location*: The Copper Canyon area of northwestern Mexico, primarily Sonora and western Chihuahua.

*Project type*: Providing health care services and education in rural villages in remote locations.

*Project costs*: $300 to $400.

*Project dates*: Generally the second weekend of each month, plus two days.

*How to apply*: Call the above number for an application.

*Work done by volunteers*: Patient scheduling and nonskilled assistance (for example, "Hold the flashlight, please"). Projects are four-day trips in which volunteers fly in small planes from the San Francisco Bay area to a small town, set up a clinic, and provide optometry, medical, and dental services and education. Saturday night is free, and volunteers return Sunday.

*Special skills or requirements*: Sense of humor, adaptability, and "no excess dignity."

*Commentary*: Thursday and Friday volunteers eat and sleep in villages where accommodations are simple; Saturday night is spent in a large town with more comfortable accommodations.

# Los Niños

7825 Fay Ave, Suite 200
La Jolla, CA 92037
(619) 456-3552

*Project location*: Tijuana and Mexicali, Mexico.

*Project type*: An educational program that involves teaching in a summer school and receiving lectures and workshops about daily life in Mexico.

*Project costs*: $900 per summer, which includes housing, food, and programming costs.

*Project dates*: The Tijuana program is six weeks long, from early July to mid-August. Weekend and weeklong programs are available between September and June.

*How to apply*: Contact the office listed above for an application. Application deadlines are late April each year.

*Work done by volunteers*: Teaching in a summer school and sharing responsibilities while living in a community setting.

*Special skills or requirements*: Participants should have cultural sensitivity, the ability to communicate in Spanish, the ability to work in a team as well as independently, and good health.

*Commentary*: Los Niños was formed in 1974 and offers short-term volunteer development training through the Development Education Program.

# Macon Program for Progress, Incorporated

38½ E. Main Street
PO Box 700
Franklin, NC 28734
(704) 524-4471

*Project location*: Franklin, North Carolina, which is in the mountains of western North Carolina and surrounded by the Great Smoky Mountains National Park.

*Project type*: MPP is a local social service organization.

*Project costs*: Volunteers are responsible for all expenses.

*Project dates*: Year-round, but the summer is the busiest time.

*How to apply*: Write to the Volunteer Coordinator at the above address for information.

*Work done by volunteers*: Wide variety of activities, from summer day care for children and adult day care, to building homes for the needy.

*Special skills or requirements*: A desire to work.

*Commentary*: Volunteers get an opportunity to do needed work in one of the most scenic vacation spots in the U.S.

# Malta Youth Hostels Association Work Camps

17, Triq Tal-Borg
Pawla PLA 06 Malta
Tel/Fax 356-693957
E-mail: myha@keyworld.mt

*Project location*: Malta.

*Project type*: Repair and maintenance projects.

*Project costs*: Volunteers pay for transportation plus a refundable $45 deposit to prove goodwill.

Volunteers enjoy a break from painting the roof of the Paceville Youth Hostel in Malta. Photo courtesy of Malta Youth Hostel Association.

*Project dates*: Year-round for two weeks to three months.

*How to apply*: Write to the above address for more information, enclosing three international postal reply coupons.

*Work done by volunteers*: Manual, administrative, and clerical. Volunteers work at least three hours a day to help provide inexpensive accommodations in youth hostels, as well other youth and charitable organizations.

*Special skills or requirements*: An interest in working with people in a cross-cultural setting. Anyone between the ages of 16 and 50 may apply.

# Mar de Jade

Las Varas
Nayarit 63715 Mexico
Tel/Fax (327) 20184 or
PO Box 423353
San Francisco, CA 94142
(415) 281-0164

*Project location*: Oceanfront on Chacala Beach near Puerto Vallarta.

*Project type*: A combined language-volunteer program in Spanish and community development projects.

*Project costs*: $865 for a twenty-one-day program for shared room, board, and Spanish instruction.

*Project dates*: Year-round.

*How to apply*: Send request for application forms to the U.S. address.

*Work done by volunteers*: Work in community health clinics, construction, teaching, and more.

*Special skills or requirements*: Interest in learning Spanish and helping others.

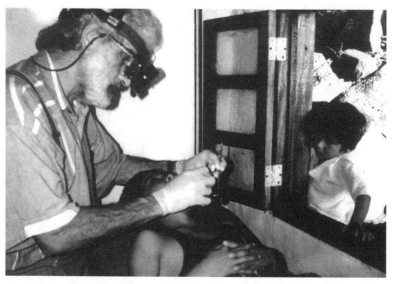

A volunteer dentist for Mar de Jade examines a Mexican youth. Photo courtesy of Mar de Jade.

# Mellemfolkeligt Samvirke
Studgade 20
Arhus 8000 Denmark
(86) 19-77-66

*Project location*: Denmark and Greenland.

*Project type*: Work camps.

*Project costs*: All volunteers receive boarding and lodging but are responsible for all transportation costs. Contact Council of International Educational Exchange (see Index) for registration costs.

*Project dates*: From June through September.

*How to apply*: Contact CIEE (see Index) for application if in the U.S. Contact the above address if in Denmark.

*Work done by volunteers*: Manual labor and social work. Camps are organized in cooperation with local municipalities and institutions. Typical projects consist of constructing playgrounds, building community centers, restoring local sites, and participating in nature conservation.

*Special skills or requirements*: No special skills are required, but volunteers must be able and willing to work in a multicultural setting. The minimum age is 18.

# Mencap's Holiday Services

119 Drake Street
Rochdale OL16 1PZ United Kingdom
(01706) 54111; Fax (01706) 43179

*Project location*: Throughout England.

*Project type*: Programs for mentally disabled people of all ages who live at home or in hospital settings.

*Project costs*: Volunteers are reimbursed up to £25 for travel. Room and board are provided.

*Project dates*: Annually for two weeks.

*How to apply*: Write to the above address for details and an application.

*Work done by volunteers*: Volunteers are responsible for all the personal care of disabled vacationers. This ranges from washing, dressing, or changing diapers to helping them enjoy their vacation setting. The work is long and hard. The days are often as long as fourteen hours, and on a two-week project volunteers can expect to have only one half day plus late evenings off.

*Special skills or requirements*: A strong commitment to helping the disabled. Special skills such as music and arts and crafts are a plus. Volunteers must be over 18, but there is no upper age limit. If you are healthy, persevering, and have a responsible attitude toward demanding work, you are welcome.

*Commentary*: While volunteers don't have much time off to tour the countryside, they do have an opportunity to make many friends while doing valuable work. This can be a true change of pace, and the vacation can come afterward.

# The Mendenhall Ministries
PO Box 368
Mendenhall, MS 39114
(601) 847-3421

*Project location*: Mendenhall, Mississippi, in the delta region of the state.

*Project type*: Outreach work in a Christian community organization.

*Project costs*: Volunteers are responsible for all travel costs and some of the room and board.

*Project dates*: Year-round, as needed by TMM.

*How to apply*: Write to the Volunteer Coordinator at the above address for more information and an application.

*Work done by volunteers*: Presently, short-term and summer volunteers take part in Bible training, farm work, legal internships, office work, recreation, research, photography, and tutoring.

*Special skills or requirements*: TMM is a nondenominational, community-based organization, but it has strong connections to a local fundamentalist church and expects all volunteers to join in group activities, which are based on a strong Christian faith. TMM is a cross-cultural organization with strong ties to the local Black community as well as the Christian community, and volunteers should be able to participate willingly in both.

# Mennonite Central Committee Ca

134 Plaza Drive
Winnipeg, Manitoba R3T 5K9 Canada
(204) 261-6381; Fax (204) 269-9875
E-mail: mcc@mennonitecc.ca

*Project location*: Throughout Canada.

*Project type*: Mostly social service assignments, which may include child care, community service, disabled service, justice advocacy, offender ministries, or youth work.

*Project costs*: Volunteers receive food, housing, and a $50 monthly allowance. They are responsible for their transportation costs, although limited transportation allowances are given for certain isolated sites.

*Project dates*: Summer assignments run from the beginning of May until the end of August, with projects lasting two to four months.

*How to apply*: Write to the Mennonite Central Committee Canada, Summer Service, at the above address for more information and a personnel information form.

*Work done by volunteers*: Promoting gardening, day-camp counseling, assisting in a global gift shop, coordinating playground activities, working with youth in a group home, and assisting people with disabilities are all activities done by volunteers.

*Special skills or requirements*: Most assignments require at least completion of high school. A flexible, curious, caring, and adventuresome spirit is a definite asset. All MCC summer service volunteers are expected to exhibit a commitment to Christian discipleship, active church membership, and nonviolent peacemaking.

*Commentary*: The Mennonite Church began as a radical, Protestant movement in Europe in the sixteenth century. Mennonites believe that faith lives through caring for, sharing with, and serving those suffering from hardship, disadvantage, or oppression. This includes a strong commitment to actively seeking justice and making peace. Volunteers, although not required to belong to a Mennonite church, are expected to commit themselves to these perspectives.

*Sample projects*: The Native Gardening Project promotes gardening and fosters relationships in native communities that have invited the MCC's participation. Locations for this project include remote locations of

Columbia, Alberta, Saskatchewan, Manitoba, and Ontario. It s volunteers an opportunity to do more than just talk about peace; articipants can join Native Canadians in rediscovering what it means to make peace with the earth. Participants are also given the opportunity of seeing their own culture through the eyes of others.

# Michigan Nature Association

7981 Beard Road, Box 102
Avoca, MI 48006-0102
(810) 324-2626

*Project location*: One hundred and forty nature sanctuaries in fifty-one counties throughout Michigan. MNA projects take place in natural areas, including woods, prairie, waterfall, dune, swamp, and bedrock beach. Twenty-nine of Michigan's thirty native habitats are represented superbly on MNA lands.

*Project type*: Ecology and conservation.

*Project costs*: Minimal.

*Project dates*: May through August.

*How to apply*: Call or write the MNA Volunteers Director, Bertha Daubendiek, at the office listed above.

*Work done by volunteers*: Sanctuary maintenance, trail work, exploration for new land preservation projects, photography, leading field trips.

*Special skills or requirements*: Interest in preservation of natural areas.

*Commentary*: Volunteers with the MNA get to explore some of the most beautiful regions of Michigan.

# Midwest Medical Mission, Incorporated

c/o Dr. Michael Rench
5757 Monclova Road
Maumee, OH 43537
(419) 389-1239

*Project location*: Dominican Republic.

*Project type*: Medical care.

*Project costs*: Approximately $1,000 for physicians and somewhat less for nonphysician medical personnel.

*Project dates*: Various times during the year for three or four weeks.

*How to apply*: Write to the above address for current information and an application.

*Work done by volunteers*: Teams of medical personnel work in the Dominican Republic, one of the poorest nations in the Northern Hemisphere.

*Special skills or requirements*: Most volunteers are licensed doctors, nurses, or technicians, but there are a limited number of positions for people who are willing to work as gofers to help the medical team work smoothly during their short but extremely busy stay.

*Commentary*: Medical help is always needed in Third World countries, and this is one program that uses nonmedical volunteers.

# Mingan Island Cetacean Study, Incorporated
address from November to June:
285 Green Street
Lamber, Quebec J4P 1T3 Canada
(514) 465-9176
address from June to November:
124 Bord de la Mer
Longue-Pointe-de-Mingan, Quebec G0G 1V0 Canada
(418) 949-2845

*Project location*: Mingan Island, in the Gulf of St. Lawrence, and Loreto, in Baja, California.

*Project type*: Marine mammal research with emphasis on rorquals.

*Project costs*: Volunteers are responsible for transportation to the project and approximately $155 per day to cover research and living costs.

*Project dates*: Various times during the year; generally between June and October at Mingan Island, and around March in Baja, California.

*How to apply*: Write or call the offices listed above.

*Work done by volunteers*: Assisting scientists in research as required.

*Special skills or requirements*: Some experience handling or working on boats. A degree in biology is required for full assistants.

*Commentary*: MICS is best known as the first organization in the world to carry out long-term studies on the blue whale.

*Sample projects*: In the past, volunteers have conducted a photo identification of blue, fin, humpback, and minke whales to help determine the distribution, migration patterns, population estimates, behavioral attributes, and genetic makeups of the various populations.

# 🌐 Missionaries of Charity

c/o Sister Priscilla
54A Lower Circular Road
Calcutta 700016 India

*Project location*: Calcutta.

*Project type*: Loving care to the poorest of the poor.

*Project costs*: Transportation to and from the site.

*Project dates*: Year-round.

*How to apply*: Volunteers should not show up without having previously written to the sister in charge of volunteers at the above address. Upon arrival volunteers can meet the sister in charge between 5:00 P.M. and 6:00 P.M. daily except Thursday and Sunday.

*Work done by volunteers*: Whatever work is needed in any of the homes operated by the Missionaries of Charity.

*Special skills or requirements*: An interest to serve the poor.

*Commentary*: Mother Teresa of this organization is known worldwide for her work with the sick and dying, the poor, and everyone in need. In recognition of her work she was awarded the Nobel Peace Prize in 1979.

# Missouri Department of Natural Resources
Division of State Parks
PO Box 176
Jefferson City, MO 65102
(573) 751-2479 or (800) 334-6946; Fax (573) 526-7716

*Project location*: Throughout Missouri state parks and state historic sites.

*Project type*: Campground host, interpreter, park aide, and trail work.

*Project costs*: Volunteers are responsible for their travel and living expenses, although they may stay in park-owned housing or camp at no cost if facilities are available.

*Project dates*: March to October for hosts. Park aides, interpreters, and trail workers may be year-round.

*How to apply*: Contact the Volunteer Program Coordinator at the office listed above.

*Work done by volunteers*: The jobs are done by volunteers, who are expected to perform at the same standards as paid employees. Volunteers are scheduled according to availability and park needs.

*Special skills or requirements*: Physical ability to perform assigned tasks. Campground hosts serve a minimum of four weeks.

*Commentary*: Many of Missouri's state parks are located in the Ozark Mountains or near large man-made reservoirs, and the campground host program offers the best volunteer opportunity.

# 🌐 Mobility International U.S.A.
PO Box 10767
Eugene, OR 97440
(841) 343-1284 (voice and TDD)

*Project location*: Sponsors work camps in Oregon. Helps place people with disabilities in work camps in the U.S. and abroad.

*Project type*: Normal work camp experiences, plus social service organizations. International educational exchange programs with the intention of increasing international understanding of the disabled are also part of MIUSA's program.

*Project costs*: Vary according to the program.

*Project dates*: Work camp dates vary, but most are for two to four weeks.

*How to apply*: Send a stamped, self-addressed envelope to the above address for information on work camps and other programs.

*Work done by volunteers*: Exchange programs usually include a community service component. Service projects have involved making trails in national forests, a city park in Costa Rica, and a retreat center accessible to wheelchair users and visually impaired people. Volunteers also work in agencies and organizations offering services to people with disabilities.

*Special skills or requirements*: Prefers people with an interest in and/or expertise in independent living for people with disabilities, whether able-bodied or disabled. Specific requirements vary with each project.

*Commentary*: Mobility International was founded in London in 1973 to integrate persons with disabilities into international educational and travel programs. Today it has offices in more than twenty-five countries, and the American branch became active as national headquarters in 1981. MIUSA also publishes travel books for people with disabilities and produces videos that document the experiences of former volunteers.

# Monkey Sanctuary

Looe, Cornwall PL13 1NZ United Kingdom
(01503) 262 532

*Project location*: Looe, Cornwall, in southwestern England.

*Project type*: Winter work includes maintenance of enclosures as well as general duties in the sanctuary. During the summer when the sanctuary is open to the public, volunteers work in the shop and at the gate.

*Project costs*: Volunteers are responsible for travel; room and board are provided.

*Project dates*: From two weeks to one month, year-round.

*How to apply*: Write to the Volunteer Coordinator at the above address.

*Work done by volunteers*: Maintenance is done during the winter, as well as cleaning enclosures. The same work is done in the summer, plus shop and gate duties.

*Special skills or requirements*: A pleasant nature and a willingness to work and mix with groups. Prefers volunteers that are at least 18 years old. An interest in animal welfare and conservation is essential.

*Commentary*: The Monkey Sanctuary is situated in a beautiful wooded setting overlooking Looe Bay. For twenty-five years the Victorian house and gardens have been the home of a natural colony of woolly monkeys. The initial aim of the sanctuary was to provide a stable setting in which woolly monkeys, rescued from lives of isolation in zoos or as pets, could live as naturally as possible. The work now focuses on the need for rehabilitation projects and public education on local and global conservation and animal welfare, including the unsuitability of captivity for primates.

# 🌐 Mount Vernon Ladies' Association

Archaeology Department
Mount Vernon, VA 22121
(703) 799-8626
E-mail: ewhite@mountvernon.org

*Project location*: Mount Vernon, Virginia.

*Project type*: Archaeological excavation and artifact processing.

*Project costs*: Participants must pay all transportation, room, and board.

*Project dates*: Most volunteer opportunities are from June through September. Volunteers are needed other months for special projects. Please inquire for specific dates.

*How to apply*: Contact Ester White, Archaeologist, at the office listed above.

*Work done by volunteers*: Excavation and recording in the field, and artifact washing, labeling, and cataloging in the lab.

*Special skills or requirements*: A willingness to work hard, and a time commitment of one day or more.

# National Audubon Society
700 Broadway, 5th Floor
New York, NY 10003
(212) 979-3000

*Project location*: Throughout the U.S.

*Project type*: Habitat restoration, trail building, guide work, and visitor center work.

*Project costs*: Depends on the individual project.

*Project dates*: Varies according to project.

*How to apply*: The national office of the Audubon Society does not place volunteers, but regional offices and local clubs often have programs in which volunteers are used. Contact the the regional offices listed below for information.

*Work done by volunteers*: Depends on the project; mainly ecological work and work in the visitor centers and as guides.

*Special skills or requirements*: Varies by project.

*Commentary*: The regional offices are as follows.

**Alaska and Hawaii**
308 G Street, Suite 217
Anchorage, AK 99501
(907) 276-7034

**Great Lakes Region**
7 N. Meridian Street, Suite 400
Indianapolis, IN 46204
(317) 631-2676

**Mid-Atlantic Region**
1104 Fernwood Avenue, Suite 300
Camp Hill, PA 17011
(717) 763-4985

**Northeast Region**
1789 Western Avenue
Albany, NY 12203
(518) 869-9731

**Rocky Mountain Region**
4150 Darley, Suite 5
Boulder, CO 80303
(303) 499-0219

**Southeast Region**
928 N. Monroe Street
Tallahassee, FL 32303
(904) 222-2473

**Southwest Region**
2525 Wallingwood, Suite 1505
Austin, TX 78746
(512) 327-1943

**West Central Region**
200 Southwind Place, Suite 205
Manhattan, KS 66502
(913) 537-4385

**Western Region**
2631 12th Court SW, Suite A
Olympia, WA 98502
(206) 786-8020

# National Park Service

Interior Building
PO Box 37127
Washington, DC 20013-7127
(202) 343-6843

*Project location*: Throughout the U.S.

*Project type*: Depends on the individual project. Some positions include research, archaeology, natural science, campground hosting, visitor center guides, and administrative support.

*Project costs*: Depends on the individual project. In some cases NPS pays for some out-of-pocket expenses, but volunteers are responsible for most housing and transportation costs. Housing is furnished with some positions.

*Project dates*: Varies according to project.

*How to apply*: The national office of the National Park Service has some individual entries for national park units, but you may contact any of the offices below for a listing of volunteer openings in the various field areas, a Prospective Volunteer Application, and a list of parks within the region. The abbreviations in parentheses indicate which states the regional office serves.

*Work done by volunteers*: Depends on the project. Often volunteers provide visitors with information on what to see and do during their visits, assist park staff in continuing research, participate in wildlife surveys, and do regular maintenance work.

*Special skills or requirements*: Varies by project. Generally volunteers should have experience or interest in camping, hiking, history, geology, or archaeology. Many parks are willing to help train volunteers for specific needs.

*Commentary*: The regional offices are as follows.

**Alaska Field Area (AK)**
2525 Gambell Street, Room 107
Anchorage, AK 99503-2892
(907) 261-2690

**Intermountain Field Area (AZ, CO, MT, NM, OK, TX, UT, WY)**
12795 W. Alameda Parkway
Denver, CO 80225-0287
(303) 969-2638

**Midwest Field Area**
**(AR, IL, IN, IA, KS, MI, MN, MO, NE, ND, OH, SD, WI)**
1709 Jackson Street
Omaha, NE 68102
(402) 221-3458

**National Capital Field Area (DC)**
1100 Ohio Drive SW
Washington, DC 20242
(202) 619-7224

**New England System Support Office (CT, ME, MA, NH, NJ, NY, RI, VT)**
15 State Street
Boston, MA 02109
(617) 223-5101

**Northeast Field Area**
**Chesapeake/Allegheny System Support Office (DE, MD, PA, VA, WV)**
U.S. Customs House
200 Chesnut Street, Suite 306
Philadelphia, PA 19106
(215) 597-4971

**Pacific West Field Area (CA, ID, HI, NV, OR, WA)**
600 Harrison Street, Suite 600
San Francisco, CA 94107-1372
(415) 744-3885

**Southeast Field Area (AL, FL, GA, KY, LA, MS, NC, PR, SC, TN, VI)**
75 Spring Street SW
Atlanta, GA 303039
(404) 331-3799

# National Trust for Scotland Thistle Camps
5 Charlotte Square
Edinburgh EH2 4DU United Kingdom
(0131) 226-5922

*Project location*: Throughout Scotland.

*Project type*: Practical conservation management.

*Project costs*: Currently about $40 per week for food and accommodations.

*Project dates*: March to October, for one or two weeks.

*How to apply*: Write to the above address. Projects frequently fill by April each year, so foreign applicants must apply early.

*Work done by volunteers*: Building fences, mountain footpath maintenance, building drystone dykes, woodland management, and farm work.

*Special skills or requirements*: Volunteers must be at least 16 years old, healthy, and prepared for hard physical work.

*Commentary*: Thistle Camps are organized by the National Trust to help in the practical management of National Trust properties.

# National Trust of Northern Ireland

Rowallane
Saintfield, County Down BT24 7LH United Kingdom
(01238) 510 721

*Project location*: The base camp, Castle Ward, in County Down, Northern Ireland.

*Project type*: Conservation work.

*Project costs*: Depends on the project.

*Project dates*: Various, usually during the summer months, for one-week placements.

*How to apply*: Write to Beryl Sims, National Trust, PO Box 12, Westbury, Wiltshire, BA13 4NA, United Kingdom.

*Work done by volunteers*: A variety of conservation tasks, including weed control and maintenance.

*Special skills or requirements*: Must be physically fit.

*Commentary*: This organization is affiliated with the National Trusts of England, Wales, and Northern Ireland, but does conservation work in Northern Ireland only.

# National Trust Working Holidays

PO Box 84
Cirencester, Gloucestershire GL7 1ZP United Kingdom
(01285) 651 818

*Project location*: Fifty-two locations throughout England, Wales, and Northern Ireland.

*Project type*: Outdoor conservation, archaeology, construction, and botany.

*Project costs*: About $85 for most weeklong projects, inclusive of full board.

*Project dates*: Year-round. Projects generally last for one week, but some are weekend projects.

*How to apply*: Write to the above address for a brochure, enclosing five international postal reply coupons.

*Work done by volunteers*: Outdoor conservation, archaeology, botany, and construction.

*Special skills or requirements*: Some botany and some construction skills, depending on the project.

*Commentary*: The working holidays sponsored by the National Trust include Acorn Projects that are for general outdoor conservation work, Construction Projects for volunteers interested in building, and Oak Camps for volunteers over 35 years of age. You may join the projects that most fit your needs and interests.

# The Nature Conservancy
1815 N. Lynn Street
Arlington, VA 22209
(703) 841-5300

*Project location*: Varies by the individual project.

*Project type*: Habitat restoration and giving guided tours.

*Project costs*: Depends on the individual project.

*Project dates*: Varies according to project.

*How to apply*: The Nature Conservancy asks that you contact its national headquarters only about volunteer opportunities at the headquarters. The state chapters and regional offices listed below often need volunteers at various preserves, and you are welcome to apply to the states and regions of your choice.

*Work done by volunteers*: Depends on the project; mainly ecological work and work in the visitor centers and as guides.

*Special skills or requirements*: Varies by project.

*Commentary*: The state chapter and regional offices are as follows.

**Alabama Field Office**
2821C 2nd Avenue S
Birmingham, AL 35223
(205) 251-1155

**Alaska Field Office**
601 W. 1st Avenue, Suite 200
Anchorage, AK 99501
(907) 276-3133

**Arizona Field Office**
300 E. University Boulevard
Suite 230
Tucson, AZ 85705
(520) 622-3861

**Arkansas Field Office**
601 N. University Avenue
Little Rock, AR 72205
(501) 663-6699

**California Regional Office**
201 Mission Street, 4th Floor
San Francisco, CA 94105
(415) 777-0487

**Colorado Program**
1244 Pine Street
Boulder, CO 80302
(303) 444-2950

**Connecticut Field Office**
55 High Street
Middletown, CT 06457
(203) 344-0716

**Delaware Field Office**
319-323 S. State Street
Dover, DE 19901
(302) 674-3550

**Eastern Regional Office**
201 Devonshire Street, 5th Floor
Boston, MA 02110
(617) 542-1908

**Florida Regional Office**
222 S. Westmonte Drive, Suite 300
Altamonte Springs, FL 32714
(407) 682-3664

**Georgia Field Office**
1401 Peachtree Street NE
Suite 236
Atlanta, GA 30309
(404) 873-6946

**Hawaii Field Office**
1116 Smith Street, Suite 201
Honolulu, HI 96817
(808) 537-4508

**Idaho Field Office**
PO Box 165
Sun Valley, ID 83353
(208) 726-3007

**Illinois Field Office**
85 S. Michigan Avenue, Suite 900
Chicago, IL 60603
(312) 346-8166

**Indiana Field Office**
1330 W. 38th Street
Indianapolis, IN 46208
(317) 923-7547

**Iowa Field Office**
431 E. Locust, Suite 200
Des Moines, IA 50309
(515) 244-5044

**Kansas Field Office**
820 S.E. Quincy, Suite 301
Topeka, KS 66612-1158
(913) 233-4400

**Kentucky Field Office**
642 W. Main Street
Lexington, KY 40508
(606) 259-9655

**Latin America and Caribbean Division**
1815 N. Lynn Street
Arlington, VA 22209
(703) 841-5300

**Louisiana Field Office**
PO Box 4125
Baton Rouge, LA 70821
(504) 338-1040

**Maine Field Office**
14 Maine Street, Suite 401
Brunswick, ME 04011
(207) 729-5181

**Maryland Field Office**
Chevy Chase Metro Building
2 Wisconsin Circle, Suite 410
Chevy Chase, MD 20815
(301) 656-8673

**Massachusetts Field Office**
79 Milk Street, Suite 300
Boston, MA 02109
(617) 423-2545

**Michigan Field Office**
2840 E. Grand River, Suite 5
East Lansing, MI 48823
(517) 332-1741

**Midwest Regional Office**
1313 5th Street SE, Suite 314
Minneapolis, MN 55514
(612) 331-0700

**Minnesota Field Office**
1313 5th Street SE
Minneapolis, MN 55414
(612) 331-0750

**Mississippi Field Office**
PO Box 1028
Jackson, MS 39215-1028
(601) 355-5357

**Missouri Field Office**
2800 S. Brentwood Boulevard
Saint Louis, MO 63144
(314) 968-1105

**Montana Field Office**
32 S. Ewing
Helena, MT 59601
(406) 443-0303

**Nebraska Field Office**
1722 St. Mary's Avenue, Suite 403
Omaha, NE 68102
(402) 342-0282

**Nevada Field Office**
1771 E. Flamingo, Suite 1111B
Las Vegas, NV 89119
(702) 737-8744

**New Hampshire Field Office**
2½ Beacon Street, Suite 6
Concord, NH 03301
(603) 224-5853

**New Jersey Field Office**
200 Pottersville Road
Chester, NJ 07930
(908) 879-7262

**New Mexico Field Office**
212 E. Marcy, Suite 200
Santa Fe, NM 87501
(505) 988-3867

**New York Adirondack Chapter**
PO Box 65
Route 73
Keene Valley, NY 12943
(518) 576-2082

**New York Central and Western Chapters**
315 Alexander Street, 2nd Floor
Rochester, NY 14604
(716) 546-8030

**New York Eastern Chapter**
251 River Street
Troy, NY 12180
(518) 272-0195

**New York Long Island Chapter**
250 Lawrence Hill Road
Cold Spring Harbor, NY 11724
(516) 367-3225

**New York Lower Hudson Chapter**
41 S. Moger Avenue
Mt. Kisco, NY 10549
(914) 2444-3271

**New York Regional Office**
91 Broadway
Albany, NY 12204
(518) 463-6133

New York South Fork/
Shelter Island Chapter
PO Box 5125
East Hampton, NY 11937
(516) 329-7689

North Carolina Field Office
4011 University Drive, Suite 201
Durham, NC 27707
(919) 403-8558

North Dakota Field Office
2000 Schafer Street, Suite B
Bismark, ND 58501
(701) 222-8464

Ohio Field Office
1504 W. 1st Avenue
Columbus, OH 43212
(614) 486-4194

Oklahoma Field Office
23 W. 4th, Suite 200
Tulsa, OK 74103
(918) 585-1117

Oregon Field Office
821 S.E. 14th Avenue
Portland, OR 97214
(503) 230-1221

Pacific Region Office
1116 Smith Street, Suite 201
Honolulu, HI 96817
(808) 537-4508

Pennsylvania Field Office
1211 Chestnut Street, 12th Floor
Philadelphia, PA 19107-4122
(215) 963-1400

Rhode Island Field Office
45 S. Angell Street
Providence, RI 02906
(401) 331-7110

South Carolina Field Office
PO Box 5475
Columbia, SC 29250
(803) 254-9049

South Dakota Field Office
405 S. 3rd Avenue, Suite 102
Sioux Falls, SD 57104
(605) 331-0619

Southeast Regional Office
PO Box 2267
Chapel Hill, NC 27515-2267
(919) 967-5493

Tennessee Field Office
50 Vantage Way, Suite 250
Nashville, TN 37228
(615) 255-0303

Texas Field Office
PO Box 1440
San Antonio, TX 78295-1440
(210) 224-8774

U.S. Virgin Islands Program
14B Norre Gade, 2nd Floor
Charlotte Amalie, USVI 00802
(809) 774-7633

Utah Field Office
559 E. South Temple
Salt Lake City, UT 84102
(801) 531-0999

**Vermont Field Office**
27 State Street
Montpelier, VT 05602-2934
(802) 229-4425

**Virginia Field Office**
1233A Cedars Court
Charlottesville, VA 22903-4800
(804) 295-6106

**Washington Field Office**
217 Pine Street, Suite 1100
Seattle, WA 98101
(206) 343-4344

**Western Regional Office**
2060 Broadway, Suite 230
Boulder, CO 80302
(303) 444-1060

**West Virginia Field Office**
723 Kanawha Boulevard E., Suite
500
Charleston, WV 25301
(304) 345-4350

**Wisconsin Field Office**
633 W. Main Street
Madison, WI 53703
(608) 251-8140

**Wyoming Field Office**
258 Main Street, Suite 200
Lander, WY 82520
(307) 332-2971

# Nevada Division of State Parks

Capitol Complex
Carson City, NV 89710
(702) 687-4384

*Project location*: Throughout Nevada.

*Project type*: Trail workers, campground hosts, interpretive assistants, and other common park jobs.

*Project costs*: Volunteers are responsible for their transportation and living costs.

*Project dates*: Year-round, for varying lengths of stay.

*How to apply*: Send for the "Volunteer in Park" bulletin at the above address. The bulletin contains information on what positions are available and an application.

*Work done by volunteers*: All types of work are done by volunteers, from hosting campgrounds and surveying archaeological digs to patrolling the backcountry.

*Special skills or requirements*: Some positions require special skills, and these are specified in the bulletin.

*Commentary*: As with most state park systems, Nevada depends a lot on volunteers to keep their system going.

# New York–New Jersey Trail Conference

232 Madison Avenue, Suite 401
New York, NY 10016
(212) 685-9699; Fax (212) 779-9699
E-mail: nynjtc@aol.com

*Project location*: Northern New Jersey to southeastern New York, from the Delaware Water Gap to the Catskills and Taconics.

*Project type*: Trail building, repair, management and maintenance, and advocacy.

*Project costs*: Volunteers are responsible for their food and transportation costs.

*Project dates*: Year-round, usually for one day, but sometimes for the weekend.

*How to apply*: Contact the office listed above.

*Work done by volunteers*: Clipping and clearing trails, painting blazes, cleaning waterbars and bridges, draining ditches, rehabilitating trails, and monitoring land.

*Special skills or requirements*: Should be reasonably fit, and a knowledge of trail tools is helpful.

*Commentary*: This is one of several hundred regional trail groups around the nation that are responsible for maintaining trails.

# Nicaragua Solidarity Network

339 Lafayette Street
New York, NY 10012
(212) 674-9499

*Project location*: The five boroughs of New York City.

*Project type*: Activist.

*Project costs*: Participants are responsible for travel, room, and board expenses.

*Project dates*: Year-round.

*How to apply*: Send a résumé and cover letter to the above address.

*Work done by volunteers*: Media networking, outreach, street theater, fundraising, and producing a weekly newsletter and radio show.

*Special skills or requirements*: Volunteers should be familiar with Latin American issues and interested in the progressive solidarity movement. Knowledge of Spanish helpful but not necessary.

*Commentary*: This organization has broadened its area of interest since the end of the civil war in Nicaragua and produces *Weekly News Update on the Americas*, a publication covering news and information from all of Latin America and the Caribbean, and the *Radio Update on the Americas*, which is broadcast on local radio.

# Northern Cambria Community Development Corporation (NORCAM)

PO Box 174
Barnsboro, PA 15714
(814) 948-4444; Fax (814) 948-4449

*Project location*: Western Pennsylvania.

*Project type*: Housing rehabilitation.

*Project costs*: $120 per week for housing and lunch.

*Project dates*: Year-round, generally for one week.

*How to apply*: Write to above for more information.

*Work done by volunteers*: Various types of construction work.

*Special skills or requirements*: Most volunteers come in groups of up to twenty-five people. Some individual volunteers are merged into other groups.

*Commentary*: This is an organization that does on a local level what Habitat for Humanity does internationally.

# Northern Ohio Archaeological Field School

Cuyahoga Community College/Cleveland Museum of National History
11000 Pleasant Valley Road
Parma, OH 44130
(216) 987-5492

*Project location*: Northeast Ohio.

*Project type*: Archaeological excavation.

*Project costs*: From $60 per week, plus room and board.

*Project dates*: From late June to early August, for two to six weeks.

*How to apply*: Write to the above address for an application.

*Work done by volunteers*: Archaeological excavation of prehistoric Native American sites and class training.

*Special skills or requirements*: None, but an interest in archaeology is necessary.

*Sample projects*: One recent project of the field school was an excavation of a late prehistoric (ca. A.D. 1300) village site in northeast Ohio. This work recovered numerous prehistoric refuse and storage pits, cooking pits, structural remains, food residue, and artifacts representing a settled, horticultural way of life.

# North York Moors Historical Railway Trust
Pickering Station
Pickering, North Yorkshire YO18 7AJ United Kingdom
(01751) 472 508

*Project location*: Along an eighteen-mile, mainly steam-operated railway in northern England.

*Project type*: All aspects of railway operation and maintenance.

*Project costs*: Basic accommodations are available in hostel-style facilities and converted railway carriages for a small charge—about £7.50 per night—to cover cleaning costs and upkeep. Volunteers are responsible for food and travel costs (self-catering facilities are provided).

*Project dates*: The main railway operating season is from the beginning of April to the end of October. Maintenance and engineering work takes place throughout the year.

*How to apply*: Write to the Volunteer Liaison Officer at the above address.

*Work done by volunteers*: Painting, drainage, lineside clearance, building repairs, shop and on-train sales, ticket inspecting, locomotive cleaning.

*Special skills or requirements*: All volunteers should be physically fit. Anyone with technical and/or railway experience, or who is able to give sufficient time to gain experience (and be trained), may be given opportunities to become involved in skilled work.

*Commentary*: Visiting groups may undertake special projects by arrangement.

# Nothelfergemeinschaft der Freunde e.v.

Leschaftsstelle
Postjack 0 5 0, 5235
Duren, Germany
Fax (0242) 176668

*Project location*: Throughout Germany and Europe.

*Project type*: Work camps.

*Project costs*: Approximately $80 registration fee, plus transportation costs.

*Project dates*: Spring and summer for U.S. volunteers who are already in Germany.

*How to apply*: Write to Gerhard Fleming at the above address for more information and an application. The application should arrive between March 1 and May 30.

*Work done by volunteers*: Volunteers spend three to four weeks working in social institutions like homes for the elderly or farms where handicapped and non-handicapped people live and work together. They help with construction or housekeeping and accompanying old people during their daily activities. Volunteers are often supervised by group leaders who are former work camp volunteers and have attended work camp leadership seminars.

*Special skills or requirements*: A knowledge of English or German, an interest in people, and an interest in international exchange.

# Oceanic Society Expeditions
Fort Mason Center, Suite E-230
San Francisco, CA 94123
(415) 441-1106 or (800) 326-7491; Fax (415) 474-3395

*Project location*: The Bahamas, Belize, Midway Atoll, California, Peruvian Amazon, and Suriname.

*Project type*: Research social and family structure, distribution, and abundance of free-ranging dolphins, primates, and manatees. Monitor sea turtle nesting success, and help assess the impact of human activities on whales and dolphins. Determine survival and movement patterns of seals and help rehabilitate seal pups to the wild; conduct seabird population counts and monitor chick hatchlings. Investigate an archaeology site, or restore native plant species. Scuba surveys of tropical coral reefs and temperate submarine canyon ecosystems.

*Project costs*: Costs vary from $280 to $2,190.

*Project dates*: Most trips last for one week. Refer to the listing of individual projects in the Commentary section at the end of this entry.

*How to apply*: Contact the office listed above for an application.

*Work done by volunteers*: Participants photograph animals and record behaviors, location of sightings, and habitat size. They also assist archaeologists and other scientists with investigations.

*Special skills or requirements*: No research experience is needed. An adventurous spirit, patience, respect of wildlife, and the ability to follow instructions are necessary. Basic swimming skills for water-based studies, snorkeling for Bahamas and Belize dolphin studies, and scuba certification for scuba programs are required.

*Commentary*: The specific programs and dates are as follows.

Amazon River Dolphins: Two eight-day trips in August and December.

Bahamas Dolphins: Weekly, May through September.

Bahamas Dolphins for High School: One eight-day trip in July.

Belize Archaeology: Weeklong trips in March, April, June, July, August, and October.

Belize Coral Reef Scuba: Weeklong trips in February, March, April, June, August, and December.

Belize Dolphins: Weeklong trips in February, March, June, August, and December.

Belize Howler Monkeys: Weeklong trips in March, May, November, and December.

Belize Manatees: Weeklong trips in February, March, July, October, and November.

Belize Turtles and Manatees: Weeklong trips in August.

Midway Dolphins: Weeklong trips in March through December.

Midway Habitat Restoration: Weeklong trips in January, March, May, July, September, and November.

Midway Monk Seals: Weeklong trips year-round except for May.

Midway Reef Monitoring: Weeklong trips year-round except June and July.

Midway Seabirds: Weeklong trips year-round except May, September, and October.

Monterey Bay Dolphins and Whales: Eight-day trips in September and October.

Monterey Scuba: Four-day trips in July, August, September, and October.

Suriname Sea Turtles: Nine-day trips in February, April, June, and July.

# Old Fort Churchill Archaeological Project

121 Cunnington Avenue
Winniper, Manitoba R2M 0W6 Canada
Tel/Fax (204) 231-8190

*Project location*: Churchill, Manitoba.

*Project type*: Archaeological excavation, with educational tours to various sites.

*Project costs*: About $1,700 Can. for room, board, and boat travel. Participants are responsible for travel expenses to the project.

*Project dates*: Twelve days in July and August.

*How to apply*: Contact the office listed above for more information as far in advance as possible. Only ten volunteers are accepted per season.

*Work done by volunteers*: General excavation work.

*Special skills or requirements*: Enthusiasm and commitment for twelve days of hard work.

# One World Work Force

Route 4, Box 963A
Flagstaff, AZ 86001
Tel/Fax (520) 779-3639
E-mail: one.world@racebbs.com

*Project location*: Jalisco and Baja, Mexico.

*Project type*: Sea turtle conservation, bird research, and endangered crocodile research.

*Project costs*: $535 for the first week, and $435 per week thereafter.

One World Work Force volunteers remove turtle eggs for safe hatching. Photo courtesy of One World Work Force.

*Project dates*: Year-round.

*How to apply*: Contact the office listed above for more information.

*Work done by volunteers*: Everything from cleaning captive turtle tanks to digging new pipelines and feeding captive turtles. Volunteers also protect turtle nests on beaches, digging up nests and transplanting young into safe nurseries, and censusing crocodile populations and locating nests.

*Special skills or requirements*: Volunteers can work as much or as little as they like. There is a wide range of abilities needed from walking many miles at night in soft sand to sewing together netting to hold hatchlings.

*Commentary*: This is a new organization in the conservation field, but they appear very organized. Volunteers returning from expeditions write glowing reports of their experiences.

# Operation Crossroads Africa

475 Riverside Drive, Suite 830
New York, NY 10027
(212) 870-2106

*Project location*: Africa.

*Project type*: Work camp projects for high school and college students.

*Project costs*: $3,500.

*Project dates*: Summer.

*How to apply*: Contact the office listed above for more information.

*Work done by volunteers*: Variety of work camp duties, including construction and day camp counseling.

*Special skills or requirements*: Must be interested in cross-cultural experiences.

*Commentary*: Operation Crossroads Africa was one of the first organizations contacted for the first edition of this guide. Several years ago they encountered financial difficulties and suspended operations. They are scheduled to be back in operation for this edition. It was from this organization that the Kennedy administration got the idea for the Peace Corps.

# Operation Osprey—Royal Society for the Protection of Birds

c/o Grianan Tulloch
Nethybridge, Inverness-shire PH25 3EF United Kingdom
(01479) 831 694

*Project location*: Abernethy Forest Reserve, Loch Garten, in the Scottish Highlands.

*Project type*: Bird protection and conservation.

*Project costs*: Currently about $35 per week for food, but this may increase.

*Project dates*: End of March to early September.

*How to apply*: Write to the above address for details and an application.

*Work done by volunteers*: Twenty-four-hour watch on an osprey nest and talking to visitors.

*Special skills or requirements*: Ability to approach and talk to visitors about ospreys and the work of RSPB.

*Commentary*: The fate of ospreys in Scotland has been cause for worry in recent years. In 1993 there were only ninety nesting pairs in the entire country, and one of those pairs was at the Loch Garten forest reserve.

# Oregon River Experiences, Incorporated
2 Jefferson Parkway, Suite D7
Lake Oswego, OR 97035
(503) 697-8133
E-mail: ore@teleport.com

*Project location*: Various rivers in the Northwest, including the Klamath in California; the Lower Salmon in Idaho; and the Deschutes, Grande Ronde, John Day, Owyhee, and Rogue rivers in Oregon.

*Project type*: Educational white-water river trips, many for senior citizens through the Elderhostel Program.

*Project costs*: Volunteers must pay their own transportation to and from the program site and provide their own sleeping bags, tents, and personal gear.

*Project dates*: The weeklong Elderhostel programs begin Sundays from mid-May through September. Other programs of three to five days are scheduled from April through August.

*How to apply*: Send a letter and a résumé to the above address, summarizing your qualifications, background, and experience.

*Work done by volunteers*: Volunteers teach college-level mini-courses in subjects directly related to the river and the surrounding area. Typical subjects include geology, botany, ornithology, river ecology, local history, American Indian lore, archaeology, and astronomy. Lectures should be supported by appropriate handouts that the volunteers furnish for twenty-five students.

*Special skills or requirements*: Volunteers should have excellent verbal teaching skills and must be able to demonstrate thorough knowledge of the subject. These are wilderness camping programs, so all participants should be in good physical condition.

*Commentary*: Oregon River Experiences has been conducting educational river trips in the Northwest since 1977. They began doing Elderhostel programs in 1986.

# Pacific Crest Trail Association

1350 Castle Rock Road
Walnut Creek, CA 94598
(510) 939-6111

*Project location*: Along the 2,638-mile Pacific Crest Trail from Manning Provincial Park in Canada to the U.S.–Mexican border east of San Diego.

*Project type*: Trail building and maintenance.

*Project costs*: Minimal.

*Project dates*: Contact the above office for dates of work weekends.

*How to apply*: Write to the above address for information.

*Work done by volunteers*: Heavy physical labor building and maintaining trails in cooperation with the U.S. Forest Service, National Park Service, and private landowners.

*Special skills or requirements*: Good physical condition and willingness to follow instructions while performing physical labor.

*Commentary*: The Pacific Crest Trail is one of the longest of the eight national scenic trails that are officially recognized in the U.S. and runs along a high altitude route on the ridges of mountain ranges along the west coast.

# Pacific Northwest Trail Association

1361 Avon Allen Road
Mt. Vernon, WA 98273
(360) 424-0407

*Project location*: Various points along the Pacific Northwest Trail between
northwest Montana and the Pacific Ocean in Olympic National Park.

*Project type*: Construction of new segments of trail, repair and maintenance of existing trails, and other related work such as mapping and
preparing a guidebook.

*Project costs*: Responsible for transportation to the project site and food.

*Project dates*: Summer.

*How to apply*: Write to Joan Melcher at the above address.

*Work done by volunteers*: Volunteers both work at the site and maintain
their camp.

*Special skills or requirements*: Knowledge of trails and backcountry living, guidebook writing and map making, and map and compass skills.

*Commentary*: The purpose of the PNTA is to develop and maintain a
1,100-mile foot and horse trail as a showcase of the region.

# Pacific Whale Foundation

101 N. Kihei Road, Suite 21
Kihei, HI 96753
(808) 879-8860

*Project location*: Maui, Hawaii, and Australia.

*Project type*: Research on humpback whales in and around Hawaii and Australia and tropical reef study in and around Maui, Hawaii.

*Project costs*: $1,395 and transportation costs.

*Project dates*: From December through April and June through October.

*How to apply*: Contact the office listed above for an application.

*Work done by volunteers*: All aspects of field study.

*Special skills or requirements*: Participants must be 16 years old or older with a basic knowledge of marine biology and good swimming skills.

*Commentary*: Pacific Whale Foundation is a research, conservation, and educational organization that specializes in the study of marine mammals and their ocean environment.

# Parks Canada Research Adventure

Box 99
Yoho National Park
Field, British Columbia V0A 1G0 Canada
(604) 343-6324; Fax (604) 343-6758
Web site: http://www.worldweb.com/ParksCanada-Yoho/

*Project location*: Currently in Yoho and Banff national parks, but soon to be expanded into other parks.

*Project type*: Scientific research.

*Project costs*: Between $200 and $1,350 (Can).

*Project dates*: Between March and October for two to ten days.

*How to apply*: Contact above for application and list of upcoming projects.

*Work done by volunteers*: Assist wildlife biologists as they study flora and fauna of Canadian parks. The studies include alpine meadows, Rocky Mountain forests, beavers, bluebirds, and wolves.

*Special skills or requirements*: Good physical condition, ability to closely follow instructions, interest in the natural world, and desire to help.

*Commentary*: Canadian parks are somewhat behind U.S. parks in the utilization of volunteers, but this pilot program may be the beginning of a rapid expansion of other volunteer programs in the Canadian parks' systems.

# assport in Time
PO Box 31315
Tucson, AZ 85751-1315
(520) 722-2716 or (800) 281-9176; Fax (520) 298-7044
E-mail: SRIArc@aol.com

*Project location*: National forests throughout the U.S.

*Project type*: Heritage resource management, including archaeological survey, excavation, restoration, lab work, and archival work.

*Project costs*: Volunteers are responsible for travel costs to the projects and for their food.

*Project dates*: Vary.

*How to apply*: Write to the above address for a newsletter and an application.

*Work done by volunteers*: Volunteers work directly with archaeologists on excavations, surveys, lab work, building, restoration, and oral history. PIT also uses volunteers as actors in living history presentations at some national forest sites.

*Special skills or requirements*: No special skills needed in most cases.

# Pax World Service

1111 16th Street NW, Suite 120
Washington, DC 20036
(202) 293-7290; Fax (202) 293-7023
E-mail: paxwldsvc@aol.com

*Project location*: Locations in 1996 included the Middle East, Cuba, Nicaragua, Haiti, and Mexico.

*Project type*: All trips involve extensive personal contact with local development, human rights, and peace organizations. On some of the trips participants take part in various agriculture and building projects.

*Project costs*: Vary according to destination and type and length of tour.

*Project dates*: Two-week projects at various times of the year, but usually during the winter.

*How to apply*: Send for an application at the above address.

*Work done by volunteers*: Various types of social, manual work, including tree seedling planting with local farmers and schoolchildren, building a tool shed for an agroforestry nursery, planting seeds in a shadehouse, and working with local villagers on a community irrigation project.

*Special skills or requirements*: Must be able to do strenuous work in the hot sun and live in less-than-resort conditions.

*Commentary*: Pax World Friendship Tours reflect the commitment of Pax World Service to peace and reconciliation and the development of all people. Hands-On Tours emphasizes the need to take action toward solving a problem. Hands-On Tours work on basic needs by planting trees in Antigua or installing water purification systems in the Dominican Republic. Participants learn about basic development issues and share what they've learned with groups back home. Fact-Finding Tours focus on the need to learn from the people involved in areas of conflict, such as Central America, Cuba, and the Middle East. By "stepping behind the headlines," participants learn firsthand about the people's concerns and positions. All sides of an issue are examined. Participants are encouraged to speak and write about their experience after they return home.

# Peacework

305 Washington Street SW
Blacksburg, VA 24060-4745
(540) 953-1376; Fax (540) 552-0119

*Project location*: Latin America, Pacific region, and countries of the former Soviet bloc.

*Project type*: Community service projects.

*Project costs*: $700 to 1,500 for a two- to four-week program.

*Project dates*: Usually summer, winter, and spring breaks.

*How to apply*: Contact the office listed above for application forms and information.

*Work done by volunteers*: A wide variety of construction and community development tasks.

*Special skills or requirements*: None other than a real interest in helping those in need.

*Commentary*: This program was begun to help bring residents of the former Soviet Union together with those of the U.S. on peaceful projects. Current programs have expanded to bring volunteers from different countries who work together on a variety of community development projects.

# Peruvian Safaris

Garcilazo de la Vega 1334
PO Box 10088
Lima (1) Peru
(14) 313 047

*Project location*: Explorer's Inn Lodge in the Tambopata Reserve in the Amazon Jungle of southeast Peru.

*Project type*: Biology or ecology research projects and construction and maintenance of trails, bridges, docks, and bungalows.

*Project costs*: $36 per day for room and board.

*Project dates*: Year-round, for a minimum of thirty days.

*How to apply*: Write a letter of interest to Max Gunther at the above address.

*Work done by volunteers*: Assisting the researchers in ongoing programs; designing and producing displays and posters for educational purposes; and doing maintenance and construction work on trails, bridges, and bungalows.

*Special skills or requirements*: Applicants should be between 20 and 40 years old. Construction, farming and gardening, arts and crafts, recreation, and previous group experience are all useful.

*Commentary*: Peruvian Safaris owns the Explorer's Inn Lodge at the edge of the Tambopata Reserve, which boasts the highest count of bird species (572) and butterfly species (more than 1,200) on Earth. The Explorer's Inn keeps a minimum of four resident naturalists (biologists and ecologists) doing research.

# Plenty U.S.A.
The Farm
156 Drakes Lane
Summertown, TN 38483

*Project location*: Africa, the Caribbean, Central and South America, and the U.S. Locations vary from year to year.

*Project type*: Projects commonly involve primary health care, small-scale agriculture, light construction, nutrition education, microeconomic development, creating potable water systems, and alternative technologies.

*Project costs*: Volunteers pay their travel and living expenses, which vary depending on the location of the project.

*Project dates*: Two to four weeks at various times of the year.

*How to apply*: Send a letter or postcard to the above address.

*Work done by volunteers*: Work ranges from building, gardening, and providing health care to organizing and fund-raising for projects.

*Special skills or requirements*: Cultural sensitivity, flexibility, patience, and compassion.

*Commentary*: Plenty is a nonprofit, nongovernmental, nonsectarian organization for relief, development, and education. Plenty works around the world promoting cooperation among people of widely varying resources to enhance the self-determination of disadvantaged societies while strengthening trust and respect between cultures.

*Sample projects*: Previous volunteers have helped native Caribs in Dominica build an office for the tribal council, started a community garden on the Round Valley Reservation in California, and taught business management to a Mayan ecotourism association.

# Projects for People
## The Great Earth Travel Company
RR 2, Box 352
Newport, PA 17074
(717) 567-9816

*Project location*: The Bahamas and Belize.

*Project type*: Community service projects.

*Project costs*: $1,000 and up.

*Project dates*: There are eight- and fifteen-day projects in January and February for the Bahamas and in October and November for Belize.

*How to apply*: Contact the office listed above for more information.

*Work done by volunteers*: Volunteers work with social service agencies, schools, and community projects on construction and rehabilitation of buildings and playgrounds.

*Special skills or requirements*: None, but an interest in cross-cultural exchange is necessary.

# QUEST
3706 Rhode Island Avenue
Mt. Rainier, MD 20712
(301) 277-3594; Fax (301) 277-8656

*Project location*: Los Angeles, Tijuana, New York, and Washington, DC.

*Project type*: QUEST collaborates with agencies to provide assistance to homeless men and women, children with AIDS and their families, abandoned children living in an orphanage in Tijuana, women and children living in shelters, and programs aimed at gang prevention.

*Project costs*: Volunteers pay for their transportation to and from the QUEST site.

*Project dates*: The summer program is from late June to early August. The yearlong program is September through August.

*How to apply*: Send a letter requesting information to the above address.

*Work done by volunteers*: Child care workers, recreational-tutorial personnel, teachers, nurses, community organizers, translators, and clinic and shelter workers are all needed.

*Special skills or requirements*: Single men and women. Some sites are limited to women. All volunteers must have a high school diploma, and some positions require college, professional training, or work experience. Fluency in Spanish is required for the Tijuana site. A personal interview is required.

*Commentary*: QUEST, established in 1971, provides summer and yearlong opportunities for lay and religious volunteers to live together in community and collaborate in ministry among the poor and marginalized. The goal of QUEST is to provide concrete, realistic, and ongoing work with the poor in the context of a faith community, so that volunteers develop a critical social consciousness that will enable and enhance their effective work for justice.

# Railway Preservation Society of Ireland
Castleview Road
Whitehead, County Antrim BT38 9NA United Kingdom

*Project location*: Whitehead, County Antrim, Northern Ireland, and Mullingar, County Westmeath, Republic of Ireland.

*Project type*: Restoration of locomotives—mostly steam, although there are a few diesel—and carriages for railways throughout Ireland.

*Project costs*: Volunteers are responsible for room, board, and transportation.

*Project dates*: Any weekend year-round.

*How to apply*: Write to the above address for information and an application.

*Work done by volunteers*: Volunteers are involved in all restoration and upkeep of the rolling stock on the railways, including major overhauls on the engines.

*Special skills or requirements*: A willingness to work hard and follow instructions.

*Commentary*: The society, formed in 1964, is actively engaged in restoring locomotives and carriages for use on excursion trains. To date, its collection of restored items is comprised of nine steam locomotives, two diesels, more than thirty coaches, and a number of rail cars.

*Sample projects*: The society is currently restoring two locomotives. Number 461 is the last survivor of 54 locomotives of the mogul (2-6-0) wheel arrangement that ran in various parts of Ireland. Most of its life was spent hauling heavy freight trains on the steeply graded Wexford-Dublin Line. Number 27 was the last conventional steam locomotive built for the Irish Railways, and is one of only two locomotives with a 0-6-4T wheel arrangement left in the United Kingdom.

# Religious Society of Friends
Friends Weekend Workcamps
1515 Cherry Street
Philadelphia, PA 19102
(215) 241-7236

*Project location*: Philadelphia.

*Project type*: Inner-city work camp.

*Project costs*: $35 for a weekend work camp. Volunteers are responsible for all transportation costs.

*Project dates*: Weekend camps run monthly from January through May.

*How to apply*: Write to Michael Van Hoy, Friends Workcamps, at the above address for more information and an application. Weekend camps are limited to eighteen participants, so apply early.

*Work done by volunteers*: A wide variety of activities from preparing meals and taking care of children at a shelter for homeless women to visiting elderly people and helping people repair their homes.

*Special skills or requirements*: Anyone 15 or older can apply for either camp. The Friends attempt to bring together as many people from different backgrounds, races, countries, and states as possible, so applicants from outside the Philadelphia area are encouraged to apply.

*Commentary*: The weekend work camps are an excellent way for volunteers to find out about the work camp experience without making a commitment to go to a foreign land for a longer stay.

# Rempart

1, rue des Guillemites
75004 Paris, France
(1) 42-71-96-55

*Project location*: Throughout France at more than 150 sites.

*Project type*: Archaeological restoration of historical monuments and sites in France.

*Project costs*: Vary by site. Most of the sites provide room and board. Volunteers are responsible for transportation costs.

*Project dates*: Most projects are in July and August. Some sites accept volunteers for as little as one weekend, while some allow two-week stays, and others require volunteers to stay for the entire three-week session.

*How to apply*: Write to Delegation Nationale de l'Union Rempart at the above address for more information and an application. Rempart has a page of information about their organization in English.

*Work done by volunteers*: A wide variety of restoration work is done at each site. Some sites also include archaeological excavations.

*Special skills or requirements*: Volunteers should know at least rudimentary French and be interested in hard work and the cultural heritage of France.

*Commentary*: This is the largest organization in France that coordinates the excavation and restoration of historical monuments.

# Rothberg School for Overseas Students

Hebrew University of Jerusalem
11 E. 69th Street
New York, NY 10021
(212) 472-2288

*Project location*: Israel.

*Project type*: Archaeological digs.

*Project costs*: Approximately $600 plus transportation to Israel.

*Project dates*: Summer classes during July and August.

*How to apply*: Write to the above address for summer school registration information.

*Work done by volunteers*: Normal archaeological dig work conducted during the hottest time of summer.

*Special skills or requirements*: The projects offered in this program are field schools that are part of the regular summer classes, and all participants must register as summer school students.

*Commentary*: This program represents students from several hundred U.S. and European universities each year.

# Royal Society for the Protection of Birds, Reserves Management

The Lodge
Sandy, Bedfordshire SG19 2DL United Kingdom
(01767) 680 551; Fax (01767) 692 365

*Project location*: England, Scotland, and Wales.

*Project type*: Voluntary reserve warden.

*Project costs*: Participants are responsible for their food and for transportation to and from reserves.

*Project dates*: Year-round for a minimum of one week and a maximum of four weeks for first-time volunteers.

*How to apply*: Write a letter to the above address for a Voluntary Wardening Scheme booklet and an application.

*Work done by volunteers*: Varies by reserve, but all volunteers are normally expected to perform physical work as needed at the reserve and to assist reserve visitors with questions.

*Special skills or requirements*: Volunteers should have an interest in birds and their conservation and be physically fit and at least 16 years old.

*Commentary*: Volunteers gain practical experience in the day-to-day operations of the Royal Society for the Protection of Birds reserves and have excellent opportunities for unparalleled bird watching.

# Royal Tyrrell Museum

Box 7500
Drumheller, Alberta T0J 0Y0 Canada
(403) 823-7707

*Project location*: The Alberta Badlands, east of Calgary.

*Project type*: Dinosaur dig.

*Project costs*: $800 per week.

*Project dates*: June through August.

*How to apply*: Write to the Volunteer Coordinator at the above address.

*Work done by volunteers*: Normal paleontology dig jobs, most of which are hot and dusty. The workday is from 6:00 A.M. to 2:00 P.M.

*Special skills or requirements*: No special skills are required other than a sincere interest in the subject, although paleontology students are given priority. Volunteers range in age from 18 to 55. Summers in Alberta can be hot, so volunteers should be able to withstand the rigors of working in midday heat.

*Commentary*: Programs are run at various sites in the Dinosaur Provincial Park, and volunteers are selected as the need arises. Although not part of the Tyrrell Museum program, the University of British Columbia Center for Continuing Education offers a field study program in the Badlands during the fall when there is sufficient demand. Write to the University of British Columbia Center for Continuing Education, Field Studies and Educational Travel Program, 5997 Iona Drive, Vancouver, British Columbia, Canada, V6T 2A4, or call (604) 222-5207 for more information.

# Samaritans

5666 La Jolla Boulevard
La Jolla, CA 92037
(619) 456-2216

*Project location*: Baja, California; Guadalajara, Jalisco, Mexico; Guatemala; Mindanao, the Philippines; Nairobi, Kenya; Rome, Italy.

*Project type*: Work camps, medical ministries, and evangelistic ministries.

*Project costs*: Generally between $200 and $500, plus transportation.

*Project dates*: Mostly in the summer for one or two weeks.

*How to apply*: Write to Dr. Harold Jones at the above address for more information and an application.

*Work done by volunteers*: Most projects involve building churches and chapels. Evangelism is a second major activity.

*Special skills or requirements*: Volunteers must be Christians who are interested in evangelism in the Third World.

*Commentary*: Although the Samaritans' ministry has been completely reorganized recently, they have been in service since 1967. With reorganization they may be expanding their volunteer programs.

# Saskatchewan Archaeological Society Field School

5-816 1st Avenue N
Saskatoon, Saskatchewan S7K 1Y3 Canada
(306) 664-4124; Fax (306) 665-1928

*Project location*: Lake Diefenbaker near Birsay, Saskatchewan, Canada.

*Project type*: Archaeological excavation.

*Project costs*: Registration is $30 per four-day session and $25 to $40 per day for room and board.

*Project dates*: Late June to mid-July for four to eight days.

*How to apply*: Write to the office listed above for a brochure and an application.

*Work done by volunteers*: General excavation work.

*Special skills or requirements*: None. Participants receive complete instruction in excavation techniques.

*Commentary*: This field school has operated since 1983 and has been at Lake Diefenbaker since 1986.

# Scottish Conservation Projects Trust

Balallan House
24 Allan Park
Stirling FK8 2QG United Kingdom
(01786) 479 697

*Project location*: Throughout Scotland, including Orkney, Shetland, and the Hebrides.

*Project type*: Practical conservation work, seven- to fourteen-day residential projects doing tree planting, restoration of traditional buildings, pond construction, footpath construction, and habitat management.

*Project costs*: About $10 per day. Insurance, tools, training, accommodations, and food are provided.

*Project dates*: Between March and November each year.

*How to apply*: Contact the office listed above for a free program of projects.

*Work done by volunteers*: Volunteers work in groups of eleven with an experienced leader from 9:00 A.M. to 5:00 P.M. each day with breaks. Evenings and one day each week are free. All food is provided, and volunteers take turns cooking.

*Special skills or requirements*: No special skills, just fitness and health. The minimum age is 18; the maximum is 70.

*Commentary*: SCP is a charity established in 1984. Each year more than eighty Action Breaks and sixty Weekend Training Courses are held. Volunteers come from all over the United Kingdom and abroad.

# 🌐 Service Civil International/IVS U.S.A.

5474 Walnut Level Road
Crozet, VA 22932
(804) 823-1826
E-mail: sciivsusa@igc.apc.org

*Project location*: The U.S. and Europe.

*Project type*: Work camps.

*Project costs*: From $50 for U.S. camps to $100 for European and $250 in the former Soviet Union, plus transportation to the site.

*Project dates*: During the summer for two to four weeks.

*How to apply*: Send $5 to the above address for a list of summer work camps. For general information about the organization send a stamped, self-addressed envelope to the above address.

*Work done by volunteers*: Physical or social work, but varies by camp.

*Special skills or requirements*: Campers in U.S. work camps must be at least 16 years old, and in others at least 18. There is no upper age limit.

*Commentary*: SCI/IVS provides a way for people of different countries to develop close friendships in the process of doing valuable community service. Through practical and enjoyable work, volunteers live the challenge of international cooperation on a personal level.

# Servizio Volontariato Giovanile

8.10 Piazza Vantitelli
Caserta 81100 Italy
(0823) 322 518

*Project location*: Caserta, Italy.

*Project type*: Archaeology, environmental protection, forest fire fighting, and other civil work projects.

*Project costs*: None, other than transportation to Italy.

*Project dates*: July to August for eight weeks.

*How to apply*: Write to the above address for information and an application. This organization only accepts five volunteers from the U.S. each year.

*Work done by volunteers*: Varies.

*Special skills or requirements*: Interest in working in a multicultural environment.

# Severn Valley Railway Company Limited
The Station
Bewdley, Worcestershire DY12 1BG United Kingdom
(01299) 403 816; Fax (01299) 400 839

*Project location*: At six stations along the railway, which is located to the west of Birmingham in the birthplace of the Industrial Revolution.

*Project type*: Operation of a steam railway.

*Project costs*: Volunteers are responsible for all travel expenses, arrangements, and meals. Lodging in old railway coaches is available at a nominal cost.

*Project dates*: April through September.

*How to apply*: Write to P. V. Edkins, Volunteer Liaison Office, at the above address for information on volunteering and becoming a member of the railway.

*Work done by volunteers*: Every aspect of operating a railway, from working as engineer to painting the bathroom.

*Special skills or requirements*: A strong interest in railways and a desire to work under supervision.

*Commentary*: Volunteers can visit a number of museums and historic sites associated with the Industrial Revolution before or after volunteering.

# Sierra Club Outing Department

730 Polk Street
San Francisco, CA 94109
(415) 776-2211

*Project location*: Throughout the U.S.

*Project type*: Cleanup, trail maintenance, and wilderness restoration.

*Project costs*: $250 to $450 for registration, food, and insurance. Volunteers are responsible for all transportation.

*Project dates*: Between March and September for seven to ten days.

*How to apply*: Write to Sierra Club Outings at the above address for more information and an application. The Sierra Club begins processing applications for trips in January each year.

*Work done by volunteers*: Volunteers generally do manual labor such as trail building and maintenance, wilderness area cleanup and revegetation, archaeological work, and campsite restoration.

*Special skills or requirements*: Volunteers must be in good physical condition. Some trips require backpacking experience.

*Commentary*: The Sierra Club has the largest service program of any of the outdoor and ecologically oriented organizations and is able to charge somewhat less for their trips than some of the others because they are subsidized by public agencies and private donations. While there have been very few work-related accidents on the trips, team leaders are trained in first aid and survival skills, and the Sierra Club tries to have a volunteer physician on every trip. These physicians volunteer their time in exchange for a waiver of the trip price and are not required to work on the project, although many do. Physicians interested in joining a project should contact Dr. Bob Majors, 3508 Williamsborough Court, Raleigh, NC 27609.

*Sample projects*: Some projects that Sierra Club volunteers have worked on in recent years include Coyote Gulch, Glen Canyon Recreation Area in Utah, where volunteers helped backcountry rangers clean up thirteen miles of trails in this isolated area of sandstone canyons with arches, alcoves, oases, and Native American ruins. Other volunteers have worked within site of Mount McKinley attempting to eradicate evidence of past mining activities in Denali Park. The project ended with a twenty-five-mile cross-country hike back over the tundra. Volunteers also have helped repair the most popular trail in Cranberry Wilderness, Monongahela National Forest, West Virginia, which is a 35,550-acre wilderness area that is designated as a black bear sanctuary. Still other volunteers worked on the Salmon River Work and Raft project in Klamath Forest, California. The volunteers, all of whom could swim and had previous rafting experience, built a steep trail down to the Cascade Rapids and roughed out a trail to the Last Chance/Freight Train rapids—both of which are Class 5 white water. These were the first trails to one of the most technically difficult rivers in the country.

# Sioux YMCAs

PO Box 218
Dupree, SD 57623
(605) 365-5232; Fax (605) 365-5230

*Project location*: Sioux Reservation communities in North and South Dakota.

*Project type*: Community development, youth projects, and camping.

*Project costs*: Volunteers are responsible for travel and personal expenses. Room and board are provided.

*Project dates*: Volunteers are accepted quarterly for periods of no less than ten weeks. Call for starting dates. (Starting dates are set by the YMCA.)

*How to apply*: Write or call for an application.

*Work done by volunteers*: Community recreation and support, youth projects, and fund-raising projects. Volunteers operate youth centers, organize community recreational events, assist in schools and Head Start programs, and serve as a camp counselors.

*Special skills or requirements*: Past experience working with children is required. Must be flexible, mature, creative, and able to work independently.

*Commentary*: These projects are sponsored by the only YMCAs operated by and serving primarily Native American people, and volunteers must realize that all projects entail a twenty-four-hour, seven-days-per-week commitment. Because of problems caused by alcohol abuse on the reservation, all volunteers are required to abstain from drinking and drug use during their service. Persons of all religious faiths are accepted as volunteers, but they will be asked to respect and participate in the Christian religious life of the community.

# Sisson-Callahan Trail

Mount Shasta Ranger District
Mount Shasta, CA 96967
(916) 926-4511

*Project location*: Mount Shasta, which is in northern California near the Oregon border.

*Project type*: Trail reconstruction.

*Project costs*: Volunteers are responsible for transportation to the project and may be responsible for room and board.

*Project dates*: To be set.

*How to apply*: Write to the above address for more information.

*Work done by volunteers*: All aspects of building trails, most of which will be six thousand to eight thousand feet long.

*Special skills or requirements*: Interest in the outdoors and physical stamina.

*Commentary*: This is a new project that is expected to last between five and ten years. It offers an opportunity to work on the reconstruction of a trail originally built as a fire access trail between Sisson (now Mount Shasta City) and Callahan around 1909.

# Société Archéologique de Douai

191, rue Saint-Albin
59500 Douai, France
(27) 96-90-60

*Project location*: Douai and surroundings.

*Project type*: Archaeological excavations.

*Project costs*: Volunteers are responsible for all travel expenses, plus Fr100 for insurance and registration fees. Room and board are provided.

*Project dates*: Excavations are open during summer holidays.

*How to apply*: Write before June 1 to the above address for more information and an application.

*Work done by volunteers*: Archaeological excavation work.

*Special skills or requirements*: No special skills are required, although experienced workers are welcome and will be assigned more complex tasks. Volunteers must be at least 18 years old.

*Commentary*: These two excavations are of medieval urban and small town sites. The work is an attempt to gain a better understanding of everyday life in towns during the Middle Ages.

# Sousson Foundation

3600 Ridge Road
Templeton, CA 93465
(805) 434-0299

*Project location*: The Channel Islands off California's southern coast, and Kings Canyon, Sequoia, and Yosemite National Parks. Other parks will be added in the near future.

*Project type*: Restoring everything from antiquated park service facilities to high alpine meadows.

*Project costs*: $195, depending on the trip, which includes food and camping sites.

*Project dates*: June through September for eight days.

*How to apply*: Contact the office listed above for an application and information.

*Work done by volunteers*: Projects vary depending on the park. Typically volunteers work on revegetation, construction, and maintenance of campgrounds and facilities.

*Special skills or requirements*: No special skills are needed, although construction skills are always useful. Sousson Foundation will accept groups and individuals of any age or background.

*Commentary*: Currently volunteers are needed for a four-year project to install a landscaped, educational trail system designed to protect the General Sherman Tree in Sequoia National Park. This giant sequoia is the largest living tree on Earth.

# South Devon Railway Association
The Railway Station, Buckfastleigh Station
Devon TQ11 0DZ United Kingdom
(01364) 643 536; Fax (01803) 556 516

*Project location*: Buckfastleigh, Staverton, and Totnes railways in south-west England.

*Project type*: Restoring and operating the railway between Totnes and Buckfastleigh.

*Project costs*: Volunteers must provide their room, board, and travel expenses.

*Project dates*: Year-round, but the railway is fully operational only between Easter and October.

*How to apply*: Write to Hon. Secretary, SDRA, 15 Barton Avenue, Paignton, Devon, TQ3 3JQ, United Kingdom, for an application and dates of current projects.

*Work done by volunteers*: All aspects of of restoring, maintaining, and operating a steam railway.

*Special skills or requirements*: None required, but some positions may only be available after special training.

*Commentary*: Both men and women are welcome at this friendly, volunteer-operated steam railway in the heart of the Devonshire countryside. Applicants should join the South Devon Railway Association to be covered by insurance.

# Southern Steam Trust

Swanage Railway
Station House
Swanage, Dorset BH19 1HB United Kingdom
(01929) 425 800

*Project location*: Swanage, in western England.

*Project type*: Railway restoration.

*Project costs*: Volunteers are responsible for their transportation, food, and lodging.

*Project dates*: Year-round.

*How to apply*: Write to F. E. Roberts at the above address for further information and an application.

*Work done by volunteers*: Everything connected with the restoration and operation of a railway line, from building maintenance to laying tracks.

*Special skills or requirements*: Any skill can be used, but volunteers skilled in conservation, engineering, and administration are appreciated.

*Commentary*: The Swanage Railway was closed in 1972 over the opposition of many local residents as well as railway buffs around the country. The Southern Steam Trust is attempting to preserve the services offered by the railway, as well as the historical aspects of it.

# Student Conservation Association

High School Program
PO Box 550
Charlestown, NH 03603
(603) 543-1700

*Project location*: National parks, national forests, wilderness areas, and other sites throughout the U.S.

*Project type*: Conservation and management of public lands and natural resources.

*Project costs*: There is a $45 application fee; $5 for low-income applicants. SCA provides all food and group camping equipment during the project. Financial aid is available to assist with travel expenses. Participants must provide their own individual camping gear and hiking boots. Those who are selected to participate must have a physical examination at their own expense.

*Project dates*: June, July, and August, typically for five weeks. There are also some non-summer programs.

*How to apply*: A listing of projects is published in December and includes an application. This is available for $1.00 from SCA at the above address. The application deadline for projects is March 1.

*Work done by volunteers*: The work is usually physically challenging and may include trail or bridge construction, ecological restoration and revegetation, stream bank stabilization, or wildlife and fish habitat improvement.

*Special skills or requirements*: Applicants must be 16 to 19 years old and in high school (including graduating seniors), physically fit, and willing to undertake the challenges of hard work and rustic living conditions as part of a group.

*Commentary*: Through this program, SCA currently fields approximately five hundred volunteers each year with the National Park Service, the U.S. Forest Service, and other agencies. Volunteers serve in crews of six to ten students and one or two trained adult SCA supervisors. They live in a tent camp, feeding and caring for themselves, usually in a remote location, for the duration of the work period. The work is followed by a one-week recreational trip, most often a hike, allowing the crew to explore its surroundings. This program is not for everyone, but for those willing to work hard and to contribute to the success of a self-sufficient crew, it offers unique rewards and opportunities for personal growth.

*Sample projects*: Projects change from year to year. In the past, volunteers have restored campsites and maintained trails on a roadless island on Lake Superior in Isle Royale National Park, Michigan. Others built a walkway for visitors inside Cottonwood Cave while camping on the surface in the Lincoln National Forest, New Mexico. Still others have worked in the Pike/San Isabel National Forest, Colorado, constructing a segment of the Continental Divide Trail.

# Student Conservation Association

Resource Assistant Program
PO Box 550
Charlestown, NH 03603
(603) 543-1700

*Project location*: At national and state parks, national forests, wildlife refuges, and other sites throughout the U.S., including Alaska and Hawaii

*Project type*: Conservation and management of lands, wildlife, and natural and cultural resources.

*Project costs*: Volunteers receive free housing and money for travel and food expenses. There is a $10 application fee. Those selected for positions may be required to have a physical examination at their own expense.

*Project dates*: Year-round, typically for twelve weeks.

*How to apply*: Listings of positions, which include an application, are published in July (for winter/spring) and December (for summer/fall). They are available from SCA at the above address for $1.00 to help cover postage and mailing.

*Work done by volunteers*: Volunteers assist professional staff. Duties vary and can include wilderness trail patrol, wildlife research, archaeological surveys, environmental education, and forest management.

*Special skills or requirements*: Applicants must be at least 18 years old and high school graduates; there is no upper age limit. Most applicants are college students, but this is not a requirement. Each position has more specific qualifications shown in the listing of positions.

*Commentary*: Founded in 1957, SCA is now one of the nation's largest source of full-time volunteers for conservation work. The Resource Assistant Program fields more than 1,100 volunteers annually with the National Park Service, U.S. Forest Service, Bureau of Land Management, U.S. Fish and Wildlife Service, the U.S. Navy's Natural Resources Program, and a number of state agencies and private organizations. Volunteers receive on-site training for their assignments and may be offered other relevant training, such as CPR, first aid, and fire fighting. Positions change from year to year but some currently available are trail construction and maintenance and mountain patrol in Baxter State Park, Maine; patrolling canoe and foot trails and providing information to visitors at the Kenai National Wildlife Refuge, Alaska; preparing and presenting programs, walks, and guided tours for visitors, conducting visitor surveys, and providing visitor assistance at the Tonto National Forest, Arizona; and assisting with censusing and observing a population of reintroduced bighorn sheep at Yosemite National Park, California.

# Tahoe Rim Trail, Incorporated

PO Box 4647
Stateline, NV 89449
(702) 588-0686; Fax (702) 588-8737
Web site: http://www.yaws.com/Lake Tahoe/TRT.shtml

*Project location*: Around Lake Tahoe in California and Nevada.

*Project type*: A wide variety of volunteer positions are available for trail building, construction and maintenance, fund-raising, office work, writing, and photography.

*Project costs*: Volunteers pay for all transportation and other expenses. On some of the trail-building crews, food is provided.

*Project dates*: Trail-building projects are held from May 1 to October 15. Other volunteer opportunities are year-round.

*How to apply*: Write to the above address for information and an application.

*Work done by volunteers*: Seven separate committees use volunteers, and they need everything from photographers and writers for publicity to attorneys and fund-raisers. Volunteers working on the trail itself do everything from surveying to hauling rocks.

*Special skills or requirements*: An interest in seeing the completion, before the year 2000, of a 150-mile trail around one of the most scenic lakes in the country. Data entry volunteers are needed for developing a master database.

*Commentary*: There is no single uninterrupted trail around Lake Tahoe, and Tahoe Rim Trail, Incorporated is attempting to rectify that by using volunteers to plan and build 150 miles of trail. This is a grassroots effort that is being joined by interested people throughout the country.

# Talyllyn Railway Company
Wharf Station
Tywyn, Gwynedd LL36 9EY United Kingdom
(01654) 710 472; Fax (01654) 711 755

*Project location*: Central Wales along the coast.

*Project type*: Running a narrow-gauge railway.

*Project costs*: Volunteers are responsible for their transportation and living expenses. The railway will provide volunteers with a list of recommended places to stay nearby.

*Project dates*: Year-round.

*How to apply*: Write to the above address for more information and an application form for membership to the Preservation Society.

*Work done by volunteers*: All jobs necessary to running a railway, from running and repairing steam locomotives to working in the gift shop.

*Special skills or requirements*: None. Training is given on the job, if necessary.

*Commentary*: This was the world's first preserved railway. The Talyllyn Railway Preservation Society—also the first railway society in the world—was formed in 1951 to rescue this fine example of Victorian engineering. More than sixty-five thousand people travel on the line each year, and thousands of others help by volunteering work and money.

# Third World Opportunities

1363 Somermont Drive
El Cajon, CA 92021
(619) 449-9381

*Project location*: Tijuana and Tecate, Mexico.

*Project type*: Awareness programs about the realities of poverty and hunger in the Third World and short-term work projects.

*Project costs*: $20 for a one-day awareness trip; the six-day Servant Event house-building project with Habitat for Humanity (see separate entry) is $200 per person, plus transportation costs to the site.

*Project dates*: Awareness trips are year-round, and house-building projects are in spring and summer.

*How to apply*: Send an inquiry to the above address.

*Work done by volunteers*: Most projects are involved with house building in Tijuana and Tecate.

*Special skills or requirements*: Construction skills and knowledge of Spanish are helpful but not necessary.

*Commentary*: Most of the work projects are done in conjunction with other groups working in Tijuana and Tecate. Habitat for Humanity is one program that TWO is currently assisting, and they plan to begin several "straw-bale" house-building projects, particularly in Tecate.

# TOC H

1 Forest Close
Wendover
Aylesbury, Buckinghamshire HP22 6BT United Kingdom
(01296) 623 911; Fax (01296) 696 137
E-mail: nah@rivers.dra.hmg.gb
Web site: http://www.demon.co.uk/charities/toc h

*Project location*: Germany and the United Kingdom.

*Project type*: Social service work with children and the elderly.

*Project costs*: A registration fee of about $10.

*Project dates*: Year-round.

*How to apply*: Write for a project program at the above address.

*Work done by volunteers*: Working on children's camps and play programs, elderly and disabled vacations and care, and environmental projects.

*Special skills or requirements*: None except energy and enthusiasm.

*Commentary*: Social service agencies such as this appear to be more popular, and better supported by volunteers, in Great Britain than in the U.S.

A group of TOC H volunteers examines a rock out-
cropping at one of their work sites. Photo courtesy
of TOC H.

# Travelers Earth Repair Network

PO Box 1064
Tonasket, WA 98855

*Project location*: Throughout the U.S. and the world.

*Project type*: Vary from reforestation to erosion control and forest preservation.

*Project costs*: Volunteers pay their travel and living expenses.

*Project dates*: Vary.

*How to apply*: Write to the above address for a TERN application. There is a $50 registration fee.

*Work done by volunteers*: Hands-on reforestation, erosion control, farming, and education and training of others.

*Special skills or requirements*: Depends on the project. Various skill levels are accepted according to project needs.

*Commentary*: TERN is a networking service that links travelers with various projects around the world.

# Turicoop

Rua Pascoal de Melo 15-1-DTO
1100 Lisboa, Portugal
(804) 539247; telex 13566 Turcop P

*Project location*: Throughout Portugal.

*Project type*: Work camps for construction projects to help the less fortunate.

*Project costs*: Esc 5,000 registration fee.

*Project dates*: July and August, for two or three weeks.

*How to apply*: Write to the above address for registration information.

*Work done by volunteers*: Heavy manual labor, such as painting a school, repairing local paths, and constructing a playground.

*Special skills or requirements*: No special skills are required. For most camps, volunteers must be at least 18 years old, but a few camps will accept volunteers as young as 15.

# University of Alaska, Anchorage, College of Continuing Education
3211 Providence Drive
Anchorage, AK 99508
(907) 786-1344

*Project location*: Confluence of Shaw Creek and Tanana Rivers, twenty miles north of Delta Junction, Alaska.

*Project type*: Archaeological excavation.

*Project costs*: Participants are responsible for transportation to Anchorage and $15 per day for food and miscellaneous expenses.

*Project dates*: Generally in July and August for five or six weeks.

*How to apply*: Write to David Yesher, Department of Anthropology, at the above address for an application. Applications must be received by May 1.

*Work done by volunteers*: Excavation of an eleven thousand-year-old site containing mammoth bones and human artifacts.

*Special skills or requirements*: Must be 18 years old, have a high school diploma, and be in good health. An introductory knowledge of archaeology is helpful but not mandatory.

*Commentary*: The project may be canceled if the field school does not have a minimum of twelve students registered.

# University Research Expeditions Program
Desk M-03, University of California
Berkeley, CA 94720-7050
(510) 642-6586; Fax (510) 642-6791
E-mail: urep@uclink.berkeley.edu

*Project location*: Worldwide.

*Project type*: Scientific research expeditions.

*Project costs*: Costs vary from $600 to $1,600, plus round-trip transportation to the point of departure.

*Project dates*: Most projects are held between June and September, but a few are held from January through March. Most are two to three weeks in length.

*How to apply*: Write to the address above for a catalog and an application.

*Work done by volunteers*: Volunteers work alongside a project leader and staff, collecting and cataloging information. Fieldwork is often hard, tiring, and repetitious, but can be very rewarding and exciting.

*Special skills or requirements*: Previous fieldwork experience is not usually necessary, but some general skills and experiences are helpful in getting accepted by this program. Project leaders often ask for wilderness, photographic, drawing, and diving skills.

*Commentary*: UREP is unique in that it sponsors projects led only by scientists who are employed by some branch of the University of California. In other words, it is actually part of the University of California system, and there is no comparable organization in any other university system in this country. Volunteers, however, can be, and are, from anywhere in the world.

# U.S. Bureau of Land Management

1849 C Street NW, Room 3615
Washington, DC 20240
(202) 208-5261

*Project location*: Most projects are in the western states of Alaska, Arizona, California, Colorado, Idaho, Montana, Nevada, New Mexico, Oregon, Utah, and Wyoming.

*Project type*: Volunteers work in a number of areas, such as wildlife management, recreation, range management, archaeology, administration, and engineering.

*Project costs*: Occasionally volunteers are reimbursed for some expenses, but generally they are responsible for all travel, room, and board.

*Project dates*: Year-round.

*How to apply*: Write to the Volunteer Coordinator at the above address for an application. Volunteer applications also may be obtained from the Volunteer Program Coordinators of the various BLM state offices. If you are interested in serving in a specific region, you can contact the BLM office there for a listing of positions available. The various state offices are listed in the Commentary section.

*Work done by volunteers*: Work ranges from entering data on a computer to installing rainwater catchments for deer and desert bighorn sheep.

*Special skills or requirements*: Some projects require volunteers to have special skills, while others simply require that they have an interest in volunteering and the ability to follow directions.

*Commentary*: The state offices are as follows.

**Alaska**
222 W. 7th Street, Suite 13
Anchorage, AK 99513-7599
(907) 271-5076

**Arizona**
3707 N. 7th Street
PO Box 16563
Phoenix, AZ 85011
(602) 640-5504

**California**
Federal Office Building, Room E-2841
2800 Cottage Way
Sacramento, CA 95825-1889
(916) 978-4743

**Colorado**
2850 Youngfield Street
Lakewood, CO 80215
(303) 239-3669

**Eastern states**
7450 Boston Boulevard
Springfield, VA 22153
(703) 440-1713

**Idaho**
3380 Americana Terrace
Boise, ID 83706
(208) 334-1401

**Montana**
222 N. 32nd Street
PO Box 36800
Billings, MT 59107
(406) 255-2827

**Nevada**
850 Harvard Way
PO Box 12000
Reno, NV 89520
(702) 328-6390

**New Mexico**
Joseph M. Montoya Federal
Building
South Federal Place
PO Box 1449
Santa Fe, NM 87504-1449
(505) 988-6030

**Oregon**
825 N.E. Multnomah Street
PO Box 2965
Portland, OR 97208
(503) 231-6251

**Utah**
324 S. State Street, Suite 301
Salt Lake City, UT 84111-2303
(801) 539-4010

**Wyoming**
2515 Warren Avenue
PO Box 1828
Cheyenne, WY 82003
(307) 772-2326

# U.S. Fish and Wildlife Service
Washington, DC 20240
(703) 358-2043

*Project location*: Throughout the U.S.

*Project type*: Conserving, protecting, and enhancing America's fish and wildlife and their habitats.

*Project costs*: Depends on the individual project.

*Project dates*: Varies according to project.

*How to apply*: For information about current volunteer listings, contact the office nearest where you wish to volunteer. The offices and the states they serve are listed in the Commentary section.

*Work done by volunteers*: Biological and archaeological inventories, recreation planning, population censusing, habitat and facility maintenance, natural resource planning, clerical assistance, environmental education, and public outreach.

*Special skills or requirements*: Varies by project.

*Commentary*: The U.S. Fish and Wildlife Service uses thousands of volunteers for a wide range of activities. Volunteers are valuable to the management of our nation's fish and wildlife resources and play a vital role in helping the U.S. Fish and Wildlife Service fulfill its mission. The volunteer program increases public understanding and appreciation through hands-on experience. The regional offices are as follows.

**Volunteer Coordinator (AK)**
**U.S. Fish and Wildlife Service**
1011 E. Tudor Road
Anchorage, AK 99503
(907) 786-3542

**Volunteer Coordinator (CO, KS, MT, NE, ND, SD, UT, WY)**
**U.S. Fish and Wildlife Service**
Denver Federal Center, Box 25486
Denver, CO 80225
(800) 872-6277

**Volunteer Coordinator (IA, IL, IN, MI, MN, MO, OH, WI)**
**U.S. Fish and Wildlife Service**
1 Federal Drive, Federal Building
Fort Snelling, MN 55111
(612) 725-3500

**Volunteer Coordinator**
**(CT, DE, MA, ME, NH, NJ, NY, PA, RI, VT, VA, WV)**
**U.S. Fish and Wildlife Service**
300 Westgate Drive
Hadley, MA 10135
(413) 253-8000

**Volunteer Coordinator (CA, HI, ID, NV, OR, WA)**
**U.S. Fish and Wildlife Service**
911 N.E. 11th Avenue
Eastside Federal Complex
Portland, OR 97232-4181
(503) 231-6121

**Volunteer Coordinator (AL, AR, FL, GA, KY, LA, MS, NC, SC, TN, PR)**
**U.S. Fish and Wildlife Service**
1875 Century Boulevard NW
Atlanta, GA 30345
(404) 679-4000

**Volunteer Coordinator (AZ, NM, OK, TX)**
**U.S. Fish and Wildlife Service**
PO Box 1306
Albuquerque, NM 87103
(505) 248-6911

# U.S. Forest Service—Volunteers in the National Forests

PO Box 96090, Room 1010 RPE
Washington, DC 20090-6090
(202) 205-1760

*Project location*: Throughout the U.S.

*Project type*: A wide variety of projects are available, including archaeological excavation, campground hosting, office work, trail work, ski patrols, and backcountry ranger work.

*Project costs*: Volunteers are usually responsible for all transportation and living expenses, but the overall cost depends on the individual project. Some projects have tuition fees, and some provide housing and living stipends.

*Project dates*: Varies according to project.

*How to apply*: Some offices of USFS are listed individually, but they all use volunteers extensively. If you are interested in a particular region, you can use the addresses listed below to contact that region's office directly. The regional offices are listed in the Commentary section.

*Work done by volunteers*: Varies by project.

*Special skills or requirements*: Varies by project.

*Commentary*: The regional offices are as follows.

**Alaska Region**
Federal Office Building
PO Box 21628
Juneau, AK 99802
(907) 586-8863

**Eastern Region**
310 Wisconsin Avenue
Milwaukee, WI 53203
(414) 297-3693

**Forest Products Laboratory**
1 Gifford Pinchot Drive
Madison, WI 53705
(608) 231-9200

**Intermountain Research Station**
Federal Office Building
324 25th Street
Odgen, UT 84401
(801) 625-5412

International Institute of
Tropical Forestry
Call Box 25000
UPR Experimental Station
Grounds
Rio Piedras, PR 00928
(809) 766-5335

North Central Forest Experiment
Station
PO Box 6775
Radnor, PA 19087
(215) 975-4200

Northern Region
Federal Building
PO Box 7669
Missoula, MT 59807
(406) 329-3194

Pacific Northwest Region
PO Box 3623
Portland, OR 97208
(503) 221-2877

Pacific Northwest Research
Station
PO Box 3890
Portland, OR 97208
(503) 326-5640

Pacific Southwest Forest and
Range Experiment Station
PO Box 245
Berkeley, CA 94701
(510) 559-6310

Pacific Southwest Region
630 Sansome Street
San Francisco, CA 94111
(415) 556-0122

Rocky Mountain
PO Box 25127
Lakewood, CO 80255
(303) 275-5350

Southern Forest Experiment
Station
PO Box 2680
Ashville, NC 28802
(704) 257-4390

Southern Region
1720 Peachtree Road, NW
Atlanta, GA 30367
(404) 347-4191

Southwestern
Federal Building
517 Gold Avenue SW
Albuquerque, NM 87102
(505) 842-3292

# Valamo Monastery
SF-79850 Uusi-Valamo, Finland

*Project location*: Eastern Orthodox monastery in a small Finnish community.

*Project type*: Normal day-to-day work of monastery.

*Project costs*: Transportation and spending money.

*Project dates*: Year-round.

*How to apply*: Contact the office listed above for more information.

*Work done by volunteers*: Volunteers participate in daily activities such as gardening, kitchen work, and maintenance projects.

*Special skills or requirements*: Interest in exploring life in a monastery.

*Commentary*: Volunteers are given the opportunity to learn about Eastern Orthodox religion, but it is not required.

# The VIEW Foundation

13 Hazelton Avenue
Toronto, Ontario, M5R 2E1 Canada
(416) 964-1914; Fax (416) 964-3416

*Project location*: Costa Rica and Antarctica.

*Project type*: Park maintenance and environmental cleanup.

*Project costs*: Projects in Costa Rica cost between $2,000 and $2,500, including airfare from Toronto or New York. Those in Antarctica cost between $4,300 and $5,900, incuding airfare from major cities in the U.S. and Canada.

*Project dates*: Costa Rica projects are two to three weeks long and are offered year-round. The Antarctica projects are for three weeks between December and March.

*How to apply*: Write or call for a brochure and application package, which costs $5.

*Work done by volunteers*: In Costa Rica volunteers rebuild old trails, construct new ones, plant trees, and work on community and environmental projects. In Antarctica volunteers work at Polish and Russian research stations cleaning up debris left from earlier scientific projects.

*Special skills or requirements*: No special skills are required, but participants should be in good physical condition and be prepared to maintain a positive attitude in trying conditions.

*Commentary*: The VIEW Foundation is a nonprofit Canadian organization that recently received an Honorable Mention by *Conde Nast Traveler* magazine for its responsible contribution to the growing field of ecotourism. Its goal is to support local endeavors aimed at improving social and/or environmental conditions, while at the same time giving volunteers the opportunity to learn intercultural, practical, and global citizenship skills. Trips are offered for adults as well as high school students (ages 15–18).

# Voluntary Workcamps Association of Ghana

PO Box 1540
Accra, Ghana
Tel 63486

*Project location*: Throughout Ghana, with some camps in adjoining countries.

*Project type*: Work camps.

*Project costs*: $100 registration and travel to the country.

*Project dates*: For two to three weeks between June and September.

*How to apply*: Contact one of the organizations in the U.S. such as Service Civil International/IVS U.S.A. or Volunteers for Peace, Incorporated (see Index), or write to the above address for membership information.

*Work done by volunteers*: A wide variety of public service projects.

*Special skills or requirements*: Participants should be at least 16 years old and physically fit enough for heavy manual labor.

*Commentary*: Another of the many work camp associations around the world, Voluntary Workcamps Association of Ghana began in 1956 with a group of eleven men and women who wanted to direct the energies of young people in their country.

# Voluntary Workcamps Association of Nigeria
PO Box 2189
Lagos, Nigeria
(1) 862997

*Project location*: Throughout Nigeria.

*Project type*: Community development projects.

*Project costs*: $100 placement fee.

*Project dates*: Between June and January each year.

*How to apply*: Request more information from the National General Secretary at the above address.

*Work done by volunteers*: Manual labor for construction and agricultural projects.

*Special skills or requirements*: Volunteers must be able to live in simple, rough conditions, work forty hours per week, and speak English. Volunteers must have smallpox, malaria, and cholera vaccinations prior to entering Nigeria.

*Sample projects*: Previous volunteers have helped with construction of a multipurpose community center in the northern part of Bendel State and the construction of roads in the eastern part of Ondo State and in the southern part of Oyo State.

# Voluntary Workcamps Association of Sierra Leone

PO Box 1205
Freetown, Sierra Leone
26501, ext. 221

*Project location*: Rural areas of Sierra Leone.

*Project type*: Community development projects.

*Project costs*: $150 per project and transportation to and from the site.

*Project dates*: For two weeks between July and September.

*How to apply*: Write to the above address for an application, or contact one of the U.S. work camp organizations, such as Service Civil International/IVS U.S.A. and Volunteers for Peace, Incorporated (see Index).

*Work done by volunteers*: Clearing brush, digging trenches, transplanting seedlings, repairing health centers, and other community service projects.

*Special skills or requirements*: No special skills are necessary, except for medical projects where volunteers should either be medical students or practitioners.

*Commentary*: This is a nonprofit, nongovernmental organization that is promoting international contact, cultural exchange, and rural development.

# Volunteers for Israel

330 W. 42nd Street, Suite 1818
New York, NY 10036
(212) 643-4848; Fax (212) 643-4855
E-mail: vol4israel@aol.com

*Project location*: Throughout Israel.

*Project type*: Work in hospitals, Israel Defense Forces bases, archaeological digs, and Jerusalem Botanical Gardens.

*Project costs*: Between $700 and $1000.

*Project dates*: Year-round. Participants depart weekly for three-week programs.

*How to apply*: Call the above phone number for an application and information.

*Work done by volunteers*: Volunteer work may include general labor, maintenance and repair, patient care, kitchen or laundry duties, gardening, warehousing, and carpentry.

*Special skills or requirements*: Good character and good mental and physical health, as well as enthusiasm. Volunteers should be between 18 and 80 years old.

*Commentary*: Over thirty thousand volunteers from the U.S. and ten thousand from other countries have joined Volunteers for Israel since 1982. These volunteers have provided moral support to the State of Israel while gaining great insight into the culture and daily life of the Israeli people.

# Volunteers for Outdoor Colorado

600 S. Marion Parkway
Denver, CO 80209
(303) 715-1010; Fax (303) 715-1212

*Project location*: Throughout Colorado.

*Project type*: Trail building, tree planting, revegetation, carpentry, improving wildlife and river habitats, and constructing boardwalks and wildlife viewing blinds.

*Project costs*: None.

*Project dates*: Various weekends during the spring, summer, and fall.

*How to apply*: Call or write the office listed above for project schedule.

*Work done by volunteers*: Trail building, tree planting, revegetation, and carpentry.

*Special skills or requirements*: None.

*Commentary*: Volunteers for Outdoor Colorado is a nonprofit organization of volunteers working together to improve public lands. In both cities and remote wilderness they've built miles of trails, planted thousands of trees, constructed whole-access boardwalks and nature trails, and improved wildlife and river habitats. VOC projects take place on weekends in the spring, summer, and fall with 125 to 300 volunteers per project.

# 🌎 Volunteers for Peace, Incorporated— International Work Camps

Tiffany Road
Belmont, VT 05730
(802) 259-2759; Fax (802) 259-2922
E-mail: vfp@vermontel.com
Web site: http://www.vermontel.com/~vfp/home.htm

*Project location*: In sixty foreign countries and throughout the U.S.

*Project type*: Work camps.

*Project costs*: A $12 membership contribution that is deductible from future registration fees. Membership includes a newsletter and an international work camp directory that contains over eight hundred work camps and is updated each year. Registration is $175 per camp, plus the cost of transportation to the camp.

*Project dates*: Most camps run for two to three weeks between May and September. A few camps run year-round.

Campers at a Volunteers for Peace work camp take a break from renovating a house in Wichita, Kansas. Photo courtesy of Volunteers for Peace.

*How to apply*: Write or call for information and an application.

*Work done by volunteers*: A wide variety of community services.

*Special skills or requirements*: Most programs are for ages 18 and up. A few are for ages 15 and up. No special skills or foreign languages are required, but an interest in learning new customs, willingness to live and work in an international group, sometimes under difficult conditions, and a cooperative spirit are all desirable.

*Commentary*: VFP is an organization with one activity—finding funding and volunteers for work camps around the world. They are not a travel agency and do not book flights or tours of any kind. They probably have the largest selection of work camps of any of the organizations in this guide.

# Volunteers for TAU

900 N. 90th Street
Omaha, NE 68114-2769
(402) 391-4300

*Project location*: Mainly in the central, southeast, and southwest U.S.

*Project type*: Various types of ministry.

*Project costs*: $10 registration fee, and transportation to and from the project site.

*Project dates*: Determined by the volunteer.

*How to apply*: Request an application from the office listed above.

*Work done by volunteers*: Depends on the work site. Volunteers work on any number of social service projects in communal settings.

*Special skills or requirements*: Work sites are selected to match the volunteer's interests and abilities.

*Commentary*: Volunteers for TAU is a program sponsored by the School Sisters of St. Francis. It is an invitation to be a source of new life, new meaning, and new hope to women, men, and children throughout the U.S.

# eers in Overseas Cooperative Assistance

eet NW, Suite 1075
Washington, DC 20001
(202) 383-4961

*Project location*: Countries throughout Africa, Asia, emerging European democracies, and Latin America.

*Project type*: Agricultural technical assistance.

*Project costs*: VOCA pays all expenses for volunteers if the project lasts thirty days or longer.

*Project dates*: Year-round, for thirty to ninety days.

*How to apply*: Call for an application.

*Work done by volunteers*: Providing technical assistance to host organizations.

*Special skills or requirements*: Agricultural expertise. Volunteers are highly experienced individuals from U.S. agriculture, agribusiness, cooperative, farm credit, extension service, and land grant university communities with fifteen to thirty years of experience in their fields of expertise.

*Commentary*: VOCA is a private, nonprofit organization that provides short-term technical assistance to cooperatives, agricultural enterprises, and agribusiness in developing countries and emerging democracies upon request from host country organizations. VOCA sends more than one thousand volunteers abroad each year.

# Volver a Casa Fundacion
Cra. De Girona 24
Bascara 17483 Spain
(3) 55-16-90; Fax (3) 55-16-90

*Project location*: Bascara, Spain.

*Project type*: Rebuilding a fifteenth-century farmhouse.

*Project costs*: The foundation provides room and board in exchange for fourteen hours of work per week.

*Project dates*: Reconstruction is scheduled between January and June, and participants must stay for one month minimum.

*How to apply*: Send fax or letter to above at least two months in advance of the time you wish to work.

*Work done by volunteers*: Carpentry, painting, landscaping, gardening, and general maintenance and reconstruction work.

*Special skills or requirements*: Some skills in general maintenance and reconstruction are helpful, and a sensitivity to terminally ill people is necessary.

*Commentary*: The foundation received the farmhouse from the estate of the former owner and is renovating it as a care facility for seriously or terminally ill people.

# Washington State Parks and Recreation Commission

7150 Cleanwater Lane
PO Box 42650
Olympia, WA 98504-2650
(206) 753-5759

*Project location*: One hundred and twenty-eight parks throughout Washington State, from the Pacific Ocean through the Cascades into the dry eastern side of the state.

*Project type*: A wide variety of park enhancement programs, including public relations projects, winter recreation projects, and assistance in a variety of programs.

*Project costs*: Volunteers are responsible for all travel and personal expenses, but campground fees are waived. Most parks have full or partial RV hookups.

*Project dates*: Year-round. The length of stay varies with each project, but campground hosts must stay for one to four weeks.

*How to apply*: Write a request to Volunteer Programs at the above address for an application.

*Work done by volunteers*: Assisting at the office; trail building; park cleanup; acting as interpretive, campground, or marine park hosts; instructing boating safety; and general park maintenance. Volunteers do not collect fees or enforce park rules.

*Special skills or requirements*: Varies by project.

*Commentary*: State parks offer opportunities for volunteers of all ages and walks of life. Applications from families, singles, couples, groups, disabled individuals, and employed or unemployed people are welcome. Washington state parks offer one-time projects as well as long-term and annual volunteer opportunities.

# Welshpool and Llanfair Light Railway

The Station
Llanfair, Caereini on Powys SY21 0SF United Kingdom
(01938) 810 441; Fax (01938) 810 861

*Project location*: Mid-Wales.

*Project type*: Operation of a narrow-gauge, steam railway.

*Project costs*: Small membership fee and free camping; hostels are available for about £10 per week.

*Project dates*: Year-round.

*How to apply*: Write or phone in advance, or simply go to the office listed above and ask for the manager.

*Work done by volunteers*: The railway is run entirely by volunteers under a full-time manager. Unskilled work is always available, and training for skilled jobs, which includes locomotive operation, signaling, and crossing guards, can be arranged in advance.

*Special skills or requirements*: None.

*Commentary*: This line is eight miles long and was built at the turn of the century as a cheap branch line. It has been run as a museum line for the past thirty years and has locomotives and coaches from around the world.

# The Welsh Wildlife Centre

Cilgerran
Cardigan SA43 2TB United Kingdom
(01239) 621 600; Fax (01239) 613 211

*Project location*: On the banks of the River Teifi in western Wales.

*Project type*: Environmental education and general maintenance.

*Project costs*: Participants are responsible for transportation to and from the site, but there is no charge while there.

*Project dates*: Environmental educators are needed particularly between April and July, and other volunteers are needed for varying periods of time throughout the year.

*How to apply*: Contact the Centre for current programs.

*Work done by volunteers*: Educators work with small groups at all levels, and other volunteers do a wide variety of work.

*Special skills or requirements*: An interest in wildlife and willingness to be trained by the Centre staff. No previous teaching experience or working with children is required.

*Commentary*: This wildlife center is the newest of some seventy nature preserves owned and managed by the Dyfed Wildlife Trust (see Index) and is located on former industrial land that has been reclaimed for wildlife.

# Wildland Adventures, Incorporated

3516 N.E. 155th
Seattle, WA 98155
(800) 345-4453

*Project location*: Nepal and Peru.

*Project type*: Trail cleanup and restoration.

*Project costs*: Airfare to project sites, plus $1,495 for the Nepal project and $1,525 for the Peru project.

*Project dates*: The Nepal project is in late October or early November, and the Peru project is generally held in August.

*How to apply*: Contact the office listed above for reservation forms.

*Work done by volunteers*: Trail cleanup and maintenance on the Inca Trail in Peru and the Annapurna Trail in Nepal.

*Special skills or requirements*: None, but all volunteers are expected to be in good physical condition and able to work at high altitudes.

*Commentary*: These are new expeditions to help maintain trails that are hiked by as many as six thousand people annually but receive little maintenance from local governments.

# Wildlands Studies

3 Mosswood Circle
Cazadero, CA 95421
(707) 632-5665

*Project location*: Alaska, Canada, Hawaii, Nepal, New Zealand, Tennessee, Thailand, and the U.S. western mountain regions.

*Project type*: Resource management, wildlife studies, cultural ecology, conservation biology, studies of endangered species, and studies of the impact of tourism.

*Project costs*: $385 to $825 for U.S. programs, and up to $1,900 for non-U.S. programs.

*Project dates*: Year-round.

*How to apply*: Contact the office listed above for information.

*Work done by volunteers*: Full participation in research activities.

*Special skills or requirements*: None.

*Commentary*: Participants can earn college credit for participation.

*Sample projects*: Volunteers have worked on endangered wolf and whale species studies, studied ecological problems in wilderness areas and national parks, studied wild rivers in Montana, and examined cultural ecology and the impact of tourism in the South Pacific.

# Willing Workers on Organic Farms Australia

Mount Murrindal Co-Op
Buchan, Victoria 3885 Australia
(051) 550-218

*Project location*: Throughout Australia and all other countries that do not have an existing WWOOF group.

*Project type*: Organic farming and living and working with a family on a cultural exchange.

*Project costs*: Volunteers are responsible for travel costs. WWOOF membership now includes accident insurance while with a WWOOF host in Australia. Membership fees for Australian projects are $25 for individuals and $30 for couples; overseas is $15.

*Project dates*: Year-round.

*How to apply*: Contact the office listed above for information or for list of farms and other organizations.

*Work done by volunteers*: All types of farm work, including reforestation of unused land, conservational plantings, weeding, harvesting, and stock handling.

*Special skills or requirements*: None.

*Commentary*: In Australia there are over 450 organic farms whose aim is to give organic farming experience, and another 400 where visitors can work.

# Willing Workers on Organic Farms Canada

RR 2 (Carlson Road), S.18, C.9
Nelson, British Columbia V1L 5P5 Canada
(604) 354-4417

*Project location*: Throughout Canada, plus a few farms in the U.S (including Hawaii).

*Project type*: Farm work.

*Project costs*: $25.

*Project dates*: Year-round.

*How to apply*: Send a request for information with two international postal reply coupons to the above address.

*Work done by volunteers*: Various farm or homestead chores; anything is possible from milking goats to weeding gardens and chopping wood.

*Special skills or requirements*: A willingness to help and try as best as one can.

*Commentary*: WWOOF—the largest farm volunteer coordinating service in Canada—is a very successful and wonderful way to see Canada, experience Canadian culture, and gain a wealth of personal experience. The booklet you receive includes addresses of other international WWOOF organizations.

# Willing Workers on Organic Farms Ireland

Harpoonstown
Drinaugh
County Werford, Ireland

*Project location*: Throughout Ireland.

*Project type*: Organic gardening and farming.

*Project costs*: Volunteers are responsible for travel costs to and from the host farm.

*Project dates*: Year-round.

*How to apply*: Write to Annie Sampson at the above address for information, and include two international postal reply coupons.

*Work done by volunteers*: Volunteers work at all aspects of rural life, including farm work, craft work, and organic gardening.

*Special skills or requirements*: Volunteer should be reasonably fit, in good health, and over 16 years old.

*Commentary*: Upon membership in WWOOF, participants receive a host list. WWOOFers and can choose a farm and arrange a visit with the host. Each volunteer must become a WWOOF member. WWOOFers come from all over the world, and the host nationalities include Irish, German, Dutch, and American. Farms vary in size and work, and WWOOFers live as part of the family with their hosts, sharing their work and leisure.

# Winant-Clayton Volunteers, Incorporated

109 E. 50th Street
New York, NY 10022
(212) 751-1616, ext. 271

*Project location*: Great Britain.

*Project type*: Social service.

*Project costs*: Contact for current costs.

*Project dates*: Early June to mid-August.

*How to apply*: Contact Volunteer Coordinator at above address for information.

*Work done by volunteers*: Supervised work in various social agencies.

*Special skills or requirements*: Involvement and interest in social service and social activist work.

*Commentary*: This is an exchange program between the U.S. and Britain. Twenty volunteers from each country spend two months working abroad in a variety of social service agencies in supervised placements.

# Wind Cave National Park

RR 1, Box 190 WCNP
Hot Springs, SD 57747
(605) 745-4600; Fax (605) 745-4207

*Project location*: Wind Cave in the Black Hills, South Dakota.

*Project type*: A variety of volunteer and intern positions are available that involve interpretation, campground hosting, visitor contact, and cave resource management.

*Project costs*: Volunteers are responsible for food, but housing is provided by the park. There are some stipends available for the intern positions.

*Project dates*: Year-round.

*How to apply*: Write to the Superintendent, Wind Cave National Park, at the above address for more information about volunteer and intern positions.

*Work done by volunteers*: Ranges from interpretive work in the visitor center to assisting resource management with cave- and prairie-related projects.

*Special skills or requirements*: An interest in people, prairie, and caves.

*Commentary*: As with most national and state park units, Wind Cave desperately needs volunteers to enhance their offerings to the public.

# Winged Fellowship Trust
Angel House
20-32 Pentonville Road
London N1 9XD United Kingdom
(0171) 833-2594; Fax (0171) 278-0370

*Project location*: Five vacation centers for severely physically disabled people in the United Kingdom.

*Project type*: Respite care.

*Project costs*: Room and board are provided; travel within the United Kingdom is reimbursed.

*Project dates*: Volunteers are needed for one to two weeks from February to December. Vacations for the disabled run throughout the year. Special weeks are offered for those interested in fishing, music, drama, outdoor pursuits, riding, and shopping.

*How to apply*: Write or phone the office listed above to request a brochure and an application.

*Work done by volunteers*: Personal care of disabled guests, pushing wheelchairs on outings, and providing general companionship.

*Special skills or requirements*: Enthusiasm is important, and the Trust feels that the greatest requirement for a volunteer is sensitivity to and awareness of a disabled person's needs.

# Wisconsin Department of Natural Resources

Bureau of Parks and Recreation
PO Box 7921
Madison, WI 53707
(608) 266-2152

*Project location*: All Wisconsin state parks and forests.

*Project type*: Parks, forests, trails, campgrounds, visitor centers.

*Project costs*: Minimal.

*Project dates*: Year-round, length varies. Ski trail patrols are in the winter.

*How to apply*: You must apply to the Superintendent of each park or forest. You can obtain a list of parks and forests by writing to the above address.

*Work done by volunteers*: Campground hosts; nature interpretation; ski, bike, or horse trail hosts and patrols; trail, building, and grounds maintenance; habitat improvement; species inventories; prairie restoration; historical research; visitor information; construction; litter control; and clerical work.

*Special skills or requirements*: Ability to do the work.

# World Horizons International

PO Box 662
Bethlehem, CT 06751
(203) 266-5874 or (800) 262-5874

*Project location*: Rural Alaska, Africa, the Caribbean, Central America, and Western Samoa in the South Pacific.

*Project type*: Community service programs.

*Project costs*: $3,450 inclusive.

*Project dates*: Late June to late July.

*How to apply*: Contact the above for application information.

*Work done by volunteers*: Work in day camps, with the elderly, or repairing and building local community facilities.

*Special skills or requirements*: Must be a high school student with an interest in intercultural exchange.

World Horizons International volunteer helps residents of Carriacon Island in the Caribbean repair and paint their houses. Photo courtesy of World Horizons International.

# WorldTeach

Harvard Institute for International Development
1 Eliot Street
Cambridge, MA 02138
(617) 495-5527; Fax (617) 495-9120
E-mail: worldteach@hiid.harvard.edu
Web site: http://www.hiid.harvard.edu

*Project location*: Shanghai, People's Republic of China.

*Project type*: Teaching English.

*Project costs*: $3,850 for the summer.

*Project dates*: Mid-June to mid-August.

*How to apply*: Write to the above address for information and an application.

*Work done by volunteers*: Volunteers teach English at a special English summer camp for high school students in Shanghai. They live and eat with students while studying Chinese.

*Special skills or requirements*: All college students and graduates who are native speakers of English are encouraged to apply. No teaching or language experience is required. Volunteers receive a ten-day orientation, with teacher and language training involved.

*Commentary*: This program promises intensive intercultural contact. Volunteer teachers spend almost all their time with Chinese students—in the classroom, in the dorm, in the dining hall, and on outings, which occur every weekend. The classes are small with five to ten students. In addition to the summer program in Shanghai, WorldTeach also offers semester and year-long programs in a number of nations around the world.

# World Travellers Network

7350 N. Broadway
Denver, CO 80221
(303) 426-0141; Fax (303) 426-1270
E-mail: wtn@qadas.com

*Project location*: Australia.

*Project type*: Environmental work camps and organic farms.

*Project costs*: $500 to $1,000 plus transportation to Australia.

*Project dates*: Projects with the Australian Trust for Conservation Volunteers are for four to six weeks throughout the year, and work on organic farms is year-round.

*How to apply*: Contact above office for information packet.

*Work done by volunteers*: A wide variety of conservation and farm work is done by volunteers.

*Special skills or requirements*: None but the desire to work hard and learn new skills.

*Commentary*: This is a full-service travel organization that is the U.S. representative of ATCV and WWOOF Australia.

# Wyoming Dinosaur Center

PO Box 868
Thermopolis, WY 82443
(307) 864-2997; Fax (307) 864-5762
E-mail: bronznrocks@aol.com
Web site: http://www.wyoming.com/~WDC

*Project location*: Wyoming.

*Project type*: Digging for dinosaurs.

*Project costs*: Dig-for-a-Day costs $100 per person or $250 per family. Kids' Digs costs $30 for a two-day session.

*Project dates*: Dig-for-a-Day is offered year-round, weather permitting. Kids' Digs are offered occasionally during the summer.

*How to apply*: Contact above for information on current offerings.

*Work done by volunteers*: Normal excavation work.

*Special skills or requirements*: None but an interest in dinosaurs.

*Commentary*: This is a great introduction to excavating for the family, and the center is located in a small town only two hours from Yellowstone National Park and has plenty of facilities, including a hotel.

A family digs for dinosaurs at the Wyoming Dinosaur Center. Photo courtesy of the Wyoming Dinosaur Center.

# Wyoming Recreation Commission

122 W. 25th Street
Cheyenne, WY 82002
(307) 777-6314

*Project location*: Throughout Wyoming at state parks and historic sites.

*Project type*: Outdoor and recreational projects.

*Project costs*: Volunteers are responsible for all travel and living expenses, although there are free campsites, and some have utilities.

*Project dates*: Year-round. Volunteers are most needed from May to September.

*How to apply*: Contact Sharon Bollinger at the above address for an application.

*Work done by volunteers*: Campground hosts, trail workers, simple maintenance, visitor information services, and interpretive programming, including living history.

*Special skills or requirements*: Ability to work with the public, mechanical and craft skills, and an interest in the outdoors or history. Many volunteer positions in this park system are tailored to suit the particular needs and skills of the volunteers.

# YEE Office
Oude Gracht 42
3511 AR Utrecht, The Netherlands
(30) 2311-537; Fax (30) 2343-986
E-mail: yee@antenna.nl

*Project location*: Throughout Europe.

*Project type*: Environmental and nature studies.

*Project costs*: Vary, but are moderate in general.

*Project dates*: Year-round. Larger camps operate mainly during the summer months.

*How to apply*: Write to the above address for the camp list. Send two international reply coupons and a self-addressed envelope.

*Work done by volunteers*: Various duties in conducting nature studies and environmental projects.

*Special skills or requirements*: Most of these camps are for youth between the ages of 12 and 30, but some accept older participants. Campers should be interested in nature and environmental studies.

*Commentary*: YEE exists through the efforts of about forty-five youth organizations throughout Europe concerned with nature and environmental studies. YEE attempts to spread information and knowledge about the environment through work camps and seminars and is actively involved in lobbying and actions on behalf of the environment.

*Sample projects*: Current projects include lobbying for political decisions on behalf of the global climate; campaigning for the preservation of Nordic Forests; and projects on marine studies and conservation, and environmental education.

# Youth Charitable Organization
20/14 Urban Bank Street
Yellamanchili 531 055, Vizag Dt. (A.P.) India
(8924) 31122; Fax (8924) 31231

*Project location*: Over ninety villages thorughout India.

*Project type*: Community development.

*Project costs*: About $10 per day.

*Project dates*: Volunteers must stay a minimum of fifteen days and a maximum of six months and may come anytime during the year with fifteen days' notice.

*How to apply*: Write to above for information packet.

*Work done by volunteers*: Work includes activities in agroforestry, watershed management, building, agriculture, health education, teaching English, and other community development activities.

*Special skills or requirements*: None but a willingness to learn and participate in a different culture and the flexibility to adapt to new situations.

# Youth Service International

301 N. Blount Street
Raleigh, NC 27601
(800) 833-5796 or (919) 733-9366; Fax (919) 733-0309

*Project location*: Central America and Eastern Europe.

*Project type*: Community development and environmental preservation.

*Project costs*: $3,800 per session. Most volunteers raise this money in their communities by promising volunteer work when they return.

*Project dates*: Various times of year, for three months.

*How to apply*: Contact the office listed above for more information on the selection process, which is more complicated than that of most organizations in this book.

*Work done by volunteers*: Various types of physical labor, while helping local people develop sustainable human service and environmental protection projects.

*Special skills or requirements*: Candidates must be between the ages of 17 and 25, and pass a rigorous selection process where they participate in a forty-hour weekend involving strenuous activities. This weekend provides candidates an opportunity to learn what an expedition will entail and gives the staff an opportunity to evaluate the candidates' abilities to work within the confines of a team effort.

*Commentary*: YSI has one of the most intensive programs in this book. Their four-stage program includes a rigorous team selection process, an intensive training program before the team leaves for their project, the project itself, and a requirement that participants perform one hundred hours of volunteer service in the community that supported their participation.

# Zoetic Research

PO Box 2424T
Friday Harbor, WA 98250
(206) 378-5767

*Project location*: The San Juan Islands near the Washington State-Canada border.

*Project type*: Whale research.

*Project costs*: $599 for the five-day trips and $399 for the three-day trips, plus room, board, and transportation to the site.

*Project dates*: Between June and September for five or three days.

*How to apply*: Write to the above address for an application.

*Work done by volunteers*: Whale research helping to mitigate the impact on orca (killer) whales by boat traffic in the San Juan Islands. Waterborn education and public outreach are performed in the presence of wild whale pods.

*Special skills or requirements*: None but seaworthiness and an interest in whale research.

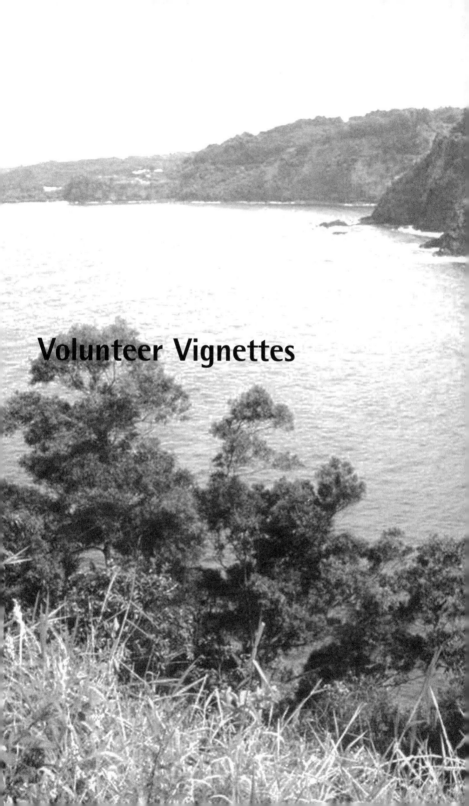

# Volunteer Vignettes

# Croatia: A Volunteer's Experience

*Amy Irwin*

I wanted to spend my summer doing something for the good of others. Luckily at this time I stumbled upon Service Civil International. When I received their spring listing out of curiosity, how could I turn away from the plea "volunteers badly needed in refugee camps," a reference to the Suncokret project in Croatia to work with Bosnian and Croatian refugee children?

At first the idea of going scared me. I pictured long rows of tents, no running water, a lack of food, and bombs in the near distance. In the viewpoint of friends and family I would be "noble but crazy" to go, and to others just plain stupid. Anyhow, with a little time, research, hard consideration, and prayer I made the first step to spending a part of my summer in a refugee camp in Croatia.

After my decision to go was finalized with Suncokret and in my own life, I pursued informing area churches of my plans, They were very receptive with donations to bring to the refugees. In fact I had so many donations I could barely lift the suitcase I had put them all into.

Arriving in Zagreb was anything other than what I expected. I was a small-town American girl there to spend time with victims of a war I couldn't understand and that countries everywhere were twiddling their thumbs over, practically turning their backs on. Zagreb did not fit the picture I had of the capitol of a country at war. It was a city full of discos, cafes, and tourist attractions, but unfortunately not many tourists. The only sign of war was the UN troops driving around and the occasional soldier on the street or train.

One by one the volunteers in my group arrived. There were seven of us in all. Before our departure to Varazdin, where our camp was located, we spent a day in preparation. This was a very impressive and enlightening experience. Through a day of talks and role playing, we all came to realize what we would face and why, and how we fit into it all.

We arrived on a Tuesday, greeted by a pack of restless children awaiting our arrival in front of our barracks. Day by day I would get to know these children, their names, families remaining, habits, gestures of affection, favorite activities, and ways of communicating without language. We were to plan out activities as a group in scheduled times that had been previously set up by Croatian volunteers and our co-leader. Many people felt it was important to give the children a scheduled time to play. If the kids had it their way, we would have been outside from dawn till dusk with them every day.

While there, we organized activities, including an Olympics day, sewing times, painting, drawing, discos, games, lots of football, English lessons, and flute lessons with flutes donated by a Danish volunteer. We also did adult activities including weekly bingo and our daily family visits. Here was where we heard all of the horrible war tragedies people desired to share. I found myself wordless at many of these visits. I knew, however, they were glad we were there and that even just listening could help.

The conditions of the camp were adequate. Living space was crowded but it was evident the refugees did the best they could with what they had left or had received. There was always enough food, but the food itself was lacking in nutrients and sometimes flavor. Every so often someone would arrive bearing outdated chocolate or other things that would go like mad. Varazdin was the camp of the journalists and TV crews, and it was just one step from the line of tents I had pictured.

I stayed in Varazdin for two months in three different groups of volunteers. All of the volunteers were motivated, empathetic people. Although none of us ever had the perfect idea of how to do things, something always turned out in the end. Leaving the camp was the hardest part of the work. I tried to be a stoic, but of course I failed. I cried with every family I visited to say good-bye. I felt close to some of them and I didn't know what would become of their future. They cried also, not only because I was leaving, but also for their own situations. I'll never forget one woman who said, "You can go home now, but when can we?" Again I had no words to appease her, only my own tears and a hug.

(This article was originally published in the *SCI/IVS News* and is reprinted with the permission of SCI/IVS and the author.)

# With Global Service Corps in Kenya
*Carrie Re*

This afternoon, while sitting in front of the computer drinking a cup of cappuccino, I did something that would make most people wince, or perhaps even blurt out a hasty "Yuck!" As I lifted the cup to my lips, I noticed a black speck doing the backstroke in the froth. Without a moment's hesitation I swiftly dipped my index finger into the foam and gracefully extracted the tiny critter. Upon examining it, I casually verified that yes, it was a bug, and promptly flung it into the wastebasket without even a wrinkle of my brow or a look of disdain. Then, the pièce de résistance, I peered into the cup again, and with a mumbled "ah, well," took another sip. After my volunteer vacation to Kenya, I'm a different person in many ways.

Will going on a volunteer vacation change you? You bet it will. You'll now shoo away spiders the size of small cars as if they were flies, be able to assemble your mosquito netting in under ten seconds, and eat with your fingers with such grace even Miss Manners would approve. Most important, however, you'll receive lessons in daily life in the developing world; a life that is drastically different from your own. Your rewards will be great and your memories fond, but it will not be easy. You'll be asked to give of yourself, to put comfort aside, to work as a team, and to open your mind. You'll be asked to put all your preconceptions about life in a developing country aside to experience that life, not to compare or contrast or even ponder, just to experience. It is the experience of a volunteer vacation—the people and places, the culture ingested, the hardships endured, the friendships born, and, most important, the awareness awakened within oneself—that spawns a desire to learn and contribute that will change you in many subtle, wonderful ways.

My own experience began with Global Service Corps's Project Kenya. Eight of us traveled to Kenya from February 18 through March 13 to assist a local organization, Manor House Agricultural Center, in spreading bio-intensive gardening technology to the rural areas of western Kenya. We received training at Manor House and then moved on to our village placements to live with local families and initiate garden plots, seedling nurseries, and compost sites. Manor House, an agricultural training center funded in part by the Ford Foundation, has been providing bio-intensive training to Kenyan farmers and community development leaders for the past ten years. The Global Service Corps represented the first group of American volunteers to receive this training.

There is one small incident in particular that I recall as having been quite significant in instigating a change in attitude in all of us. It was an experience of humility, education, perseverance, and good humor. After the Manor House staff had taught us the basics of bio-intensive gardening such as how to double dig a planting bed, layer a compost pile, and correctly space the fragile seedlings, we set about learning the proper way to swing the African gardening tool of the trade, the jembe. The jembe is a short-handled, heavy hoe that requires a certain grace and deftness to swing; our initial clumsy efforts brought stifled chuckles and outright belly laughs as we attempted to turn the dusty red earth with the awkward and much cursed tool. We laughed too, in between gasping for breath. Again and again, each person attempted to execute the maneuver effectively and with a bit of dignity as the staff shouted tips and encouragement. Finally, drenched in perspiration and covered in a light coating of fine, red dust, we had successfully turned over a few square feet of earth without amputating any body parts or causing grievous damage to each other, our instructors, or the indestructible jembe. The work was hard, the sun was hot, and we all quickly came to respect the enormous effort exerted by the local farmer in coercing the dry, unyielding soil to feed his family.

Crawling beneath my mosquito net that night and recounting that afternoon's activity, the feeling of being unskilled and somewhat useless in this faraway land washed over me. I then realized what a gift that was. I had been given the opportunity to be a student—to try something new, to fail, to learn, and to finally succeed. Throughout the rest of the trip, I realized that our Kenyan hosts are the experts on their country, their lifestyle, and their difficulties.

How have I changed? I went to Kenya expecting to teach and was reminded that to teach, one must first learn. Through this awareness, I returned home ready to learn more, share my experience, and take further action. To paraphrase a good friend: "Your experience will influence a thousand others." Is he a prophet? No. Does he know what he's talking about? Absolutely. There is a chain that is created by one volunteer relating his or her experience on to coworkers, family members, and friends, who in turn pass on the story in their own circles. The links of this human chain are slowly formed as more and more people are drawn in and asked to consider the needs of others and confront their own responsibility as global citizens of a shrinking planet. It is a slow process, but a steady one. As another friend, a Kenyan by the name of Emmanual, told me, "If everyone wanted to see results in a short length of time, no one would plant trees." Being a volunteer vacationer helps you plant the seed of awareness in yourself and in those around you.

(This article was written especially for this book.)

# Eco-Service in Costa Rica

*Marya Glass and Joshua Bruce*

How do several thousand villagers live sustainably within a small rainforest area? Can educational travel, or ecotourism, help save these forests, while supporting the needs of local residents? What is appropriate development? Volunteers from the Global Service Corps (GSC) recently traveled to Monteverde, Costa Rica, to answer these and other vital questions. Their goal is to work with the citizens of Monteverde to create sustainable communities in this ecologically sensitive region.

Located forty-five hundred feet above the Pacific Ocean in northwestern Costa Rica, Monteverde is a mountainous tropical region containing several small towns and farms and, most notably, thousands of acres of lush forests. This dense rainforest provides habitat for hundreds of plant, insect, and animal species, including green- and red-plumed quetzal birds and many endangered species.

Last December, GSC intern Joshua Bruce led a small group of volunteers on a three-week community-service expedition to the Monteverde region. The group worked in cooperation with the Monteverde Conservation League (MCL), a local organization that manages the 42,500-acre International Children's Rain Forest. The MCL's challenge is to expand conservation and reforestation in the area, sponsor biological research and environmental education, and simultaneously work with local residents who subsist in this delicate ecosystem. The dilemma facing Monteverde is common to many natural areas throughout the world: how to balance the needs of the local population with the need to preserve the rainforest environment.

Ecotourism, seen by some as an essential revenue generator, has increased steadily in Monteverde over the past decade. With it have come increased infrastructure development to accommodate increasing numbers of tourists and cultural changes within local farming villages.

Many residents of the Monteverde region are wary of the negative impacts that overdevelopment and reckless tourism have on their communities, families, and natural resources. They do not want to encourage the usual travel tourism. They do, however, want to accommodate those who are interested in environmental education and biological research.

According to Bruce, "People who have lived in the outlying countryside for many years don't want tourism to take over." He added that many residents do not oppose tourism, as long as the number of visitors is limited.

The GSC volunteers split their time between two sites: the San Gerardo Field Station, located within the International Children's Rain Forest park boundaries, and The Association of Buen Amigo, a farming cooperative in the nearby village of San Luis.

Many an environmentalist hailed the creation of the Children's Rain Forest in 1988 as a victory for the Earth. But because of their location within the environmentally protected zone, the people of San Gerardo Arriba found their lifestyles affected. No longer could they graze and farm in their traditional manner. They were compelled to relocate, driven away by the same environmental restrictions that were designed to save the forest.

Some villagers, however, are working with the MCL to develop a more environmentally sustainable community called the San Gerardo Project. GSC volunteers assisted residents and staff with preparations for organic gardening plots, new housing construction (using lumber from fallen trees), and reliance on renewable energy sources. The project intends to provide jobs and income for the people in the community, and the field station will furnish facilities for researchers and student groups. Most importantly, the villagers will be able to return to their original environment, within the boundaries of the forest.

In San Luis, GSC volunteers, with guidance from the MCL, assisted the Association of Buen Amigo with the development of its ecological research station. Designed as a small-scale ecotourism site, it ∧ intended to provide income and employment for impoverished local co-op residents. Ongoing work includes trail maintenance, organic gardening, and further construction of the research station.

The Buen Amigo residents face competition from foreign (mainly U.S.) groups and individuals who run high-priced research facilities that do not necessarily benefit the local community. Villagers complain that these "gringos" trespass across their land and present an unwanted cultural intrusion.

According to Bruce, the Association of Buen Amigo would "allow only groups who have a research project or want to help the small community. They will not give in to providing a place where anyone can come simply to visit and walk in the rainforest—there are other locations in the area for this type of visitation."

He added that the MCL and GSC are interested in helping the village run itself, which requires hard work and a willingness to assist on the villagers' terms.

As pressure to develop land increases, so does the need for sustainable strategies in accordance with local culture. The thrust behind Global Service Corps is to provide volunteers with a first-hand experience of the complex problems of, and appropriate solutions to, human impacts on tropical forests.

(This article was originally published in the *Earth Island Journal* and is reprinted with the permission of the Earth Island Institute and the authors.)

# Guatemala's Unbelievable Situation

*Roya Rafei*

Like most Americans, Helen Lindsay planned a summer trip last year. But the sixty-eight-year-old chose to travel to refugee camps in the far-flung rural villages of Guatemala.

She was part of a seventeen-member delegation that went to the Central American country bordering Mexico for two weeks in late July to become familiar with the situation of the forty thousand Indian refugees who were kicked out of Guatemala in the eighties. The mostly American group, whose members ranged in age from twenty-five to seventy-three, met with U.S., United Nations, and Guatemalan officials and representatives from human rights groups. They climbed mountains, took long rides in cramped buses, and traveled in trucks with wooden seats to visit the refugee camps.

The trip was sponsored by the nonpartisan Peace Brigades International (PBI) and the Interreligious Fellowship of Reconciliation, two pacifist organizations that send unarmed teams of volunteers to various strife-torn regions of the world. The volunteers provide protective accompaniment for labor union leaders, human rights activists, and peasant organization members whose lives have been threatened. The delegations also attempt to foster a dialogue between conflicting parties and provide training in human rights.

The volunteers, however, are not allowed to become involved with rebuilding the camps, according to Lindsay, who is on PBI's national board.

"You can't go in there and help them sow the corn, for example, because it's a nonpartisan group, and it has to guard that very seriously," she said.

Once they return to the United States, the delegation members are expected to call their local representatives and inform them of the refugee situation in Guatemala, recounting the conditions they witnessed at refugee camps, Lindsay added.

"You see poverty here, but poverty there . . . ," she paused, lowered her head, searching for the right words, and said, "is so unbelievable." There is no electricity, running water, or plumbing at the camps in rural Mexico, which are supervised by UN officials. The refugees live in primitive wooden shacks that they have constructed themselves. They grow their own crops and have slowly built schoolhouses and health clinics.

"What they have is just a roof over their heads," Lindsay said. "They can come and go from the camps—it's not like there's barbed wire around them. But where would they go?"

In the late seventies and throughout most of the eighties the Guatemalan army had a "scorch-the-earth policy," said Lindsay. They destroyed hundreds of rural villages where the indigenous Indians lived, and killed thousands of civilians.

"The army wanted to control the area. It destroyed the villages and people fled," Lindsay said. "[The army] pushed the Indians further and further away and into marginal land. Some migrated to the coast to survive."

"To me, the early eighties in Guatemala was the same kind of 'ethnic cleansing' that's going on in Bosnia right now," she continued. "They just wanted to wipe [the indigenous population] out."

After more than a decade, with human rights groups and UN intervention, the Guatemalan government is now willing to take the refugees back. Under an agreement, before they can return the refugees must locate land, purchase the land through Guatemalan government loans, and then prove that they will have enough income to pay back the loan. Lindsay's job now is to work for the refugees from here.

"I'm an activist," she said. "I've always participated in some way to improve things. Human rights is an issue we can't avoid—no matter where violations occur. Somalia, China, Sri Lanka, Guatemala, Bosnia . . . maybe I can make a difference."

(This article is reprinted by permission from the Interfaith Office on Accompaniment.)

# One Volunteer's Story or How I Spent My Summer Vacation

*Francoise Yohalem*

When Global Volunteers asked me to serve as a team leader on a July trip to Vietnam, I was both intrigued and excited. My previous experiences with Global Volunteers had been in Central America (Guatemala and Costa Rica) and I could not resist the opportunity to discover a totally different culture in a part of the world I had never visited.

Global Volunteers's involvement in Vietnam started in the fall of 1994 when the organization was invited by the Vietnamese government to work hand-in-hand with local people in the village of Tan Hiep, located in Tien Giang Province, two hours south of Ho Chi Minh City. Our work and stay in Tan Hiep were arranged through the People's Committee, with the provincial People's Committee coordinating our program at the local level. We were the fifth team to work in Tan Hiep.

Vietnamese officials asked us to work at two schools. At the local high school we would teach conversational English, and at the kindergarten we would help build a security fence.

Our team was made up of eight people; a small but remarkably diverse group. There were two couples in their fifties (among them two university professors, one psychotherapist, and a businessman), and Shizuko, an octogenarian from Hawaii whose daughter was one of the teachers. For two of the other volunteers, Dan and Kate, this was a special "return" trip. Dan, a career military man, had been an advisor in Vietnam in 1968 and had been obsessed with the desire to go back there in peace. Kate, a twenty-one-year-old Vietnamese-born Princeton student had been adopted from a Saigon orphanage by an American couple when she was four months old, and grew up in Florida. For her, too, this was a very intense and emotional pilgrimage. Dan and Kate had not felt comfortable going to Vietnam as tourists, but returning with Global Volunteers seemed the perfect venue. For me who grew up in France and remembers both the French and the American experiences in Vietnam, this promised to be a fascinating journey.

As diverse as our team was, we soon found out we were all well-traveled, idealistic, and open-minded. We also shared curiosity, enthusiasm, and a desire to make friends and learn. After our first orientation meeting in Ho Chi Minh City, as our van took us south into the Mekong Delta we felt that we had already bonded as a team.

Upon our arrival in My Tho, the capital of Tien Giang Province, we were welcomed by the provincial People's Committee and settled in a modest but comfortable guesthouse along a busy street. From there we could experience the very pulse of the city. The day would start at dawn with hundreds of people, young and old, jogging by, children playing badminton on the sidewalk, and peasants carrying precarious loads of fruits and vegetables in enormous baskets to nearby markets. We saw people carrying whole families, furniture, mattresses, and screaming pigs on a bicycle. All day and well into the night the street swelled with this constant flow of people and their wheels. It seems that in Vietnam everyone is busy. There is a feeling of great energy, of a whole country looking and pushing forward.

To our surprise, we found few people wanting to discuss the past, nor did we detect any feelings of resentment or bitterness. As we ventured into the flow of the street on foot or on bikes, or as we visited the market, we were immediately approached by curious but always friendly and smiling people, and received countless invitations to modest homes where the warmth and hospitality were overwhelming.

Our day started early in the morning when we were driven to the village of Tan Hiep twenty minutes away. There we became amateur construction workers helping build a masonry wall for the kinder-

Team leader Francoise Yohalem of Global Volunteers shares a rest period with a local Vietnamese worker. Photo courtesy of Global Volunteers.

garten. We worked at our own pace, with plenty of time to rest or play with the children swarming around us. Shizuko was a favorite of the children, with whom she played educational games, while Kate fascinated the teenagers. Mr. Va Lao, our foreman, directed us and the local people working with us. (Global Volunteers has a one-to-one policy and the volunteers contribute funds to purchase essential materials for the projects.)

One step out of the school grounds and we found ourselves in the midst of a poor village, surrounded by crowded homes, ancestors' tombs, rice paddies, water buffaloes, temples, and many, many people.

Later in the afternoon we went to the Language Center located within the local high school where we worked with the teachers and students. Most of them had only heard English spoken by their Vietnamese teachers and we found that we could be most helpful by concentrating on listening and pronunciation skills. Even though most of us had very limited teaching experience or none at all, we found that we could make a substantial contribution by just speaking slowly and correcting pronunciation. The teenagers were extremely polite, very respectful of their teachers, and very eager to learn.

On our weekend off, we took a trip down the Mekong River, exploring several small islands nearby. The imposing river is a lifeline to the area and is filled with activity, just like main street. Along the shores the vegetation is lush with exotic fruit trees. As we glided into smaller canals that took us more deeply into the mysterious recesses of the land, we had trouble imagining that twenty years ago this area was totally destroyed by napalm and defoliants. Another excursion took us to the famous Cu Chi tunnels, now open to visitors.

While we were in Vietnam, Washington announced the re-establishment of diplomatic ties with Hanoi. The Vietnamese expressed to us their pleasure and hope that this would lead to more opportunities and growth. At our last meeting, we were thanked by the chief economic advisor to the provincial government, a former Viet Cong, who proposed a toast to Dan ("the other soldier"), wishing for a future filled with peace and friendship.

As we parted from our new friends, we were sad. In our short stay we had gained tremendous respect for the Vietnamese people. More important than building the school wall, our goal as "unofficial diplomats" had been to help build a bridge of understanding and friendship. We felt that we had accomplished our mission, but as we returned home, we also felt that we received much more than we gave, and learned much more than we taught.

(This article was originally published in *Destination: Vietnam* and is reprinted with the permission of Global Volunteers and the author.)

# Trail Building in Colorado

*Joyce Downey*

I departed, complete with backpack, sleeping bag, two-person tent, and everything but the kitchen sink, from a sweltering New York summer day, to arrive exhausted but excited in the beautiful, fresh Colorado sunshine. I was met in Denver by a group member and six other international volunteers. Our main destination was the base of Mount Yale, known to the experts as a tough fourteen-footer (fourteen thousand feet) and to the layperson as a rather large mountain with incredibly steep sides. This remote wilderness, a common stomping ground for bears and coyotes, was our base camp for the first week. Our project was sponsored by the Colorado Trail Foundation and involved the construction and maintenance of a five hundred-mile nonvehicular trail that loops between Denver and Durango, in the southern part of the state.

After the seven international volunteers became acquainted (two each from Germany, France, and Britain, and myself from Ireland), we met the twenty-nine American volunteers, all members of the Colorado Trail Foundation. Many were experienced trail builders, this being their third or fourth crew, and we quickly realized we had a lot to learn from them.

Work began each morning with breakfast at 6:00 A.M. and a "quick" hour-long hike up a steep mountainside. Because of the high altitude and intense heat, work was demanding physically. Three o'clock never came too soon when the descent down the mountain began. Our shower water was heated by the sun in shower bags, which were in high demand after a hard day's work. The meal chores were divided up among all crew members. This worked very effectively and the ravenous masses were fed at 6:00 P.M. each evening.

After dinner we sat around our campfire and tried to come up with ingenious ways to entertain ourselves. As most of the American volunteers were retirees and most of the international volunteers were students, it was interesting to see the rapport that developed between the two groups, considering the age gap. They enlightened us with stories about the many trail crews they had worked on throughout Colorado and the United States, and we explained what brought us to Colorado and what our expectations were before we arrived. We delighted them with national songs and homespun stories.

As we lacked transportation, we relied heavily on the goodwill of other mobile volunteers to transport us into town on our days off. We managed to visit Mount Princeton Hot Springs on two occasions, a welcome relief for the shower alone, and we also enjoyed whitewater rafting on the Arkansas River. Merle McDonald, our incredibly organized, experienced trail crew leader, made our camp outstanding. With his tremendous energy, he was an inspiration to us all.

We left our Mount Yale base camp early at the start of the second week and headed to our next destination. Our second base camp was set in a magnificent valley, close to Lake Ann, about thirty miles south of Leadville. Here we met our new crew members, twenty-three Americans, who had traveled from as far as Michigan, Texas, and Louisiana. This was their first week of work, so their high spirits and relentless energy lifted us just as the tiredness was beginning to set in. Our new group leader, Ernie Waring, woke us each morning at 7:00 A.M. to his yodeling of "Europeano, breakfast time"—having Swiss parents he took a special liking to us. Our main work was building a thirty-foot-long bridge over Clear Creek. We manually sawed down trees (we didn't have a chain saw), and twelve people dragged them with ropes to the bridge site and maneuvered them into position. Not an easy task, but one we accomplished with incredible teamwork and some muscle. We finished our bridge on the last day with just enough time to put the handrail in place and take the final scenic photograph with it in the background.

Sadly, we took down camp for the last time and departed, each of us happy with the memory that we'd accomplished something and in some small way did our bit for nature. I've promised to return next year to help maintain a different section of trail and I'm sure it will be an easy promise to keep.

(This article is reprinted with permission of Council on International Educational Exchange.)

# Discovering Italy and So Much More

*Helen Yuen*

It was a rather gloomy day. Pellets of rain dropped from the sky, and the sun remained hidden by a layer of clouds. The gray weather was out of the ordinary for summertime in Italy, but then, it was a unique day for myself as well. I had just arrived in Milan's International Airport, ready to begin my work as a volunteer for Service Civil International (SCI). For the next six weeks, Italy would be my home as I volunteered at three different work camps. These international camps bring youth and older people together from around the globe to participate in service projects. For two to three weeks, the volunteers live and work together in one of hundreds of sites in the world. The service project ranges from site to site, but the emphasis in each camp remains the same: community service and increased global understanding.

I had chosen Italy because it had always fascinated me as a country rich in history, art, and music. Working abroad also gave me a chance to be immersed in a different language and culture. I wanted to experience living as an outsider for once and to be introduced to alternative ways of thinking and being. This was important to me, having always lived in the United States.

My first worksite was at a modest two-story building called Villa Amantea. Located on the outskirts of Milan, it serves as a center and home for underprivileged individuals. Concerned local youth founded the center in 1983. Villa Amantea initially helped those recently released from prison and the drug addicted. In the past few years, Italy's surge in immigration has created a new need. The center now concentrates its work in this area; the villa is equipped to provide low-income housing for ten occupants. There is also a legal center to help immigrants who need this kind of support. The building itself is a simple concrete structure, with a general-use room on the lower level and living quarters on the second floor. The immigrants live two to a room. Residents share a bath, kitchen, and lounge room.

During my stay at the center, there were eight adults and two youngsters (aged thirteen and fifteen) living there. They all hailed from Morocco originally, as do many immigrants in Italy. The residents were all middle-aged men currently unemployed or doing odd jobs and/or manual labor.

Our work was to help clean the center every day and the grounds around it. The surrounding gardens had become overgrown with weeds and were in need of replanting. In addition to the manual labor, we had a chance to visit two other immigrant centers in Milan, which unfortunately did not have adequate housing, as in Villa Amantea. The first center we saw consisted of a pair of row houses on a dusty lot. The hard clay beneath our feet ensured that not even weeds could grow there. A sense of melancholy filled me as I viewed the bleak surroundings. The drab landscape was matched only by the residents' expressions as they spoke of their difficulties. One man talked of his family in Senegal relying on him for support. Yet his attempts at finding a job as an electrical repairman (the field in which he was trained) had yielded nothing. His story was hardly a unique one. We had the chance to speak with many others there. The resounding message I heard that day was the desire for a job. The immigrants were willing to work, were eager to contribute to society, yet barricades such as bureaucracy prevented them. Currently, Italian law allows only those non-citizens with work permits to reside permanently in the country. However, this creates an impossible situation for immigrants. Employers can legally hire only those persons with work permits, yet such a document is issued only to those actually holding a job. In other words, one must first secure a position and a work permit before moving to Italy. Government "aid" comes in the form of immigrant centers, which provide shelter and little else. A tour inside revealed decay everywhere. Our group of volunteers had difficulty walking through the dark and narrow hallways. The floorboards, made of plywood, had long since begun to rot. In some spots one could clearly see through to the earth below. Bedrooms led off of the hallway. Approximately one hundred people lived in the cramped quarters, three to a room. There was barely enough space to accommodate the three beds and a night stand, the standard-issue furniture. Kitchen facilities were nonexistent. The entire complex smelled of urine and rot.

Poor living conditions are not the only problem facing immigrants there. Tough economic times have made finding a job all the more difficult. Furthermore, in a homogenous population like Italy's, there is bound to be resentment toward outsiders. This expresses itself in many ways. I never saw social interaction between the two races. Also, during my stay at Villa Amantea, there was a local movement to shut down the center as a possible haven for illegal residents. Policemen had threatened to occupy the building and take legal action against the villa. It is safe to say that African immigrants are marginalized from the rest of society. The combined effects of these factors means immigrants hold low-paying jobs, if any at all. In Italy, one would be hard pressed to find an immigrant in a white- or even blue-collar job. Bankers, bus drivers, waiters, salesclerks—people with whom I had regular contact—were all Italian. More often than not, I saw Africans on the streets hawking cheap plastic wares or beaded bracelets. Not once can I recall an immigrant who worked elsewhere.

I could not help but think that Italy is only beginning to experience what has already become institutionalized in America. I am speaking of racism and all of its hateful spawns. The only solution is to allow Africans a chance to compete with Italians for jobs. Let them demonstrate the skills and talents they possess. If this happens, both Italy and the immigrants benefit.

My second site was located in Bologna, a medium-sized city in central Italy. I and seventeen other volunteers worked the Molino Grande river park. The park began in 1987 as a project funded by World Wildlife Foundation (WWF). Its goal was to protect the banks of San Lazzarro River. Eventually, WWF bought the area around the river from the state, and the land is now protected as a natural environment. Our job consisted of cleaning the park and doing various repair work on signs, benches, and fences.

The third and final camp was located outside Marzabotto, in the mountains of central Italy. One would hardly know after a stroll through the small town that it played an important role in World War II. A famous and large partisan brigade operated from Marzabotto in those times. In 1944, the Nazis killed about nine hundred inhabitants of the village in retaliation against the partisans. Among the victims were 180 children. Since then, Marzabotto has become a symbolic place of international peace and solidarity.

In keeping with the themes of the town, the volunteers came together to paint a mural with an antiwar message. The project was directed by two professional artists. We worked in the local elementary school. The finished project depicted a scene in a jungle. On the right, the soldiers' boots and military hardware advance towards the left, where doves and hands poke through the bush. The hands reach out, imploring the oncoming troops to halt. This left side represents peace, while the opposing side symbolizes war. Above the chaotic scene sits the sun, trying to spread light over both sides. The painting delivers a simple message, yet its impact is powerful.

Besides the unveiling of the mural, one of the most dramatic moments during the work camp was a field trip to the partisans' stronghold in 1944. There we heard the story of how the Nazis came and murdered an entire town. We visited the ruins of the church where the townspeople of Marzabotto huddled, in hopes the approaching German soldiers would spare them. Instead, the army disregarded their own Nazi law forbidding the murder of those seeking refuge in a religious edifice. We walked the same path the townspeople tread as the Nazis had ordered them at gunpoint to do. And finally, we arrived at the cemetery where the Germans marched the people. Against those walls, the troops had lined up the civilians, then opened fire. They did not stop until the men, women, and children lay lifeless before them. It is a chilling story and beyond human comprehension how such an act of cruelty could ever happen. I was struck with irony as I took in the mountaintop view. How could such a place of physical beauty have been host to such utter brutality? Standing in the cemetery that day only reinforced the mural's message to me. In 1944, the Germans hoped the massacre at Marzabotto would serve as an example to other partisan brigades. But today, the mountain town is a lesson for us all. We should never forget the horror that is war. Looking back upon the summer I learned much more than how to repair a park bench or how to weed a garden. Certainly there were the lessons gained from the study parts of the work camps. Then there are the intangibles that come from living with a dozen or more people you have never met before. Each work camp brought me closer to understanding the history and culture of another place. Certainly there were occasions when cultural differences produced mild controversy (mostly of a culinary nature), but the curiosity about each other's background and a genuine desire to work together quickly eroded any preconceived notions we might have had about one another. It is especially uplifting to know that such a microcosm of youth could exist in the world today with its horror of genocide in the former Yugoslavia, race riots in South Africa—the list goes on. It was truly a wonderful and unique experience. It was a summer of discovery.

(This article was originally published in the *SCI/IVS Newsletter* and is reprinted with the permission of SCI/IVS and the author.)

# How We Made the Earth Move
*Tony Kelly*

I was already knee-deep in muddy water when I stumbled against the monk. I felt my body being dragged further into the mire; a second later I emerged, cold and wet to the waist, my arm around the monk as I hauled myself free.

I should explain that a monk is a wooden, stepped device used for measuring water depth, and I was on a National Trust working conservation holiday at Stowe Landscape Gardens, near Buckingham. The activity for Thursday was "clay puddling," which involved treading lumps of clay into a leaky lake in order to raise the water level. All morning we had been jumping up and down on the clay, splattering each other with mud as we enjoyed renewed permission to be children.

The Trust runs more than four hundred weekend and weeklong volunteer projects each year. Volunteers pay around £35 (about $55) for a week in a Trust base camp, helping out with tasks ranging from drystone walling and fencing to footpath construction and woodland management. No special skills are needed; the holidays are open to anyone who is reasonably fit, including people with disabilities. Anyone completing a week receives a volunteer card, which effectively gives them membership in the Trust for a year.

This trip had particular significance for me: the mansion at Stowe is now a public school, and I was a pupil here in the seventies. I had hardly been back since, and the tingling started even before I reached the gates. As I followed the straight three-mile drive from Buckingham, classrooms and cricket fields stirred long-repressed memories. And when Colin, our volunteer leader, told us we would be staying in the sanatorium, my mind went back to the two days I spent there suffering from a boil at the age of thirteen.

The sanatorium has not changed (it is as grim as it sounds), but in most respects Stowe is the luxury option for Trust volunteers. On other projects, they are expected to produce their own meals on a rota basis; at Stowe the kitchens were turning out food for the summer conference season and we simply joined in. Instead of cooking and washing up, we spent evenings in the school's swimming pool, on the tennis courts or golf course, or, one night, on a fruitless badger watch.

Daytimes were different. Work started at 9:00 A.M. and went on until 5:00 P.M., with an hour for lunch, and generous tea and coffee breaks, plus, as the week progressed, more and more time for "putting away the tools." Few of us were used to physical labor—that was why we chose it for a holiday—and the work was exhausting. We spent the first two days digging out two dry nineteenth-century ponds looking for a spring and an elusive iron grille: "The search for the holy grille."

After digging and shoveling and lifting, the most back-breaking task was carting barrow after barrow of soil from the site to a mound fifty yards away. "What will happen to all this soil?" I asked one of the gardeners. "We'll get the next lot of volunteers to put it back," he said. We were not sure he was joking.

After a half day off, which most of us spent in Oxford, we turned to clay puddling, fencing, and lighting fires. The final two days were spent in a ha-ha (a sunken ditch that acts as a barrier for livestock, without spoiling the view), chipping away at an old stone wall prior to its renovation. As chunks of limestone disintegrated under our trowels and beetles, toads, and wasps found their habitat destroyed, I wondered how much damage Trust volunteers unwittingly cause. But a school worker dispelled any guilt. "A lot of the best stones have been taken away by teachers," he told us. "They turn up in their garden walls."

We were a mixed bunch: engineers, teachers, a school matron, a cook. But the shared sense of purpose, and the hard outdoor work produced an immediate camaraderie, manifested mainly in an endless stream of puns. "Get in there, you sod!" shouted Erica, a primary teacher, as she threw a large lump of earth into a barrow. After two days of using a mattock (a type of pickax used to loosen the soil) the word has yielded more puns than I thought possible. When I was caught in the face by a lump of mud, self-inflicted after too enthusiastic a blow, I was a "mattockist"; Brad, a disc jockey, accidentally chopped a worm in two in the "mattocker of the innocents."

The puns would have been appreciated by the Temple family, owners of Stowe for three centuries from 1593. It was the Temples who commissioned what was effectively England's first landscape garden, and filled it with temples, follies, and arches, consciously evoking the world of ancient Rome.

The 750-acre gardens are described by the Trust as "England's largest work of art"—it shames me to think that in five years as a schoolboy I barely even noticed them. Capability Brown was head gardener for a decade from 1741 and was married in the small church that still stands near the main house. His creations, and those of his predecessor, William Kent, are beautiful in themselves; but the gardens also stand as a monument to the radical Whig politics of a rich and eccentric family who used their money and influence to create a lasting shrine to their liberal beliefs.

The most obviously political monuments are found to either side of the Alder River, commonly known as the Styx. To the west, the Temple of Ancient Virtue is a rotunda containing statues of Homer, Socrates, Lycurgus, and Epaminondas, all Greeks; the remains of the Temple of Modern Virtue, nearby, once contained the headless statue of the Prime Minister Walpole, a pointed and damning contrast between classical greatness and modern degeneracy.

Across the Styx, reflected in the water, the Temple of British Worthies holds busts of eight thinkers (including Shakespeare, Milton, Newton) and eight doers (including Raleigh, Drake, Elizabeth I), considered the greatest that Britain had to offer. A niche in the center contained the head of Mercury, the god who would lead the souls of the blessed across the Styx to join Homer and Socrates in the "Elysian Fields" opposite. Britain's heroes, in other words, were almost fit to be lifted to the level of the ancient Greeks; its contemporary leaders were not.

Behind the Temple of British Worthies is an almost illegible inscription to "Signior Fido, an Italian of good extraction"; this "faithful friend" and "loving husband" is in fact a greyhound. Another monument to the Temples' eccentricity is the Gothic Temple, a triangular, turreted structure built high above a meadow and looking for all the world like a haunted palace. Originally the Temple of Liberty, it represents the freedoms of Magna Carta and once contained the quotation over the door: "I thank the Gods that I am not a Roman."

"Is it haunted?" I asked Frank, the head gardener. "Only by American tourists," he replied. It is managed by the Landmark Trust and can be rented for (expensive) self-catering holidays.

The National Trust acquired the gardens in 1929 and is making efforts to restore them to the eighteenth-century design; the work is expected to take another fifty years. We couldn't pretend that our week had made much difference, yet there was great satisfaction in seeing a task, however small, completed. When we returned to our puddling pond on the last day, the monk was almost invisible because the level was two feet higher, and water was flowing over the clay and into the outlet that we had built up.

Finally, we all posed for a group picture on the massive heap of soil that we had dug. "The earth moved for us," said Erica.

(This article was reprinted by permission of the British Trust for Conservation Volunteers.)

# Holidays for Healing
*Ryan Ver Berkmoes*

Denis Radefeld, M.D., used to cruise the Caribbean while on vacation. He saw the glitzy resorts aimed at well-heeled tourists. What he didn't see was the poverty endemic to many of the islands in the region.

Dr. Radefeld doesn't take those luxury cruises anymore, but he still goes to the Caribbean. He bypasses the resorts for the parts of the islands most tourists don't see—the parts where medical care is unheard of, and the promise of a long and healthy life is slim.

Since 1983 the surgeon from Lorain, Ohio, has spent his annual vacation running clinics in impoverished parts of the Caribbean. He can't imagine a better way to spend two weeks.

"You can't appreciate the culture of these people until you smell it, touch it, and taste it. It's not about the little straw huts with souvenirs for sale. It's about good people leading hard lives. I'm disappointed I didn't get my act together earlier."

Dr. Radefeld began thinking of using his vacation time to help others after visiting physician friends doing medical volunteer work in Kenya in the seventies.

He is not alone. Organizations that specialize in placing physicians in volunteer foreign assignments of one month or less report unprecedented demand.

"Every time we make a presentation at a medical meeting, we are overwhelmed by the response," says Kate Skilman, a program coordinator for Health Volunteers Overseas, a private Washington, D.C.-based group that uses physicians to help train medical personnel abroad. Doctors discover that vacations spent helping in foreign lands are beneficial, not just to others but also to themselves.

"For some doctors, volunteering for a few weeks abroad fulfills their spirit of adventure. For others, it answers a need to do work on a humanitarian level," says Madonna Yates, who works for Medical Group Missions, the largest short-term, volunteer medical mission in the world, which places fifteen hundred volunteer medical professionals annually from North America. Although the Richardson, Texas-based group is part of the Christian Medical/Dental Society, it has no religious requirements for its volunteers.

"Many doctors are at first unsure why they volunteer, until they realize that they did it to answer a deeper need—a need to have a global view. They don't want to listen to the news the same way they always did," says Yates.

Spending a vacation helping others in a strange land also produces a kind of gratification that can't be found among the steely-eyed shopkeepers of a mainstream destination. Akron, Ohio, general practitioner Charles Castro, M.D., discovered this benefit while passing through Miami International Airport. A man stopped him and said, "You don't remember me, but I remember you. You came to Honduras and helped my son who had a bad skin rash many years ago. I have always been grateful to you."

Once physicians experience the gratitude of their new patients in these medically underserved parts of the world, many never want to waste another vacation. Yates has a favorite story that illustrates this point.

"He [a doctor] was spending his first night in Africa inside of a tent on the floor and surrounded by mosquito netting. Around him the other volunteers on his team were snoring away. He thought: 'What have I done?'

"But two days later he had his first post-op meetings with his patients and their families. One man looked at the doctor, thanked him, and offered him the only two eggs his chicken had laid that day.

"That was it. Now that doctor is one of our regular volunteers. He takes ear plugs for snoring and lotion for the bugs, and he loves it," she recounts.

And then there's the chance to know a culture as tourists never will. Aaron Bannett, M.D., a surgeon from Philadelphia, found gratification helping teach surgical residents on Sumatra, an island that is part of Indonesia.

Although semiretired, Dr. Bannett likes to travel and wants to continue using his skills. He spent three weeks this last January at a hospital in the town of Palembang.

"I've taken many trips to places like London, France, and Italy. And I will again," says Dr. Bannett. "But it is much more rewarding to have the cross-cultural experience of living, shopping, and preparing food as part of an unfamiliar culture."

Dr. Bannett also savored his time with the surgical residents. "I found a level of professional satisfaction working with them that I haven't felt in a while."

Like most volunteers, Dr. Bannett was accompanied by his spouse. By the third day, she had set up a program teaching English to students at the hospital. "I think she was as rewarded by the experience as I was," he says.

Most programs accommodate spouses, since not many married couples want to take their annual vacations apart. Yates has found an unexpected advantage to this.

"Where one spouse does not have a medical career, resentment and misunderstanding can build up because of the amount of time the other spouse spends practicing medicine. But on trips, the nonmedical spouse often works as an assistant to the medical team. This may be the first time the nonphysician spouse gets a chance to see up close what their physician spouse does. I've had a lot of people tell me that going on one of these vacations together has helped engender mutual understanding and respect."

For some physicians, spending a few weeks in a developing country can be a prelude to something more. Says Skilman of Health Volunteers Overseas: "People can go to Asia, Africa, and Central and South America. They can see the great need for health care in these places. But they don't have to close their practices and leave town. They can acquire knowledge that will help them decide if they want to make a greater commitment later."

But before rushing to take a volunteer vacation, there are certain points a physician should take into consideration. One is money. Unlike long-term volunteer commitments, short-term volunteerism typically doesn't pay a stipend of any kind. In fact, it usually costs the volunteer money.

For stints of a month or less, volunteers are expected to pay their own expenses. This includes airfare, room, and board. Volunteers are sometimes even asked to provide the medical supplies they will use.

Medical Group Missions is fairly typical. Participants pay their own airfare and a fee of $450 that covers room, board, and ground transportation during the usual two-week trip.

This can easily cost a couple over $2,000 per person. But that's still less than a two-week vacation in Europe, even at humdrum hotels. And there's much less chance of becoming encumbered with expensive trinkets.

Volunteering also brings some risk. Volunteers may end up sick, frustrated, or otherwise disenchanted. During his nine years of volunteering Dr. Castro almost died from blood poisoning one trip and got malaria on another. But he remains sanguine about those experiences, saying, "You can get sick at home."

Medical conditions and equipment can shock even the best prepared. Aleksandra Mazurek, M.D., a Chicago anesthesiologist, last year made her first trip as a volunteer to Addis Ababa, the capital of Ethiopia. "At various times during an operation, the oxygen lines would turn off," she recalls. "Because the hospital's phones didn't work, we would have to open a window and yell down to the workers in the basement to fix the oxygen."

"It took some getting used to. But then again, I grew up in Poland where you learn not to expect things to be perfect."

Yates said that volunteers should expect to be resourceful—switching to flashlights, for example, when the power fails during an operation. "It is important that people continue to remind themselves that nothing is going to be the same as it is at home."

But she says physicians can find spending their vacations helping others rewarding as long as they possess two key traits: "Flexibility and a sense of humor—that's all it takes."

(This article was originally published in *American Medical News*.)

# Karma Yoga in the Third World
*Josh Lozoff*

I didn't bring a meditation cushion, the food wasn't organic, and there wasn't a yoga facilitator in sight, but my six-week stay in a Bolivian orphanage was the most powerful "retreat" I've ever attended.

My trip was arranged through Volunteers for Peace (VFP), a non-profit organization that places Americans in locally run work camps all over the world. Each spring VFP publishes its International Workcamp Directory, a veritable yellow pages of over eight hundred hands-on volunteer opportunities. Most last just a few weeks, some longer. Last year's options included conflict resolution in Bosnia, protecting turtle eggs in Japan, and working in a battered women's shelter in Belgium. I chose the orphanage because of my interest in working with children and my passable Spanish-language skills. But, as VFP points out, no foreign language ability or previous experience is required.

I sent in the application, and in less than a week I received my acceptance letter, along with an all-too-brief description of how I would be spending the summer: "Volunteers will renovate a building and lend a hand to the little farm which belongs to the center. You are also invited to get in contact with the boys (in the orphanage) and to develop common interests with them."

With only a backpack, a copy of Lao Tzu's *Hua Hu Ching* for daily reading, and a supply of anti-malaria pills, I arrived in La Paz, Bolivia, for a week-long orientation before heading on to the orphanage. There I met the rest of my group, three from France, one from

Germany, and another American. We got acquainted as we learned about the kids, the farm on which they lived, and the work we would be doing.

From La Paz we flew to Trinidad, in the heart of Bolivia's Amazon Basin. After a short, dusty ride from the airport we arrived at the orphanage and passed through its rusty gates (which we would soon be fixing). Located on a small parcel of government land, Chetequije Orphanage is home to twenty-nine boys, ages five to seventeen. Most were orphaned or abandoned, some were found living on the streets. They live and eat together and share in the work at the orphanage, which includes tending the garden, cooking meals, and teaching Bolivian card games to the occasional gringo volunteer.

The experience was terrific, and we did a variety of work. One day might find us building a trough for the cattle, the next, harvesting lettuce to sell at the local *mercado*, or stringing a barbed wire fence with nothing but a machete.

But nights belonged to the kids, and it was my favorite time of all—telling stories, singing songs, drawing elephants with five-year-old Johnny, feeling so sad for the parents who abandoned such a beautiful little boy.

I began spending a lot of time with Wilson, a fourteen-year-old mildly retarded boy, placed at the orphanage after authorities removed him from an abusive home. Wilson's special-ed classes met in the afternoon, so while the other kids left for school around eight, he often spent the morning working with me. We became fast friends, trading T-shirts and walking into town for ice cream several times a week.

One blistering hot afternoon, Wilson set out on his daily thirty-minute walk to school, made all the more difficult by his slightly palsied feet. When I asked him why he never took one of the old bicycles, he said no one had ever taught him to ride one. And so began the most rewarding experience of the summer. We practiced each day at dusk. One week and two skinned knees later, I let go of the seat and watched as Wilson wobbled off into independence.

It amazed me how quickly the summer came to an end. My last day was especially difficult, and Wilson told me he had never seen a grown man cry before. I took inventory of what we'd accomplished. Corrals had been built, tables painted, friends made. But for me, it was much more. It had truly been a karma retreat, a chance to remind myself of the reason I meditate, practice yoga, and read holy books in the first place. As Lao Tzu says: "Only those who increase their service along with their understanding can be called men and women of Tao." I'm already planning my next "retreat."

(This article was originally published in *Yoga Journal* and is reprinted with the permission of the author.)

# Bardou: Stepping into Another World

*Alison Benney*

*"We had the choice between the 'easy life' and a Spartan existence—to move from the twentieth century into a nineteenth-century environment and have the fascination of being pioneers in the heart of Europe."*
—Klaus and Jean Erhardt

After a spectacular two-hour hike up the mountainside, around the corner of a cliff and over the hill from a waterfall, the hamlet of Bardou appears nestled in a corner of a remote valley, its stone cottages and gardens blending organically into the rocks and trees of the surrounding hills. Sheltered by the terraced mountains of the Haut Languedoc Regional Park, the village is populated each summer with seekers of tranquility and lovers of the simple lifestyle that the Erhardts, Bardou's proprietors, offer.

In 1967, after ten years of traveling, Jean, an American, and Klaus, a German, decided to settle down and concentrate on raising their three children. They found that for the price of a country home near Paris they could purchase the nearly abandoned village of Bardou, with acres of surrounding chestnut forest, in the south of France. Originally conceived as the makings for a private utopia, it has evolved into a seasonal community for city refugees.

When they moved in, the Erhardts lived in tents, as most of the houses were in ruins, filled with rubbish, overgrown with thorns and vines. According to Jean, "It was like being in a fairy land and cutting through Sleeping Beauty's hedge of thorns." After twenty-two years of renovation, there is now modest accommodation for between forty to seventy inhabitants and the work continues: cleaning out debris, rebuilding roofs, and patching walls with cement. Klaus explained that the primitive dwellings had never been designed for leisure; in fact, the lower half of each house was used as shelter for poultry and pigs, and the upper half for sleeping. Some houses still have plants creeping in through their stone walls.

Staying in Bardou reveals a sense of what life was like before modern conveniences. Visitors receive only the basics: a cottage equipped with a fireplace or woodstove for cooking, and a timber loft with a foam rubber mattress. There is no running water, no electricity, no flush toilets. People come here for life's uncomplicated basics—collecting water from the spring, gathering firewood, sharing supplies (like emergency chocolate or forgotten toilet paper), and the company over morning coffee and evening wine, and late-night conversation. Food is cooked over a fire, clothes washed on rocks, and bedtime books read by candlelight.

It's the spiritual amenities that bring people back to this tranquil retreat. Bardou is surrounded by national forest on the south edge of the Cévennes Mountains, a breathtakingly beautiful area that embraces the Gorges d'Heric, Roman ruins, waterfalls, wild sheep and boar, and very few people. The nearest food shop is three miles down the mountain (a twenty-minute drive or two-hour hike), and the closest café is an hour's trek through the woods, in the even tinier village of Heric.

The town of Bardou does possess a part-time taberna, run by the Erhardts' twenty-six-year-old son Pan, who bakes delicious bread once or twice a week for the residents. A neighbor provides home-brewed cherry wine and elderberry port, and a roofless courtyard is available for ping-pong tournaments.

One American visitor stated, "It's another world; it's hard to believe this exists." On a recent rainy day in June, art students could be seen tucked away in nooks and crannies throughout the village, sheltered in doorways and window frames with drawing pads on their laps, painting, sketching, and writing. There are also groups of musicians that visit each year. Last year flute music floated through the passageways and this summer stringed instruments will be accompanying the cries of the resident peacocks.

It's a curious but unpretentious mix of art appreciation and simple living in a community setting that makes Bardou more than just an unusual camping trip. Either the Erhardts or one of the Bardou workers organizes weekly Shakespeare readings, and everyone who wants to participate gets a role. One summer an actor visited who was a *King Lear* fan, and the community was inspired to enact the play, in improvised costumes, using the whole town as a setting and inviting neighboring farmers to the performance.

Bardou's population includes a crew of workers who exchange lodging and a weekly homestyle feast for the privilege of helping the Erhardts in their lifetime project of reanimating the town. This year's crew is a typical mix: Maureen and Perry from Holland; Oliver, a Canadian who just returned from a month's retreat in an ashram in India; and Bruce and Joanna, British traveling companions on their way to Turkey. Although there are few volunteers or residents during the winter months, and they can only accept four to six helpers at a time, the Erhardts receive as many as twenty letters a day from people wanting to work on exchange during the summer, despite the lack of modern amenities.

The work is financed partially by paying guests (Fr 40 to Fr 50 nightly per person in individual houses for two to four persons) and occasional windfalls, such as the year an Italian film crew took over the village to shoot a film about Che Guevara and provided the money to install a water system from the spring to the village. In addition, seven years ago the Erhardts started raising Bizet sheep, a rare breed of mountain sheep that suit the hilly Bardou terrain. They have since won prizes for their pedigree stock, and their sheep are chosen to represent the breed each year at the prestigious Foire de Paris.

When asked if he misses the comforts of the city, Klaus replied that he prefers country comforts—clean air, fresh water, starlight, and forest noises—to city noises and lights. What puts Bardou on the map is not the size of the population, but the quality of life it is seeking. It's this mixture of opposites, of culture in a rustic setting, a dream built on hard physical labor and beauty in simplicity, that creates the Bardou experience.

Bardou is located between Montpellier and Béziers and can be reached by a direct overnight train from the Gare de Lyon to the town of Bédarieux. At the Bédarieux station, a bus picks up passengers five minutes after the train arrives for a thirty-minute drive to Mons-la-Trivalle, where it is advised that travelers pick up provisions before hiking three miles uphill to Bardou.

It is recommended that you bring food, a flashlight, candles and plenty of matches, rain gear, sturdy shoes, a sleeping bag, something to scrub dishes with, salt and pepper, and a gas stove if building a fire isn't your forte.

(This article is reprinted with permission from Bardou.)

# From Carpentry to Rodents: A Woman's Perspective

*Andrea-Lee Cohen*

When I looked at the work chart during my second week on kibbutz, I did a double take. "This can't be right. . . ." I had thought they would need me for kitchen duty. I was a woman after all, and after being on kibbutz for two weeks I realized that "politically correct" was impossible to translate into Hebrew.

But, after staring at the chart a few more minutes, I faced the reality that I was entering where no woman had gone before . . . THE TSUBA CARPENTRY FACTORY!

On the first day, I entered the factory and approached my boss, Marc. The machinery was unbearably loud. He could not hear a word I said and, as I later grew to realize, also did not understand a word I said! But, on that first day, after five minutes of me screaming my name, he simply smiled and put me to work!

By lunchtime I was covered in glue, had become an expert drawer builder, and could not stop smiling. I was so excited about my new job that I had day dreams of returning to the States as a carpenter.

Imagine, I would learn my trade in Israel, bring it back to California, and by the time I was thirty, I would be a millionaire. Only then would I retire and donate all of my sanding equipment and carpentry tools to Kibbutz Tsuba, the place that brought my genius to light. It was a definite blow to my fantasy when my friends slammed their lunch trays down and told me how ridiculous I looked covered in glue. Though I was the only woman, let alone American, in the factory, I began to feel at home. My only "problem" was the work gloves. The smallest pair was still too big and my endless complaints were greeted by uproarious laughter. Their laughter made me smile and my "glove antics" became a daily routine, and not so much because I was truly unhappy, but rather so I could fill the factory with their laughter.

And then, one day, I walked to my machine and found a new pair of small gloves. I never found out how they got there, all I did know was that, despite the incredible language barrier and gender "division," they had accepted me. From then on, even though gloves went "missing" all of the time, mine were always sitting right where I had left them.

Over the next few months, when I was not diligently studying Hebrew or gleefully singing "Yerushalyim Shel Zehav" (all right, I didn't do that one) I could be found sanding, sawing, gluing, or drilling at the Tsuba Carpentry Factory. I even had a job title, "Assistant Director of First Stage Development." Translation: I didn't actually make anything; I prepared wood.

Working alongside me in the "wood preparation department" was my saving grace, Alec. Alec was my co-worker. He was from Russia, but his English was fantastic as was his Hebrew, therefore he became my translator, my only verbal link to my fellow carpenters. In addition, he carried the heavy wood and, despite my feminist ideals, did the really dirty work. One day as we were sweeping the factory, I came across a dead mouse. I stopped dead in my tracks and contemplated the situation. I had two choices: sweep it up or call for Alec. Within a second the choice was made; Alec appeared.

It still amazes me how those few months in the factory really changed my life. To begin with, I learned what it means to work hard. And I worked this way consistently for months, motivated not by money nor professional mobility, but by the kindness of a few men who worked just as hard alongside me and for a kibbutz that took me in and enveloped me within its home.

Looking back now, over the entire Oren experience, I know that the biggest change came with the way I feel about myself. In Israel, I learned that I could climb mountains (literally) and that they were easier to climb when I knew that someone was there to pull me up or hold my hand when I didn't think I could go on. I learned that communities are there for each other and that when we work together, we reap what we sow. I also learned that there are no language barriers when we share a common bond. So I may not have become a master carpenter, and I didn't become fluent in Hebrew, but I did become a stronger and more confident woman. And the friendships that I formed are unlike any other: they are unconditional and they are forever.

(This article was originally published in the Kibbutz Program Center newsletter and is reprinted with the permission of Kibbutz Program Center and the author.)

# Closing Out the Cold War: Joining Hands with the Old Adversary

*Ronald H. Reimann*

Scholars may argue about the date of the end of the Cold War, reckoning its demise by various political or symbolic events like the election of Boris Yeltsin or the crumbling of the Berlin Wall. But in my life, the Cold War ended palpably and decisively in May, 1993.

On May 8 my wife, Jan, and I joined six other businesspeople, most of us retired, in Moscow as part of a business education team sponsored by Global Volunteers of St. Paul, Minnesota. All but our leader were volunteers: we had paid our own way for the three-week project.

I had long harbored a desire to visit the USSR. Two decades of my professional life in one way or another had been premised on the idea that the Soviets were a likely enemy and certain adversary of the United States throughout the world. My nine years as a submariner, a graduate at Harvard in international relations, and a spell as a civilian intelligence officer dealing exclusively with Soviet national security issues engendered this unquenchable desire to see the Soviet Union firsthand.

With the dissolution of the USSR and deterioration of the economies of the former republics, it was clear from friends who had tried it that travel to those countries was not just occasioned by inconvenience, but was impossibly frustrating. So for several years my wife and I visited other countries. After retiring from Burlington Northern Railroad in December 1992, I met another retired businessman who had just returned from Tver (formerly Kaliningrad) in Russia as part of the first Global Volunteers business group to work in the former USSR. He had had an extraordinary experience: an opportunity to teach Russians about free enterprise business, occasions to meet individual Russians and enjoy the hospitality of their homes and families, and most importantly, to help shatter images about who U.S. businessmen really are. On top of all this, he had ample invitations to sample Russian culture and to visit nearby cities with minimal hassle. My decision was immediate.

The team Jan and I selected had been invited to teach at Zaporozh'ye, a Ukrainian industrial city of about one million on the Dnieper River a hundred miles north of the Crimea. The agenda—typical for Global Volunteers efforts of this kind—called for two one-week sessions of lectures delivered to classes of thirty-five to forty students each.

These two weeks were preceded by a week of orientation—part in Moscow, part in Zaporozh'ye—which alone was worth the price of the trip. For instance, in Moscow at a briefing a senior economics deputy from Yelstin's cabinet debated one of Speaker Ruslan Khasbulatov's chief economic advisors on the direction of Russia's economy and the politics of the new constitution. Eight of us were seated in a small room watching an event that would have landed one or both of those officials in Siberia or an asylum ten years before. In Zaporozh'ye we spoke with university officials, municipal leaders, bankers, and fledgling businesspeople. We visited state enterprises and were treated to cultural events. By the time classes began, we had a pretty good sense of the city, its traditions and history, and its people.

Most of the students at our business education sessions were from small- and medium-sized private firms, rather than from large state enterprises seeking to privatize. The lectures and seminars elicited questions disclosing the varying exposure of our students to Western business ideas and theories. The greatest obstacle, though, was not training Eastern entrepreneurs to be good businesspeople, but for the rest of the population to accept the idea of what free enterprise really means. For example, the idea of earning a return from an investment—that is, the creation of value from something other than human labor—is still not natural to many Ukrainians and Russians. Even more pervasive is the suspicion that the middleman is an exploiter of others' efforts rather than the key to the distributive genius of the free market system, indeed, the only possible alternative to the wretched central-planning effort that failed so completely. Marxist dogma dies hard.

Yet these people were bright, cultured, educated, and of great depth of heart and human warmth. The questions in our workshops often turned to Western attitudes, values, and customs. I had been prepared for at least a few challenges to our mores—God knows many of them merit condemnation—but among our seventy-five students there were no such comments. When I raised some of the issues facing contemporary America, the response tended to be "Sure, we know, but you'll solve that just as you have solved other problems you have encountered."

Certainly the objectives of Global Volunteers and the attitudes of our eight teammates in this experience were characteristic of America at its best: reaching out to a former adversary—an adversary whom most of us never knew as people—forgetting the past and building toward the future as friends. More than any business knowledge that we imparted (and I believe that that knowledge was substantial), the net value of this exercise for most of us was in extending a hand in friendship to good human beings after so long a time in rigid isolation from one another.

The experiences with the deepest meanings came in brief encounters with former Soviet military men. In a workshop, Vladimir, a man of about my vintage, told me that he had flown I1-38 ASW missions out of Egypt. Knowing that I had been in the submarine force at that time, he rose from his chair and shook my hand. "It is so much better that we meet like this as friends," he said. Later that evening at dinner, he presented Jan with roses and moved us both with a soulful toast about friendship between past adversaries. Vladimir's eyes were not dry, nor were ours.

During our stay Jan and I had lectured at several of the local colleges. At a reception held at one of them, the International Institute for State and Municipal Management, we were introduced to retired Colonel General Pavl Pavlovich Polyakh of the faculty. During the inevitable exchange of family photographs, when he saw that our five sons were in the U.S. Navy, four in submarines and one at the Naval Academy, he produced photos of his two sons, both Ukrainian Army officers. We toasted our seven sons, that they would never meet in battle, unless it was on the same side. At a later banquet, just before our return to the United States, General Polyakh repeated our toast and gave Jan and me a warm Slavic embrace. He put in my hand the unit identifier from his uniform—a PVO Strany device. Taken somewhat by surprise, I managed to respond with the miniature submarine dolphins from my lapel. At that moment I knew that the Cold War had come to a close with fitting symbols and quiet dignity.

I had commented several times to my teammates that virtually every one of the people whom we had met in Ukraine were the sort that would make welcome neighbors: hard working, intelligent, eager to learn and to do things right. For the sake of such neighbors, no one would think twice about spending a weekend helping to paint the house, or fixing the Ford, or bringing over dinner when times are tough. It occurred to me later when the swirl of impressions and experiences began to take their proper perspective, that neighbors are exactly who these people are, just a few thousand miles farther down the road.

When I recount the things of which I am most proud in life, just below my family stands my service to the United States during a very dangerous era, and my service to a few neighbors in Ukraine. In August I shall return to Ukraine with Global Volunteers as a team leader, to try to help some people rebuild their country and their lives, and in so doing again celebrate the end of the Cold War.

(This article is reprinted with the permission of Global Volunteers.)

# Sobering Realities on a Volunteer Vacation in Calcutta

*Jim Molnar*

Calcutta is India's largest city and home to fifteen million people. About three-quarters of them live on streets chock full of garbage and human waste, or in one-room squalor within the crush of three thousand slums built of cardboard, crates, and scrap metal.

It would take about five lifetimes for the average Calcuttan to achieve the annual income of the average American. It's a place where the lines between hope and hopelessness and between life and death have lost meaning.

"I love Calcutta," Laura Marinoni wrote in a letter home to Seattle five years ago. The statement, unqualified and without reservation, isn't something one would expect. A tourist might say it about London, Paris, Bangkok, and even New York—but Calcutta? Yet I've heard it repeated from people who have spent time there. The tone is never quite like "Wish you were here" so much as "I wish you the experience of Calcutta sometime in your life."

To understand what they mean is to understand something central to the art of traveling. It concerns a quality more basic to traveling than curiosity, adventurousness, fortitude, or perseverance. It concerns compassion. Calcutta provides a profound illustration, but compassion is no less essential to the traveler in London or Paris or our own downtowns.

Marinoni is one of about twenty people who have traveled to India from Seattle University since 1986 to work for a month or two with

Mother Teresa and the Missionaries of Charity. Members of this "Calcutta Club" work alongside hundreds of other people from around the world who arrive at places like Nrimal Hridy or Kalighat, Mother Teresa's Home for the Dying Destitute; Prem Dan, the Home for the Mentally Ill; Shiso Bhavan, the Home for Children and Mentally Ill Women; or Titagarh, the Home for Lepers.

There are no qualifications, training programs, or financial support beyond what the volunteers carry in their belt packs. They simply show up.

After finding a place to stay, volunteers ask the way to Mother Teresa. The walk through the city is filled with overwhelming sensations: the sights, sounds, and odors of mortality throbbing in muddy heat.

"[Near] Prem Dan, the Home for the Mentally Ill, there sprawls a slum built of tin cans, bits of cloth, wood, and newspapers," Marinoni wrote of her visit. "As I passed by, there was a baby boy, naked, sitting on a pile of garbage. He saw me, smiled at me, and put his little hands together in the Indian sign of greeting *namaste*.

"This baby [came to] represent the soul of Calcutta to me."

Finally, volunteers arrive at the yellow bulk and towers of Kalighat, perhaps the holiest temple to the goddess Kali in all of India. On one side of the altar wall, pilgrims mill among goats, sheep, and other sacrifices. On the other side is Mother Teresa's Home for the Dying Destitute.

"I was overwhelmed by the sensation that I was entering the city of Kali, the Devourer, the goddess of death," said Monica Gehrts, another Calcutta Club veteran. "This was her college. And I was faced with my first exam."

Some people freeze at the threshold for a moment, or an hour, wondering what to do next. But what needs to be done becomes obvious. A hundred people need to be bathed, to be fed, to be caressed. They need someone simply to be with them.

The nuns don't offer greetings or directions. They don't have time to give orders or preach. Volunteers simply must enter, put on aprons, and offer their labor and, more importantly, themselves.

"Shortly after I arrived, a baby died in my arms," Gehrts said. "More happened to me in Calcutta in two months than will ever happen to me again in my whole life."

Many of us expect to be changed by our travel experiences. Usually we are not. We return with memories, perhaps—persistent images that allow us to revisit some favorite sights and peak emotions. We are seldom altered so deeply, however, that we can't slide back neatly onto the tracks of our ordinary lives. But transformation is part of the Calcutta experience.

"Some volunteers—especially younger, less-traveled ones—go hoping to change the world," said Neil Young, the psychology professor who started the program that now operates from Seattle University Volunteer Center. "We find ourselves trying to help them prepare for something that can't be prepared for: the surprise, the shock, of living among the dying, the orphans, the poorest of the poor," Young said.

A few come back frustrated and angry.

"They hate themselves more for not being able to live up to their ideal of sainthood," he said. "But the idea isn't to help—to do something—for the dying at Kalighat. The idea is simply to be with them.

"Most volunteers can come back, though, saying, 'I didn't go to change the world; I went and the world changed me.' In Calcutta, you're always confronting your own limits, weaknesses and vulnerabilities. The real challenge is to discover compassion for yourself through compassion for others."

Young speaks of Calcutta as the "wound that heals one." He compares the process of learning to Dante's progression from Hell to Purgatory to Paradise.

The first impulse is to pity. Young's and Gehrts's descriptions of Calcutta are filled with devastating images that seem to leap from nightmares or dark fairy tales: the thirty-year-old woman at Prem Dan who looked sixty and couldn't speak, having been raised by bears in the jungle; the dying teenager who loved to sing, for whom the only help one could offer was a song; and the woman who could not feed herself because half of her jaw had been eaten away by cancer. Gehrts spoke of a three-year-old boy who always was taking care of others, who when he received his food gave it to another until everyone else had been fed.

"We couldn't speak to each other, but you learn very quickly how unimportant language is," she said. "On my last day, I wanted to tell him I wouldn't be back, but there was no way to say it. He knew.

"He followed me to the door, and for the first time in all the weeks we'd been together, he put his hands together and offered me a solemn namaste.

"The look on his face was one of acceptance. It said 'thank you,' but without sadness. It said he'd miss me, but without regret."

Pity is replaced by perseverance. The work is relentless and without glamour, in the most primitive conditions: bathing daily at courtyard fountains, hand-scrubbing floors and walls, and washing clothes in black cauldrons of boiling water.

"Your courage deepens," Gehrts said. "You begin to learn to be comfortable with what's uncomfortable."

Finally, Young said, comes a deep understanding of compassion and with it a kind of "enchantment."

"You accept who you are as a human being and you accept that other person whose hair you're stroking, whose hand you're holding, as a human being," he said. "Compassion isn't pity. It's a truthful, intimate interaction with another person—one to one.

"Sharing death, after all, is the ultimate intimacy: just you and this other person—not doing, just being.

"Samuel Johnson said something like 'Nothing so concentrates the mind as the idea of death.' In Calcutta, there's more than the idea of death. It's death itself, in your arms," Gehrts said.

"And you've never felt so alive as you come to feel there in the House of the Dying. That's what compassion is, I think: It's being truly alive with someone."

Compassion distinguishes a traveler from someone who simply goes places and sees things. Compassion—a quality of heart rather than of mind—is the root through which our humanity is nurtured. It goes beyond both pity and understanding. It allows us to recognize our connection, our essential union, with people whose difference from us seemed at first to be the attraction.

With compassion, we recognize ourselves in others. Without it, the world becomes a museum, a zoo. The people in it become exhibits that may interest or excite us, but remain separate from us behind glass and bars and cultural moats.

We don't have to visit Calcutta to learn compassion. But because they did, Laura Marinoni, Neil Young, Monica Gehrts, and the other members of the Calcutta Club can help us as tutors and guides.

"In Calcutta I learned to appreciate life, my own and others'. I learned to find my own sense of peace," Gehrts said.

"Wherever we are, we need to try to relate on a basic human level—spontaneously, without stereotypes, without ideology. . . . Just be."

(This article was originally published in the *Seattle Times.*)

# A Mount Vernon Volunteer's Vignette

*Louanne N. Wheeler*

It's been a long, cold winner, and as I sit here wondering if it will snow every month this year, my thoughts wander to warmer, happier times. In just three weeks, I'll be digging again at Mount Vernon!

Friends are fascinated when they find out I work there. But on second thought, they ask, "You mean you get up early every Saturday all summer, and work out there in the sun and stifling heat? Why?"

I am not a morning person. Most days I can barely make it to work on time. But come summer Saturdays, I spring out of bed like a seven-year-old. Who knows what we may do today?

Maybe we'll "munsell" dirt—define its color (yellowish brown, or brownish yellow?) and note the difference between clay and "silty loam." We might measure and map the site, drawing in the various strata in the wall of a dug-out square.

I might interpret what we're doing for the visitors (they're never "tourists" at Mount Vernon), or screen (not "sift") the dirt we dig through wire mesh screens to be sure we don't overlook tiny bits of glass, bone, or ceramics.

Archaeology has been part of the permanent program at Mount Vernon since 1987—I've been a volunteer since 1988. Research helps in the study of the Washington family's daily life and that of their slaves, and aids restoration efforts on the 550-acre property. The Mount Vernon Ladies Association purchased the property in 1858 from the Washington family and still runs the estate. The goal is to restore and maintain it as it was in 1799, the year that Washington died. For instance, archaeology has found evidence of posts for an eighteenth-century fence running along the South Lane, instead of the nineteenth-century brick walls now there, so that fence will be restored.

We use Samuel Vaughn's 1787 plan of the estate to help identify areas, like that of the dung repository, which we dug out two years ago. Built in 1787 across from the stable, this shed for manure and other organic materials was the earliest covered building for composting in this country. Washington's constant interest in agriculture was shown in his many letters to his farm manager, like those giving instructions about "the repository for the compost." The excitement of finding the cobblestone floor nearly intact after 200 years more than made up for all those questions (no, it doesn't smell). Demolished sometime after 1820, this building will also be reconstructed.

But my favorite site so far has been the trash "midden" near the kitchen—a depression in the ground where garbage was thrown (a common practice in the eighteenth century). Garbage can tell us about the food people ate, the clothes they wore, the tableware they used, and more. In this twenty-by-fifteen-foot oval only about one and one-half inches deep, more than 100,000 artifacts were discarded between 1760 and 1775. Talk about a treasure trove! This collection of food remains, blue-and-white china, wine bottle glass, buttons, and even bone-handled toothbrushes tells us a lot about what was being used during Mount Vernon's early years.

I've learned about the crafts of the period through work on the blacksmith shop and the carpenter's shop. I've learned about slave life through investigation of the "House for Families," a two-story structure that housed the slaves who lived on this farm. In its brick-lined root cellar (later filled with trash), we discovered 40,000 artifacts—including 25,000 animal bones—that tell us about the diet and daily lives of the slaves.

Are there drawbacks? Sure. Some days the site is like a sauna. You get dirty, and your knees hurt. There are bugs (this is Virginia, after all!). But a friend who saw me after a long day of digging said, "I never saw anybody so dirty look so happy!"

And it's not just about my trowel uncovering the occasional ceramic piece or a friendly sheep looking over our site. There's the serenity of the gardens, the friendships made over the years of digging together, the feeling of being part, somehow, of history. There have been quiet mornings when I've known how our first president must have felt, looking out at the river. His presence is still there, in the place he loved.

So let it sleet and snow today. Tonight, I'm sharpening my trowel.

(This article was written for *Volunteer Vacations* and is printed with the permission of the author.)

# But, Why Are You Doing This?

*Francoise Yohalem*

"But, why are you doing this?" "*Por qué?*" This was Francisco's question as he stopped digging the trench to address my daughter and me. Nicole and I looked at each other, our red sweaty faces and sticky, dirty clothes, our arms loaded with a shovel full of dirt, and we burst out laughing. How could we explain to Francisco and the other *campesinos* why we decided to come to this isolated farming community in the Guatemalan highlands to do this backbreaking work? After being tempted for a moment to try to remember the Spanish translation of "masochist," I explained to Francisco that we wanted to be helpful to the people of Llanos de Morales by working on this potable water system, but most importantly, that we wanted to get to know them and be friends. Francisco smiled, shook his head, and his next question was: "How come we are not allowed to come and work in your country?"

The idea of sharing a working vacation with my twenty-year-old daughter had stemmed from my recent travels to developing countries. I had returned from treks in the Himalayas and the Andes, not only awed by the spectacular unspoiled scenery, but touched by the warm welcome of the shy and gentle people I met, who live harsh lives in very isolated areas. I wanted Nicole, a senior at the University of Michigan, to accompany me on a trip where we would not just be tourists and observers, but would have a work assignment allowing us the opportunity to know another culture and gain a new perspective of the world.

After some research, we decided to join Global Volunteers, a non-profit international development organization based in St. Paul, Minnesota. Global Volunteers' programs center around a two- or three-week personal learning and work experience in remote villages on several continents. The volunteers come at the invitation of a host organization and work alongside the local people on projects the villagers themselves have initiated. Because I speak Spanish, I have always felt very much at home in Latin countries, and Global Volunteers' program in Guatemala seemed the most attractive. So I made arrangements for Nicole and myself to join a thirteen-member team scheduled to go to Guatemala for two weeks in August. Our team was assigned to Llanos de Morales, an isolated rural community located in the central highlands, two hours northeast of Guatemala City. We were told that we would be working on the construction of a health post, doing mostly masonry and carpentry work. The organization provided us with excellent predeparture training materials consisting of videotapes and manuals discussing the culture, history, politics, climate, and geography of the area. Practical dos and don'ts as well as health concerns were also addressed. Development issues and cultural sensitivity were discussed in order to better prepare us for the local people with whom we were to work hand in hand on the project, sharing our skills and energy.

Nicole and I also read several books on the political situation in Guatemala, including devastating accounts of human rights violations and persecution of the indigenous population. But Global Volunteers assured us that we would be safe, and that the area where we were going had been free of civil strife.

Since this was our first venture to Central America, and Nicole's first introduction to a Latin American culture, we added a couple of weeks of traveling to enlarge our experience. We spent the first week in Mexico, and traveled within Guatemala for one week beyond our two-week work assignment. I made all the arrangements for the touring part of our trip.

We rendezvoused with the other Global Volunteers team members in Guatemala City. The group was congenial and friendly. We ranged in age from a high school senior from Texas to a retired couple from Kentucky, and politically, from mild "Kentucky liberal" to radical activist. Our leader, Chris, a young woman in her middle thirties, had left a career as a successful executive to move to Guatemala and head Global Volunteers programs in that country. She had unbounded energy, good humor, and much needed diplomatic skills, serving as the liaison between the Institute of Cultural Affairs (ICA), our host organization, our group, and the villagers, who had their own committee. She also maneuvered our red platform truck through impossible roads, worried about our physical and mental well-being, all while working twice as hard as anyone else.

We found Guatemala City, the present capital, rather unattractive, and were happy to leave it to go to Llanos de Morales, our group's destination. We got there after a scary drive, tightly packed in our red truck, acquiring the first bruises of many more to come from our "contact" with the Guatemalan "roads." From Sanarate (the regional capital) to Llanos, we acquired two extra riders, local villagers hitch-hiking back to their farms, and we learned that "there is always room for more."

Llanos is not so much a village as an *aldea*, or farming community, spread out along a lovely green mountain ridge. The people are Ladinos, or of Indian and Spanish heritage. They are open and friendly, and have a high level of initiative. The community language is Spanish, and the people are primarily Catholic, although, because of a shortage of priests, mass is only celebrated for special occasions. Corn is the main crop and the basis of the people's diet, but the villagers grow many vegetables, including several varieties of beans and squash, as well as wonderful tropical fruit. The banana plantations also grow coffee and cacao bushes. Brilliant hibiscus and bougainvillea provide brilliant splashes of color along the dusty, bumpy roads. Altogether, I was happy to see that the village looked much better off than some of the places I had visited in Peru the year before.

The team settled down in our modest, dormitory-style quarters, a decrepit annex to the village's old church. We had an all-purpose courtyard with an ugly pink cast cement washbasin next to a curtained toilet area. For showers, we used "solar showers," plastic bags filled with water which we hung from a rusty nail behind the wall of our compound. We had electricity, but many houses did not. We jokingly called this our hacienda.

The morning after our arrival we found out that the health post project we had been told we would be working on was on hold since the building materials had not arrived. So our assignment changed to working on a potable water system, a project already started several months ago, that the villagers hoped to have finished before the end of the year. In plain terms, we would be digging ditches up and down the hills, across fields, to and from farms, across the river—and so we did!

In order to beat the heat, we would get up at 6:00 A.M. and by 7:00 A.M., armed with our picks, shovels, and hoes, we waited at the corner of the road for the team of villagers that we would be joining. Each family had to contribute a certain number of days to the project in order to get the water to their farm, so our digging companions changed frequently. Our *jefe del dia* (chief of the day), usually recognizable by the impressive machete hanging from his belt, would divide us into groups and assign us to different sections of the job. There, under very hot sun, we worked in unison with the men, digging, shoveling, carrying pipes, and burying them. The men worked very hard although they made it look so easy! The jefe would usually walk around and supervise, using his machete to clear up bushes or cut snakes in half.

Nicole and I sometimes worked on the same team, and the villagers found it amusing that we were mother and daughter. (We felt a special sense of responsibility after being told that we were the first mother-daughter team with Global Volunteers!)

As an interpreter for the group, I had the delicate task of trying to facilitate the cross-cultural exchange, explaining us to them and them to us. In spite of the hard work and oppressive heat, there was genuine friendliness and good spirit among the gringos and campesinos, and we did bury a lot of pipes (although we worried about the fact that none of them were tested before we filled in the ditches). As we mastered uphill digging we experienced a new complete body workout that, while leaving us tired and sore, also made us feel healthy and strong.

Nicole and I developed a new relationship: we worried about one another, felt proud of each other, bound together by our work, the serene surroundings, and our feeling for the people of Llanos whom we grew to admire and care about.

When we needed a rest from the digging there were other tasks to be performed: painting the wooden furniture for the preschool, or the rusting beams for the roof of the health post, accompanying the nurse on her rounds, working with the children in the preschool. By lunchtime, we collapsed at the table for what was usually a very healthy meal, prepared on a wood fire by our cook, Petrona. We especially enjoyed the black beans and tasty vegetables, although some of us did get tired of the daily tortillas! After a rest, we spent the afternoons doing gentler tasks, usually working in the homes to which we were invited, chucking or graining the corn that the women would soak, then take to the mill the next morning to be ground into a paste for the tortillas. In the one-room homes we worked with the women, surrounded by their many children. These mothers were so young, yet looked old, and it was hard to answer their questions about our own lives and careers in a way that would make sense to them. The children were wonderful and affectionate. They would cling to "Nicola" and play with her, and I was afraid she was going to adopt them all! We noticed that as soon as the husbands came into the room, the women would become quiet and almost submissive, reluctant to further participate in the conversation. So, as we acquired new callouses on our thumbs from our poor graining technique, we also acquired a real respect for these gentle yet strong women who have to care for their husbands, many children, and oftentimes parents, in-laws, and even grandparents, all in a small house that lacks potable water. After a few days, we enjoyed recognizing many familiar faces and began to feel part of Llanos.

As the region was entering the rainy season, we experienced some spectacular downpours, usually in the late afternoon and at night, when the rain would beat wildly on the not-so-waterproof metal roof above our heads. In our cramped quarters, we got to know one another quite well, banding together to organize our evening bug searches that usually consisted of gently relocating the big, ugly tarantulas, while mercilessly killing the less fierce-looking scorpions. Local mosquitos seemed quite fond of the gringos' skins. We took turns fetching purified water to drink and brush our teeth with, filling the solar showers, and burning our paper wastes that the septic tank could not accommodate. Every day in the late afternoon, we took turns teaching English to some of the eager teenagers, and they helped us with our Spanish. We had fun exchanging songs and spent some pleasant evenings serenading back and forth before bedtime.

On our last afternoon, we organized a fiesta for the children and more than one hundred came, plus the mothers carrying babies. We were amazed at how much fun we all had, without any fancy props or toys, making up silly contests and games. That night we hired a marimba band and invited the whole community to our dance. This turned out to be quite an event, and we got to dance with the same men with whom we dug ditches, dressed in their same hats and working clothes. We had been briefed on what was culturally acceptable behavior, and I hope that we did all right!

As we left for Guatemala City in our red truck early the next morning, we were sad to be leaving friends behind, and all of us felt lucky to have had this opportunity to spend a couple of weeks that, although physically demanding, seemed so uncomplicated and felt so enriching and healthful. It was a positive experience for everyone, although a few in our group felt that the hard physical labor made it difficult for them to contribute as much as they had wished.

Feeling both sad and relieved to separate from the rest of our group, Nicole and I took the bus from Guatemala City for Antigua, a wonderful eighteenth-century city surrounded by dramatic volcanoes and rich in ruins from its colonial past. From there, we explored the western highlands, populated by diverse indigenous people who still wear the traditional multicolored woven costumes and cling desperately to their history, culture, and lifestyle that is constantly under threat. We also visited beautiful Lake Atitlan and climbed Pacaya, a still-active volcano. We ended our trip by escaping to magic Tikal, the greatest of all Mayan sanctuaries in the middle of the luscious jungle of Petén, a world apart from another jungle, that of Mexico City, which we had experienced at the beginning of our trip.

(This article is reprinted with permission of Global Volunteers.)

# Lost Forest of the Andes
*Kathy Glass*

In the south of Chile, the South American continent crumbles into archipelagos and deep fjords cut the diminishing mainland. Mountain meets sea in the green cloak of the Bosque Valdiviano—the Valdivian Forest, one of the last two extensive temperate rain forests on Earth (the other edges the north Pacific coast from Washington State through British Columbia to southeast Alaska). Wild, tangled, and difficult to access, this ancient forest is almost as unknown today as when Charles Darwin first journeyed to this remote region in 1832. In the *Voyage of the Beagle* he wrote, "Among the scenes deeply impressed on my mind, none exceed in sublimity the primeval forests undefaced by the hand of man."

Darwin never saw an old-growth forest in his native land; most had been cut long before his time. The "primeval forests" of the New World were destined to suffer the same fate; only a small fraction has been protected by law or topography. Chile's magnificent coastal rain forest owes its existence today to the latter. The region's rugged mountains and convoluted coastline, along with a wet and windy climate, have combined to keep most of the lower third of Chile (from Puerto Montt to Tierra del Fuego) a little-known and seldom-traveled wilderness. Less than 3 percent of Chile's human population lives here. Thus for adventurous travelers who enjoy camping, hiking, and kayaking, southern Chile is an unspoiled paradise.

I am visiting the forest along with Chilean environmentalists to explore, document, and ultimately preserve some of Chile's old-growth forest that is slowly falling victim to multinational timber interests. Our base camp is Cahuelmo Fjord, on the coast about eighty kilometers (fifty miles) south of Puerto Montt, the southern terminus of the Pan-American Highway. The boat trip takes us past a mountainous and heavily forested coast reminiscent of British Columbia and southeast Alaska. As in the coastal areas of northwestern North America, ferries and private boats are the main mode of transportation in southern Chile. The scenic coast and innumerable islands drift past like a mural of Eden.

We are awed as we cruise into the narrow mouth of Cahuelmo Fjord. Clear water reflects the steep green walls of the fjord's confines, and further up the spectacular open valley, we see the last of the summer's snow on the glacially carved granite peaks. Cahuelmo Fjord penetrates Chile at its narrowest point. Here the Continental Divide and Argentinean border is less than fifty kilometers from the coast.

At night the southern stars burn in the Andean sky, and we form a tiny circle of fire-lit faces in this vast wilderness. We talk about *alerce* (ah-LER-say), a threatened species of giant conifer that lured us to Chile in the first place. This massive cedar is the largest tree in South America—up to four meters, or thirteen feet, in diameter—and one of the three most long-lived species on Earth, estimated to reach 3,300 to 4,000 years of age (probably edging out the giant sequoia but not the bristlecone pine, which lives up to 4,800 years).

Because of its size, its soft and fibrous bark, the rich red color of its wood when cut, and its fire and rot-resistant qualities, the alerce cedar is sometimes called the "redwood of South America." These same qualities have proven a liability for the slow-growing alerce, which today is nearly extinct from logging in its more accessible coastal lowland habitat. The alerce's patchy range is now limited to steep Andean ridges and remote hanging valleys south of Puerto Montt. It has been protected by law since 1976.

The alerce is the reigning monarch of the forest in grandeur if not in numbers. Below the canopy of these giants is a lush evergreen growth of southern beech, laurel, and myrtle trees, bright scarlet fuchsia blossoms, and numerous vines and shrubs. Few scientists or naturalists even know the names of most of these plants. This is the enigma of the Valdivian Forest, the "lost forest of the Andes." Few people even know it exists, and yet it is one of the finest ancient forests on the planet, with cathedral groves of alerce that have withstood the powerful winds of the "Roaring Forties" (along the forty degree latitude belt) since before the time of Christ.

That such a superlative tree as the alerce could be virtually unknown to most of the world outside Chile is in itself amazing. But then the media tends to focus almost exclusively on South America's tropical rain forest, not on its temperate fringe. Indeed, the temperate zone of South America, where freezing subzero temperatures commonly occur, is quite small and isolated from other climates like it in the world. It is a narrow sliver down the western slopes of the Andes from central Chile to the tip of the continent. These forests developed in near-total isolation from the extensive temperate forests of North America, Europe, and Asia.

Temperate rain forests hold the planet's densest accumulations of life per hectare, with at least twice as much biomass as an equivalent area of tropical rain forest, where plants must expend more energy on temperature regulation than on growth. Here in the midlatitudes, the climate is cooler and often wetter, and in the filtered half-light of these ancient forests grow most of the world's largest and oldest trees.

The temperate rain forest of northwestern North America was long thought to be the world's single best example of this ecosystem. Yet here at the southern end of the South American continent we are amazed to find a forest comparable in size and every bit as rich and beautiful—in many respects, a "sister bioregion" to the north Pacific coast. Increased awareness of this southern hemisphere temperate forest is opening a whole new frontier in forest research.

Near our camp on the water's edge, there is a hot spring with rough "tubs" carved in what is either a shell mound from a long vanished tribe of people or simply fossiliferous sandstone. I rise on the first full day here and head for the baños. (This will become a daily ritual for me when in base camp.) The peaks are alternately hidden and revealed by a low, sensuous mist, and steam rises from the spring. The photographers among us are out on the tidal flats, going through rolls of film.

We explore this wilderness by breaking into small groups, heading up the river that bisects Cahuelmo's main valley, or plunging directly into the rain forest up toward the high valleys. The pure essence of the forest is revealed as we push inland through prime old growth heavy with the secret and undisturbed life of plants. Tangled bamboo and the debris of centuries litter the forest floor, for in this climate deadfalls can last hundreds of years. Scrambling through the dense understory with packs is so rough that one woman pronounces it "as difficult as giving birth."

We must work hard to simply reach lone outposts of the larger stands of alerce. After struggling for two days, we finally see scattered alerce near the mouth of a box canyon. We fall upon our first specimen like a hidden treasure which, indeed, it is.

Further into the grove, we wander spellbound in its beauty. In the vertical world of the old-growth forest, even the sunlight falls in shafts to the earth. The ferns are three times a human's height, and we are tiny creatures among infinite shapes and shades of green. Hoary trees tower like benevolent giants, wrapped in moss and the peace of silent centuries. Somehow it feels like home, though we have traveled thousands of miles to be here.

It is ironic that, after so much effort to reach this place, we must wonder about the safety of this last refuge of the alerce. New roads are gradually being pushed south through the coastal mountains, opening the region to timber and mining development. Nearly a quarter of a million hectares of wilderness is for sale, some for as little as fifteen dollars per hectare.

The outlook for Chile's remaining ancient forest vis-à-vis the new "democratic" government is unclear. The country's environmental movement, long stunted under the Pinochet dictatorship, is now working more openly and urgently. But while the new regime seems sympathetic to environmental concerns, increased leeway for free enterprise could further strain exploitable resources. Wood products have long been one of Chile's major sources of foreign exchange. This is a critical time for the government to commit to the protection of key areas.

As our boat chugged back up the coast toward civilization, the forests edging the water seemed endless. I thought of the dense and nearly impenetrable forest we trekked through and knew it was but a glance off a narrow path. Yet the image of abundance is illusory. As Chile's priceless old-growth forest hangs in the balance, one can only hope it will be spared the fate of most of the earth's once-vast ancient forests.

Chilean poet Pablo Neruda, himself widely traveled, once wrote, "Anyone who hasn't been in the Chilean forest doesn't know this planet." I feel fortunate to have been there, and I realize it is a blessing that this forest in the Andes has remained lost for as long as it has.

(This article was originally published in *Great Expeditions*.)

# A New View of Africa

*Christopher Wright*

Sitting in the cool shade under the corrugated metal eaves of the Charuru Primary School, I sighed contentedly at the view of Mount Kenya rising into the clouds around its twin peaks. It provided a dramatic backdrop to the gathering of teachers and yellow-and-green uniformed children sitting in the school yard. But my attention was soon captivated by a fourteen-year-old Meru boy with a voice resembling a Vienna Boys Choir tenor who stood to sing an Elizabethan love ballad.

Before I came to this small rural village high on the verdant slopes of that ancient volcano, my conception of the Dark Continent was predominantly influenced by Hollywood and the media. Celluloid dreams, from *The African Queen* to *The Lion King*, romanticized the animal kingdom and human empires that shaped and reshaped Africa. *National Geographic* and the Discovery Channel provided glimpses of apparently endless desert and jungle wilderness teeming with critters. CNN's up-to-the-minute coverage overwhelmed me with clips of butchered bodies littering the roads and villages of Somalia and Rwanda; at the top of the hour, malnourished children with swollen bellies, their faces swarming with flies, stared balefully out at me with the same exhausted gaze as those tragic children Sally Struthers had wept over on late-night television before she went on to flog mail order trade school certificates for low-wage, dead-end jobs.

But sitting in this village with healthy children dancing around and serenading us, I realized that Africa is more than the sum of its flora

Youngsters enjoy a celebration at the end of Global Citizens Network project. Photo courtesy of Global Citizens Network.

and fauna, more than tragic news blurbs of distant drought, famine, and intertribal strife, more than a background setting for Academy Award-winning cinematography. It is a living continent full of vibrant life and mundane worries, with all the beauty and all the troubles that humans and nature can create.

The song ended and the gathered students and visitors applauded enthusiastically. Mbaabu Charles, the first grade teacher and health clinic committee chairman stood and welcomed the visitors to Charuru and thanked us for coming, his deep gentle voice challenging our lazy ears with the rolled r's and broad, full-bodied vowels of the Kenyan English accent. More speeches followed, the children grew restless and giggled, teachers scowled and waggled fingers, and we six Americans lost our shade and began to sweat as the sun passed its apex and peeked under the eaves at us. But we had been sweating all morning, digging and beveling a sloping hillside with spades, fork-like picks called jembes, and two rickety wheelbarrows with rusted-out sides, so we relished the chance to sweat while sitting and doing nothing. After all, this was our vacation.

So how did two teachers, a retired English professor, a nursing student, a retired IBM salesman, and I end up living in a stone house with no indoor plumbing or electricity, six thousand feet up an African mountainside, doing manual labor and being praised, thanked, and sung to for three weeks? Well, missionaries we weren't, as evidenced by the lineup of empty Tusker beer bottles on the cement verandah outside our rooms each morning. No, we were doing our part as Global Citizens, lending a hand on a health clinic building project while immersing ourselves in the culture and daily life of a community a world apart from our own.

"When you have the chance to learn firsthand about the livelihood of other cultures, you will feel more connected to others in ways you may never have experienced before." So said the literature from Global Citizens Network (GCN), the St. Paul-based nonprofit organization sponsoring our trip.

"By becoming a 'Global Citizen,' you will also be helping to honor, preserve, and assist developing communities around the world." Our team of six *wazungu*—Kiswahili for 'foreigners'—was the fourth GCN team to Charuru, and after three days of sweating side by side with local men, women and children, carrying stone building blocks, and excavating a hillside, we certainly felt connected to the community.

The health clinic we labored on—the fifth self-help project initiated by the community—was begun in the summer of 1993. The first GCN team helped clear the land for the first five rooms and participated in the cornerstone laying ceremony. By the time our team arrived, the walls were up, the roof was on, a rough floor had been poured and the interior walls finished in plaster. Doors and windows were being installed by skilled tradesmen, each one a volunteer like us, while we unskilled wazungus and villagers dug and moved dirt and leveled ground for the next stage. Since part of the GCN philosophy is to "do with" not to "do for," teams work only when local people work, and we were occasionally left idle when the daily work force was busy with other pressing chores. We were also bedeviled by a scarcity of tools until, using part of GCN's matching grant funds, we bought tools to donate to the community. But the delays and lack of resources that drive us type A wazungus crazy are commonplace throughout most of the world.

Fortunately, our hosts kept us busy, taking us on walking tours to the stone quarry and tea factory, guiding us through the forest on the ridges around the village in search of the elusive Colobus Monkey and inviting us to their *shambas* (as the farmsteads are called).

Peggy and Jill, our two professional teachers, spent a day in the school teaching and answering questions about themselves and our culture. They were joined by Sarah, the nurse-in-training who taught first aid, hygiene, and the Heimlich maneuver to seventh and eighth graders.

I spent an afternoon building a solar oven with Jeremiah, the local man hired to cook meals for us and who became our cultural advisor, translator, *matatu* (taxi) negotiator, and friend. Though the rainy season prevented the oven's debut, Jeremiah and the local women's group were eager to try it, since most of their fuel is wood or charcoal from the ever-receding forest.

Under Peggy's expert guidance, we all took up needle and thread and sewed curtains, along with some of the local women who giggled at the sight of a man with a needle. And one sunny afternoon when no workers were available, we were invited to learn tea-picking techniques. We joined workers plucking "two leaves and a bud," the tender new shoots that a trained eye can find and a skilled hand can pick at great speed but which we hunted and mauled with little competence until we were eventually invited to "watch and rest."

In the evenings before dinner, Mbaabu Charles or John Mithika, the committee secretary, taught us Kiswahili down at the school. Glenn, the former IBM salesman, was our best student, learning greetings and small talk through repetition whenever we were walking or working. He greeted everybody, from tiny children to the ancient elders who only understood the local Meru tribal language but responded anyway, to school children, our fellow workers, and the matatu drivers who took us grocery shopping in Meru town. It was easy to see why he was such a successful salesman!

But those days when we worked, we worked hard. I had some carpentry skills, so I helped a little with the chiseling of rock around the window into which frames would be set.

Charley, the retired English professor—"by definition, I have no skills" he told us—wielded a mean jembe by week three, tearing into the rain-sodden hillside with relish when he wasn't leaning on a shovel as adeptly as any road construction worker on Highway 394.

By the time our stay was over, we Global Citizens had come to realize that no matter how much we wanted to give the people of Charuru, they had given us much more. Sure, we left behind tools, some curtains, a solar oven, and a level spot of ground, but far more importantly, we left behind friends we will remember the rest of our lives. And we left behind the old images of Africa, taking home memories of green hills, healthy, smiling children, and warm, hard-working people who aren't all that different from ourselves. Their politicians are both caring and corrupt, their environment and wildlife are beautiful and threatened, there's trouble and strife and love and decency, just like here at home. So next time CNN reports tragedies in Africa, I think I'll turn off the TV and look at my pictures instead.

(This article was originally published in *Big World Magazine* and is reprinted with the permission of Global Citizens Network and the author.)

# They're Blazing Paths for Others
*Lucinda Dillon*

In her hometown of Portsmouth, England, twenty-three-year-old Amanda Bullion can't ride the city bus, watch a movie in a theater, or roll her wheelchair into many public buildings.

Kingstone Kelly Zimba, whose legs were amputated below the knee joints after a train accident fifteen years ago, prefers to use prostheses. People in his hometown of Lusaka, Zambia, stare mercilessly when he uses his wheelchair.

Bullion and Zimba both want to advance opportunities for people in their countries who have disabilities. They were a part of a thirty-one-person international delegation that visited Eugene, Oregon, as part of a leadership exchange program sponsored by Mobility International U.S.A.

They worked at the Broken Bowl Picnic Area in the Willamette National Forest, thirty-five miles southeast of Eugene. There they widened paths, restructured picnic areas, and otherwise made camp-sites more accessible to people with disabilities.

"I came here to see how far Eugene has come and how these other people are getting things across in their countries," said Bullion, who was born with cerebral palsy. "I've got to go back and tell other disabled people."

The delegates, most of whom are disabled, learned about themselves and each other during the four-day community project in the forest, and they shared experiences and suggestions.

Zimba camped outdoors for the first time, one of several new experiences he had in Eugene. "When I came to Eugene, I couldn't believe my eyes—I can get on the bus here and get around anywhere," said Zimba, who is deputy chief executive of administration for the Zambian Council for the Handicapped.

While Zimba and Bullion clipped, raked, and pruned back the growth along paved trails to allow passage of standard thirty-two-inch wheelchairs, other delegates worked to elevate ground-level barbecue pits to a height more accessible to people using wheelchairs.

Efforts to make the campsites "barrier free" were long overdue, said Chuck Frayer, the accessibility and engineering specialist for the U.S. Forest Service who visited the site. "Until recently, the Forest Service really hasn't done much marketing of services for the disabled," he said. "We're learning that what we thought was accessible really wasn't accessible."

So the partnership with Mobility International U.S.A. (MIUSA), which has completed several similar projects within the forest, is a valuable one, he said.

MIUSA is the Eugene-based, U.S. branch of Mobility International, a twenty-three-nation organization. The group promotes international understanding and provides opportunities for people with disabilities to exchange information that will improve their lives, said its director Susan Sygall.

The exchanges generate a "powerful connection" among disabled people who have similar challenges, goals, and experiences, she said.

"There's a real sense of solidarity," Sygall said. "They were all here with a mission—to improve services in their country."

Workshops highlighted topics including leadership skills, discrimination, and sexuality.

"Every disabled person, no matter what country they're from, has experienced some form of discrimination," Sygall said.

One woman in the group once was turned away from a resort because of her disability. Another was denied an airline reservation. Eleven people in the group use wheelchairs.

Bullion resents that she can't go to the theater and must wait for her favorite movies to come out on videotape. "We're a fire hazard," she says.

Similarly, Ryan Tu, twenty-five years old, believes business owners in Taipei, Taiwan, have passed him up for jobs because he walks with a limp.

"Sometimes you don't even get to talk to the boss because when you come in, the staff sees how you walk and thinks you can't do the job," said Tu, whose leg is affected by nerve damage that he suffered during a knee operation.

As a volunteer for the National Society of Rehabilitation for the Republic of China, Tu hopes to support laws ensuring employment equality for people with disabilities. "People think it's cruel to make the disabled do some kind of job, but it's even crueler not to let them," he said.

(This article first appeared in *The Register-Guard* of Eugene, Oregon, on July 12, 1989.)

# Volunteers (Not) Going Overboard
*Dory Devlin*

It was a normal day on the Upper Delaware River. Conditions weren't rough, and an average amount of water was flowing down Skinners Falls. Still, a canoe flipped, and a young boy washed down the river and found himself caught under a boat that was pinned by a rock.

What could have been a tragedy instead turned quickly into a well-executed rescue by staff of the National Canoe Safety Patrol who spotted the boy in trouble and saved him. One member swam out to the child, extricated him from underneath the boat and stabilized him, while another member threw out a line of rope to bring the pair to shore.

Christian Nielsen remembers observing the dramatic rescue from shore. As a founding member of the patrol, he, too, has helped bring many inexperienced canoeists who suddenly find themselves in trouble on white water to safety.

Those memories are why he finds himself out on the Delaware nearly every weekend of canoe season.

"People come out of New York City and Philadelphia looking for a weekend away doing something different," says Nielsen, sixty-seven years old and the patrol's vice president. "They get involved in something they really don't know about and are not aware of the skills needed."

Nielsen speaks from experience. He first paddled a canoe in 1973, and early on he learned that there was a lot more to canoeing than he thought. So he joined a canoe club and bought the right equipment before taking his two sons on the water.

"I got involved in canoeing like a lot of people do things—just to get my kids away from the television set," he says.

It worked. The Long Valley family became avid canoeists, and twenty years later Nielsen still finds himself in a canoe on all but the coldest weekends, paddling about one thousand miles a year on rivers like the Musconetcong in New Jersey, the Shenandoah in Virginia, and Esopus Creek in New York's Catskills.

"It's been a way to meet an awful lot of nice people over the years and a great way to see the scenery," says Nielsen, who owns an insurance agency in Flanders.

Nielsen turned his attention to helping novice canoeists in 1977 as an instructor with the Greater Trenton Area Red Cross Small Craft Safety Committee. It was a pilot program run by the Mohawk Canoe Club along the Delaware River in Lambertville, and it proved to be an immediate success.

"We decided there was a lot of inexperienced use of canoes," he recalls. As the number of people on the water rose, club members also saw initiating a patrol as a way to discourage government intervention.

"We were concerned regulation might shut down the river for us if we didn't do something to police it ourselves," he says.

The patrol shifted its locale in 1978 to the more crowded Upper Delaware and formed the National Canoe Safety Patrol, based in Skinners Falls in the National Park Service's Upper Delaware Scenic and Recreational River, headquartered in Narrowsburg, New York. The area boasts nearly seventy-three and one-half miles of the Delaware River, "the largest stretch of the wild and scenic river system administered by the park service on the East Coast," says John Hutzky, the National Park Service superintendent. The Upper Delaware begins where the east and west branches of the Delaware River converge in Hancock, New York, and runs southeastward to Sparrowbush, New York, just north of the Delaware Water Gap National Recreation Area. Last year, more than 260,000 people visited the area, and about 187,000 of them went boating, canoeing, rafting, and tubing.

Skinners Falls, one of several Class II rapids on the Delaware, is a popular spot for canoeists and therefore for the patrol. The rapids, with rushing waters and hidden obstacles, does not provide a straight run through but rather requires canoeists to maneuver from side to side to have a successful run.

Hutzky is convinced that lives that been saved by Nielsen and the other devoted patrol members, who number between seventy and ninety and last year contributed 2,240 hours on peak-season weekends. Hutzky estimates that since the volunteer program began, patrol members have put in more than 66,000 hours, which would have cost the park service more than $543,000 if they paid park rangers to do the work.

The patrol officially linked up with the park service in 1980, the year there were nine drownings on the Upper Delaware River. In 1985, there were no deaths by drowning in these waters. In 1992, the same. In every other year there have been one or two deaths, most swimming related, says Hutzky. He attributes the drop in fatalities is due in large part to the patrol.

"Undoubtedly, they have probably saved many more lives that may have been lost as a result of their not being here," says Hutzky.

Since 1980, there have been twenty-nine deaths in the area, most of them young men overestimating their physical limits versus the strong, unfamiliar currents of the river, says Hutzky. Surprisingly, only eight of them were deemed related to alcohol and drugs.

While drinking among the weekend canoeists and boaters is an acknowledged problem by the patrol and park service, the safety patrol is not out to snag drinkers, says Nielsen. They cruise the river only to find canoeists in trouble and to help them, he says.

Canoe liveries are now playing a key role in discouraging drinking on the river, Hutzky says. Some are checking every item put into the canoe or raft to ensure no alcohol is going along. One livery has even opened its own alcohol-free campground. And all twenty-two canoe liveries licensed by the park service must provide safety orientation on canoeing and rafting, he adds.

The patrol members train annually to reinforce their rescue skills as well as their knowledge of CPR and first aid before the canoe season, which runs from April through October. For most of their rescues, a rope is used to pull overboard boaters to shore.

"We use ropes extensively," says Nielsen. "Throwrope bags"—sixty-foot white, highly visible polypropylene ropes—are used alone or tied together if the imperiled canoeist is far from shore.

"It's quite effective and gets right out to people," says Nielsen. "We pull in a lot of people with those."

Sometimes patrol members must swim out to the endangered boaters, stabilizing victims by instructing them to lie calmly on their backs and to hold onto the rope while being pulled to safety. Once the canoeists are ashore, the patrol also rounds up the errant boat and gear. "The normal scenario involves somebody dumping over in the water and momentarily being terrified by it," says Nielsen.

When not cruising the Upper Delaware—the only park where the volunteers patrol—some of the members travel to prominent whitewater races to volunteer their rescue skills. Nielsen has attended Olympic trials on the Savage River in western Maryland, World Cup races, and the well-known white-water slalom races on the Tohickon in Point Pleasant, Pennsylvania.

But on the Delaware, inexperience, the patrol has found, is what leads most to injury. Not knowing basic paddling techniques or how to sit in a canoe is "like someone going to a ski area and trying to go down a hill without knowing what to do," says Nielsen. "They're going to kill themselves."

Nielsen and his fellow patrol members found a long time ago that the best time to instruct people on some of canoeing's basics and safety tips is after their first day on the river, not before.

Patrol volunteers go around to the area's campgrounds to tell the first-day canoeists what they see them doing wrong and give them pointers for the next day out. Just about all, says Nielsen, are receptive.

"They had to get involved to realize they needed more information," adds Nielsen, who also has served on the New Jersey Trails Council as the water trails representative since the 1970s. This citizen advisory council inventories and monitors hiking, biking, horseback riding, skiing, and water trails throughout the state, working to link the trails together so that they can be accessible to all residents.

It only takes about fifteen to twenty minutes to impart some of the basics needed not to get hurt. Advice on how to keep the boat pointed downstream, and warning that canoeists should always wear life jackets and kneel in a boat, not sit, are included in those brief talks. Patrol members also illustrate basic paddling techniques to go forward, stop, move to the side, and slow down.

With several thousand canoes rented on the Upper Delaware on a summer weekend, Nielsen knows the patrol's work is important and that he could be busy for a long time to come.

"There are an awful lot of people out there who just don't understand what they're doing, and we're here to help," he says.

(This article is reprinted with permission of the National Park Service.)

# The Month That Would Never End

*Emily Duggan*

"The month that I thought would never end is over, but in returning I have a heightened sense of what I am physically and mentally capable of and a new confidence of my strengths and myself as a person."

As I glance at my final journal entry from July 27, 1995, I am stung by hundreds of questions and memories shooting through my mind, refusing to be ignored. My mind is hungry for answers and yet so full of the familiar faces, smells, and voices that make up my Alaska. The experience began at C.W. Post, Long Island, with an orientation that to me is a blur of nervous, confusing, and often uncomfortable situations, as well as many wrong first impressions. I asked myself, "What have I gotten myself into? Who goes to Alaska in the middle of the summer? The twenty-two hours of daylight will drive you mad. How do you possibly survive in a village of four hundred?" Suddenly, I knew I had entered the month that would never end. I am astonished when I remember that the people I met at C.W. Post are the people whom I am now so close to, the people who acted as my surrogate family for a month. There must be something about the freedom of open expanses, the tundra and the Yukon River, that allow you to feel safe. When I think about how long it has taken me to truly feel comfortable with my friends at home, I am shocked about how quickly and seemingly easy it was for me to reach that level with the Horizons group. As easy as it feels in retrospect, I know that it is never that simple.

After a long and tiring day of flying, my group and I were in Alaska, more specifically, St. Mary's. The people of St. Mary's, especially the children, are extremely outgoing and helpful. Between our internships, the day camp, village functions (including a wedding), and the constant bombardment of the kids at our residence, I think that it is safe to say that we all grew very attached to the community. The group established a day camp for the children and worked hard trying to make it work. We soon realized that we were in a different world and we knew that for our ideas to work, we would have to adapt to the Yu'pik way of life. The day camp was an exhausting but rewarding undertaking. The response from the children to us and our efforts was often overwhelming. The children showered us with gifts, ranging from flowers to hugs, which showed the openness and attachment that had grown between us. The internships gave everyone a chance to branch out to a different part of the community and to do something that they really wanted to; between tanning hides, beading and sewing, doing various work for the elders, and fishing, the opportunities seemed endless.

The group left St. Mary's and traveled to a nearby village, Pilot Station, to work on another project for a week. I've got to say that building a foundation into rocky soil is not an easy task, but who isn't impressed by a girl who can say "Yeah, I know how to use a pick ax"? As we worked on the building's foundation, feelings of accomplishment and of pride grew inside all of us. When we returned to St. Mary's it felt to me like I had come home: I knew the people, I knew I was welcome, and I knew that this was the place where I wanted to be.

For me, the month that would never end is over, and although leaving Alaska was one of the hardest things I've ever done, I still have my associations with Alaska—the letters, as well as an open invitation to return from the people I became close with in St. Mary's. I also have my second family, who helped me get through homesickness and any other problems I had. Looking back, I realize that it was not that simple to become close with the group at first. When you live with people for a month in close quarters and share the same, amazing experiences, it is almost impossible not to become close. And for me in Alaska, whether we were fighting over whose turn it was to return the movie, helping each other over a rocky path on the Yukon or discussing religion at 4:00 A.M., we all grew. Since the group was so small, fourteen people, we grew together and were forced to give a little piece of ourselves to each other. So, to answer my own question, who goes to Alaska? People who want to work, who want to make a difference, who are willing to open themselves up to the people of St. Mary's, especially the children who want to learn and tell and know. People who can respect real, untouched beauty—not just see it, but live it. People who want to take advantage of the twenty-two hours of daylight to learn all they can about the Yu'pik culture, about the people who live in St. Mary's and about themselves. That's who.

(This article was originally written for World Horizons International and is reprinted with the permission of World Horizons International and the author.)

# Additional Resources

Below is a list of agencies, books, directories, and periodicals that are concerned with various types of unique vacations. These resources cover volunteer vacations, learning vacations, adventure vacations, or a combination of the three, and provide different perspectives for people who want to learn more about this kind of travel. Some of the books are published outside the United States and are not likely to be available in local bookstores. Their publishers can be contacted through the addresses listed.

## Agencies

**Archaeological Institute of America**
675 Commonwealth Avenue
Boston, MA 02215
(617) 353-9361; Fax (617) 353-6550

The AIA publishes an annual edition of *Archaeological Fieldwork Opportunities Bulletin*, which lists excavation opportunities for volunteers, field school students, and some paid positions throughout the world. The bulletin also includes listings of institutions and organizations affiliated with the AIA that also use volunteers. To order this publication call (800) 338-5578.

**Archaeology Abroad**
31–34 Gordon Square
London WC1H 0PY United Kingdom

Archaeology Abroad publishes three annual bulletins (in March, May, and October) that are available through subscription. These list projects and give detailed information about their staffing needs.

**Cotravaux**
**Coordination pour le Travail Volontaire de Jeunes**
11, rue de Clichy
75009 Paris, France
(1) 48-74-79-20; Fax (1) 48-74-14-01

Cotravaux publishes a brochure that lists work camps of twelve French work camp associations. This brochure is available in French only.

**Council for British Archaeology**
Bowes Norrell House, 111 Walmgate
York YO1 2UA United Kingdom
(01904) 671 417; Fax (01904) 675 384

The CBA advertises projects organized by other volunteer organizations. Subscription to its newsletter is $50 for ten issues, including postage.

**Dorset County Museum**
High West Street
Dorchester, Dorset DT1 1XA United Kingdom
(01305) 262 735

Each spring, the Dorset Natural History Museum and Archaeological Society produces a list of excavations taking place in Dorset throughout the year. This list gives information on the directors of the digs and whether they are looking for volunteers. The listing can be obtained by writing to the museum at the above address. Volunteers on these excavations are responsible for all transportation to the site and room and board while there.

**Elderhostel**
100 Boylston Street, Suite 200
Boston, MA 02116
(617) 426-8056

Elderhostel is a program of seminars and learning experiences for those over fifty-five. Held on college campuses and utilitzing campus faculty, the sessions are held throughout the year nationwide.

**Involvement Corps, Incorporated**
15515 Sunset Boulevard, Suite 108
Pacific Palisades, CA 90272
Tel/Fax (310) 459-1022

The Involvement Corps designs community involvement programs and projects, then works directly with senior management of corporations to recruit their employees for the programs. The ICI program, launched in 1968, pioneered the field of employee volunteerism. ICI has worked with management and employees of manufacturing, utility, transportation, aerospace, insurance, and financial service firms. ICI associates are experienced professionals, particularly knowledgeable in solving problems and enhancing relationships in corporate community programs. Additionally, ICI associates are informed and knowledgeable about local self-help and community service programs. Have your company contact ICI and get involved in your community.

**National Volunteer Clearinghouse for the Homeless**
1310 Emerson Street NW
Washington, DC 20011
(800) HELP-664

This organization has one purpose: to help match volunteers with local service providers who work with the homeless and need volunteer assistance. They maintain a list of providers, the services they offer, hours of operation, and volunteer needs, which is available by contacting the National Volunteer Cleainghouse.

**Volunteer—The National Center**
1111 N. 19th Street, Suite 500
Arlington, VA 22209
(703) 276-0542

Volunteer is the national clearinghouse for volunteer centers around the country. If you are interested in volunteering in a particular location and would like information concerning the closest volunteer center to it, contact the above address for information. Volunteer also has a list of books on volunteering that it has compiled for its member organizations. The list may be of interest to those who wish to learn more about volunteerism and its many forms.

**Volunteers in Technical Assistance (VITA)**
1815 N. Lynn Street, Suite 200
Arlington, VA 22209
(703) 276-1800

VITA matches volunteers who have technical expertise with Third World organizations that have requested assistance with problems encountered during the complex process of economic development. Most of the help given by the volunteers is done by mail, but frequently volunteers are required on-site. VITA asks three questions of anyone who wishes to volunteer: Do you have technical skills that would be of use to others? Are you willing to share them? Why do you wish to be a VITA volunteer? If you can answer these questions in a positive manner and are genuinely interested in sharing your expertise, call or write VITA at the office listed above.

## Books and Directories

*Adventure Holidays: Thousands of Holidays in Britain and in 100 Countries Worldwide,* David Stevens, ed., Vacation Work Publications, 9 Park End Street, Oxford OX1 1HJ, United Kingdom. Some titles from Vacation Work Publications are distributed by Writer's Digest Books in the U.S. and Henry Fletcher Services, Limited, in Canada.

*Adventure Travel Abroad,* Pat Dickerman, Adventure Guides, 36 E. 57th Street, New York, NY 10019.

*The Adventure Vacation Catalog,* Specialty Travel Index, Simon and Schuster, Simon and Schuster Building, 1230 Avenue of the Americas, New York, NY 10020.

*Adventure Vacations: From Trekking in New Guinea to Swimming in Siberia,* Richard Bangs, John Muir Publications, PO Box 613, Santa Fe, NM 87504.

*Alternatives to the Peace Corps: Changing Third World Experience,* Becky Buell, The Institute for Food and Development Policy, 145 9th Street, San Francisco, CA 94103.

*Beyond Safaris: A Guide to Building People-to-People Ties with Africa,* Kevin Danaher, Africa World Press, PO Box 1892, Trenton, NJ 08607.

La Sabranenque volunteers restore a castle entrance in southern France. Photo courtesy of La Sabranenque.

*Channels: A Guide to Service Opportunities in the Newly Independent States*, Richard Upjohn, Center for Civil Society International, 2929 N.E. Blakely Street, Seattle, WA 98105.

*Directory of Long-Term Voluntary Organizations*, Voluntary Service Publications, UNESCO, 1, rue Moillis, 75015 Paris, France.

*Directory of Low-Cost Vacations with a Difference*, J. Crawford, Pilot Books, 103 Cooper Street, Babylon, NY 11702.

*Directory of Overseas Summer Jobs*, David Woodworth, Vacation Work Publications, 9 Park End Street, Oxford OX1 1HJ, United Kingdom.

*Directory of Volunteer Opportunities*, Ellen Shenk, ed., Volunteer Directory, Career Information Center, University of Waterloo, Waterloo, Ontario N2L 3G1, Canada.

*The Directory of Work and Study in Developing Countries*, David Leppard, Vacation Work Publications, 9 Park End Street, Oxford OX1 1HJ, United Kingdom.

*Environmental Vacations: Volunteer Projects to Save the Planet*, Stephanie Ocko, John Muir Publications, PO Box 613, Santa Fe, NM 87504.

*Going Places: A Catalog of Domestic and International Internship, Volunteer, Travel and Career Opportunities in the Fields of Hunger, Housing,*

*Homelessness and Grassroots Development*, Joanne Woods, National Students Campaign Against Hunger and Homelessness, 11965 Venice Boulevard, Suite 408, Los Angeles, CA 90066.

*The Green Travel Sourcebook: A Guide for the Physically Active, the Intellectually Curious, or the Socially Aware*, Daniel Grotta and Sally Wiener Grotta, John Wiley and Sons, 605 3rd Avenue, New York, NY 10158-0012.

*A Guide to Earthtrips: Nature Travel on a Fragile Planet*, Dwight Holing, Living Planet Press, 558 Rose Avenue, Venice, CA 90291.

*Guide to Tourist Railroads and Railroad Museums: A Directory of Over 250 Railroad Attractions in North America*, George H. Drury, Kalmback Publishing Company, 1027 N. 7th Street, Milwaukee, WI 53233.

*Helping Hands: Volunteer Work in Education*, Gayle Janowitz, University of Chicago Press, 5801 S. Ellis Avenue, Chicago, IL 60637.

*Helping Out in the Outdoors*, American Hiking Society, 1015 31st Street, NW Washington, DC 20007.

*The International Directory of Volunteer Work*, David Woodworth, Vacation Work Publications, 9 Park End Street, Oxford OX1 1HJ, United Kingdom.

*International Directory of Youth Internships*, Cynthia T. Morehouse, Learning Resources in International Studies, Suite 9A, 777 United Nations Plaza, New York, NY 10017.

*International Workcamps Directory*, Volunteers for a Peace, International Workcamps, Tiffany Road, Belmont, VT 05730.

*Invest Yourself: The Catalogue of Volunteer Opportunities*, Susan Angus, The Commission on Voluntary Service and Action, PO Box 117, New York, NY 10009.

*Kibbutz Volunteer*, John Bedford, Vacation Work Publications, 9 Park End Street, Oxford OX1 1HJ, United Kingdom.

*Learning Traveler, Vols. 1 and 2*, Gail Cohen, IIE, 809 United Nations Plaza, New York, NY 10017.

*Learning Vacations: A Guide to All-Season Worldwide Educational Travel*, George Eisenberg, Peterson's Guides, PO Box 2123, Princeton, NJ 08543-2123.

*The Nature Directory: A Guide to Environmental Organizations*, Susan D. Lanier-Graham, Walker and Company, 720 5th Avenue, New York, NY 10019.

*New World of Travel*, Arthur Frommer, Prentice Hall Press, 1 Gulf and Western Plaza, New York, NY 10023.

*Open Gate: Teaching in a Foreign Country*, Chris Roerden, Edit Publications, Brookfield, WI 53045.

*The Peace Corps and More: 114 Ways to Work, Study, and Travel in the Third World*, Medea Benjamin, Global Exchange, 2141 Mission Street, Suite 202, San Francisco, CA 94110.

*Rainforests: A Guide to Research and Tourist Facilities at Selected Tropical Forest Sites in Central and South America*, James L. Castner, Feline Press, PO Box 7219, Gainesville, FL 32605.

*The Response—Lay Volunteer Mission Opportunities*, International Liaison, Incorporated, U.S. Catholic Coordinating Center for Lay Missioners, 1234 Massachusetts Avenue NW, Washington, DC 20005.

*Summer Options for Teenagers*, Cindy Ware, Explorations, PO Box 254, Acton, MA 01720.

*Teenager's Guide to Study, Travel, and Adventure Abroad*, Marjorie Adoff Cohen, IIE, 809 United Nations Plaza, New York, NY 10017.

*Travel and Learn: The New Guide to Educational Travel*, Evelyn Kaye, Blue Penguin Publications, 147 Sylvan Avenue, Leonia, NJ 07605.

*Vacation Study Abroad*, Edrice Howard, ed., IIE, 809 United Nations Plaza, New York, NY 10017.

*Volunteer*, CIEE, 205 E. 42nd Street, New York, NY 10017.

*Volunteering in Literacy Work: A Guide to National and International Opportunities*, Coordinating Committee for International Voluntary Service, UNESCO, 1, rue Miollis, 75015 Paris, France.

*Volunteerism and Older Adults: Choices and Challenges*, Mary Kouri, ABC-CLIO, Incorporated, 130 Cremona Drive, PO Box 1911, Santa Barbara, CA 93116-1911.

*The Volunteer's Survival Manual*, Darcy Campion Devney, The Practical Press, PO Box 2296, Cambridge, MA 02238.

*Volunteer Work*, Hilary Sewell, The Central Bureau, Seymour Mews House, Seymour Mews, London W1H 9PE, United Kingdom.

*What in the World Is Going On? Opportunities for Canadians to Work, Volunteer, or Study in Developing Countries*, Ingrid Knutsen, CBIE, 85 Albert Street, Suite 1400, Ottawa ON K1P 6A4 Canada.

*Working Holidays*, Hilary Sewell, The Central Bureau, Seymour Mews House, Seymour Mews, London W1H 9PE, United Kingdom.

*Work, Study, Travel Abroad: The Whole World Handbook*, Marjorie Adoff Cohen, St. Martin's Press, 175 5th Avenue, New York, NY 10010.

*A World of Options for the Nineties: A Guide to International Educational Exchange, Community Service, and Travel for Persons with Disabilities*, Cindy Lewis and Susan Sygall, Mobility International U.S.A., PO Box 3551, Eugene, OR 97403.

## Periodicals

*Archaeology*, Archaeological Institute of America, 675 Commonwealth Avenue, Boston, MA 02215.

*The Directory of Alternative Travel Resources*, Diane Brause, One World Travel Network, 81868 Lost Valley Lane, Dexter, OR 97431.

*The Educated Traveler*, PO Box 220822, Chantilly, VA 22022.

*Transitions Abroad*, 18 Hulst Road, PO Box 344, Amherst, MA 01004.

# Cross-Referenced Indexes

# Cross-Referenced Indexes

These cross-referenced indexes were developed with undecided readers in mind, such as those who may know how much vacation time they want to spend on a volunteer effort but don't know just what they want to do, or those who may have very specific ideas about what they want to do but don't know what is available. The indexes are divided by project cost, length, location, season, and project type, so that anyone can begin with the item most important to them and proceed from there to narrow their choices. While some of the indexes were easy to define, others were more difficult. Just what should be included in project costs? Where does one put the ocean in project location, especially if one year the project is in the Caribbean and the next in the South Pacific? And what should be the category for a social action project offered by a religious organization that includes an archaeological dig?

The definitions were made, and imperfect as they may be, they are a starting point for readers who need help in deciding what type of volunteer vacation is most appropriate for them. There are twenty subdivisions in the Project Type Index, thirteen in the Project Location Index, and five in the Project Season, Project Cost, and Project Length indexes.

A word about the Project Cost Index—some organizations, like Earthwatch, include many things in their costs, such as travel, room, board, and insurance expenses. Other smaller organizations don't include anything but registration costs. This makes it almost impossible to compare organizations, so estimates given in the cost index

Shawna Gibbs, a Volunteers for Peace volunteer, met many new friends in Ghana. Photo courtesy of Volunteers for Peace.

only include the amount volunteers must pay directly to the sponsoring organization. This, in effect, makes some of the organizations appear inordinately expensive, and others deceptively inexpensive. Be wary and check what is included in the charges and what extras you will have to pay. A trip to India that requires you to pay $100 to the sponsoring organization won't be as cheap when you add round-trip transportation and room and board while in India. On the other hand, a trip to the South Pacific with round-trip transportation and room and board included in the charge may end up much less expensive than it initially appeared.

# Project Cost

When using the following index, be aware that these are only estimates. The total cost of any trip varies with individuals and where they are traveling from. Transportation costs to and from the project site or departure point are not included in any totals. The costs to volunteers at the project sites and any expenses that must be paid directly to the project sponsors are included. Personal expenses can vary widely, particularly on projects where volunteers are responsible for their own room and board.

Turicoop, 229
University of Alaska, Anchorage, College of Continuing Education, 230
U.S. Bureau of Land Management, 232
U.S. Fish and Wildlife Service, 234
U.S. Forest Service—Volunteers in the National Forests, 236
Valamo Monastery, 238
Voluntary Workcamps Association of Ghana, 240
Voluntary Workcamps Association of Nigeria, 241
Voluntary Workcamps Association of Sierra Leone, 242
Volunteers for Outdoor Colorado, 244
Volunteers for Peace, Incorporated—International Work Camps, 245
Volunteers for TAU, 247
Volunteers in Overseas Cooperative Assistance, 248
Washington State Parks and Recreation Commission, 250
Welshpool and Llanfair Light Railway, 251
Willing Workers on Organic Farms, 255–257
Wind Cave National Park, 259
Winged Fellowship Trust, 260
Wisconsin Department of Natural Resources, 261
Wyoming Dinosaur Center, 266
Wyoming Recreation Commission, 267
YEE Office, 268

## $500 to $999

American Friends Service Committee, 4
Bermuda Biological Station for Research, Incorporated, 24
Caribbean Volunteer Expeditions, 37
Community Service Volunteers, 58
Crow Canyon Archaeological Center, 68
Earthwatch, 75
Global Children's Organization, 97
Global Citizens Network, 98
Insight Nepal, 117
Kibbutz Program Center, 133
La Sabranenque Restoration Projects, 136
Land and Culture Organization, 135
Los Niños, 143
Mar de Jade, 147
One World Work Force, 183
Pax World Service, 193

Peacework, 194
Rothberg School for Overseas Students, 202
University Research Expeditions Program, 231
Volunteers for Israel, 243
Wildlands Studies, 254
World Travellers Network, 265
Zoetic Research, 271

**$1,000 to $1,499**
CEDAM International, 40
Committee for the Health Rights in Central America, 57
Fellowship of Reconciliation Task Force on Latin America and the
  Caribbean, 83
Global Citizens Network, 98
Global Volunteers, 102
International families, 124
Interplast, Incorporated, 126
Kibbutz Program Center, 133
Land and Culture Organization, 135
Lisle Fellowhip, Incorporated, 139
Midwest Medical Mission, Incorporated, 154
Mingan Island Cetacean Study, Incorporated, 155
Mobility International U.S.A., 158
Oceanic Society Expeditions, 180
Peacework, 194
Peruvian Safaris, 195
Projects for People, 197
Wildland Adventures, Incorporated, 253

**$1,500 to $1,999**
Andover Foundation for Archaeological Research, 11
Caribbean Conservation Corporation, 36
Focus, Incorporated, 88
Global Service Corps, 101
Kibbutz Program Center, 133
Land and Culture Organization, 135
Old Fort Churchill Archaeological Project, 182
Pacific Whale Foundation, 190
Peacework, 194
Projects for People, 197
Winant-Clayton Volunteers, Incorporated, 258

**$2,000 and Over**

Amigos de las Americas, 9
Amizade, Limited, 10
Fudan Museum Foundation, 95
Global Routes, 100
Health Volunteers Overseas, 109
Institute for Central American Development Studies, 118
Jewish National Fund—Canadian and American Active Retirees in
 Israel, 129
Operations Crossroads Africa, 185
The VIEW Foundation, 239
World Horizons International, 262
WorldTeach, 264
Youth Service International, 270

# Project Length

## Weekend

Appalachian Mountain Club, 13
Australian Trust for Conservation Volunteers, 20
Bala Lake Railway, 21
Bristol Industrial Musuem, 26
Cholsey and Wallingford Railway, 48
Colorado Trail Foundation, 54
Dean Forest Railway Society, 70
Farm Hands–City Hands, 82
Ffestiniog Railway Company, 84
Florida Trail Association, 87
Great Western Society Limited, 104
Heritage Trails Fund, 112
Los Medicos Voladores—The Flying Doctors, 142
Los Niños, 143
Mount Vernon Ladies' Association, 160
National Audubon Society, 161
The Nature Conservancy, 168
New York–New Jersey Trail Conference, 174
North York Moors Historical Railway Trust, 178
Pacific Crest Trail Association, 188
Passport in Time, 192
Railway Preservation Society of Ireland, 199

**One to two weeks**

## Three to four weeks

**Five to six weeks**

**Over six weeks**

American Rivers, 8
California Department of Parks and Recreation, 29
Case de Proyecto Liberad, Incorporated, 39
A Christian Ministry in the National Parks, 50
Community Service Volunteers, 58
Florida Department of Natural Resources, 86
Frontiers Foundation—Operation Beaver, 94
Insight Nepal, 117
Institute for Central American Development Studies, 118
Jewish National Fund—Canadian and American Active Retirees in Israel, 129
Kibbutz Program Center, 133
Koinonia Partners, 134
Land and Culture Organization, 135
Mennonite Central Committee Canada, 151
Peruvian Safaris, 195
QUEST, 198
Rothberg School for Overseas Students, 202
Servizio Volontariato Giovanile, 209
Student Conservation Association, 219, 221
Winant-Clayton Volunteers, Incorporated, 258
World Horizons International, 262
WorldTeach, 264
Youth Service International, 270

# Project Location

In this index, organizations are sorted by where they have the majority of their projects. When an organization has its projects evenly spread throughout many regions, it is listed as worldwide. Those that have projects in several locations but are not worldwide are listed under each of the regions where they operate.

**Africa**

Christian Medical/Dental Society—Medical Group Missions, 49
Christian Movement for Peace, 51
Council on International Educational Exchange, 64
Dental Health International, 71

## Caribbean

Bermuda Biological Station for Research, Incorporated, 24
Caribbean Conservation Corporation, 36
Caribbean Volunteer Expeditions, 37
Fellowship of Reconciliation Task Force on Latin America and the
  Caribbean, 83
Midwest Medical Mission, Incorporated, 154
Pax World Service, 193
Projects for People, 197
World Horizons International, 262

## Central America

American Friends Service Committee, 4
Amigos de las Americas, 9
Andover Foundation for Archaeological Research, 11
Artimas Cloud Forest Preserve, 16
Belizian Department of Archaeology, 23
Breakaway, 25
Casa de los Amigos, 38
Centro de Estudios de Español, 43
Committee for the Health Rights in Central America, 57
Costa Rica National Park Service Volunteer Program, 63
Eco-Escuela de Español, 77
Genesis II Cloudforest Preserve, 96
Global Citizens Network, 98
Institute for Central American Development Studies, 118
Peacework, 194
Plenty U.S.A., 196
Projects for People, 197
The VIEW Foundation, 239
World Horizons International, 262
Youth Service International, 270

## Europe

APARE (Association pour la Participation et l'Action Regionale), 12
Association pour la Défense et l'Étude Canton de Levroux, 19
Bardou Restoration Project, 22
British Trust for Conservation Volunteers, 27
Chantier de Jeunes, 45
Chantiers d'Études Medievales, 46

## Great Britain

Ffestiniog Railway Company, 84
Foundation for International Education, 90
Great Western Society Limited, 104
Loch Arthur Community, 141
Mencap's Holdiay Services, 149
Monkey Sanctuary, 159
National Trust for Scotland Thistle Camps, 165
National Trust of Northern Ireland, 166
National Trust Working Holidays, 167
North York Moors Historical Railway Trust, 178
Operation Osprey—Royal Society for the Protection of Birds, 186
Railway Preservation Society of Ireland, 199
Royal Society for the Protection of Birds, Reserves Management, 203
Scottish Conservation Projects Trust, 207
Severn Valley Railway Company Limited, 210
Southern Steam Trust, 218
Talyllyn Railway Company, 224
Welshpool and Llanfair Light Railway, 251 252
Willing Workers on Organic Farms, 255–257
Winant-Clayton Volunteers, Incorporated, 258
Winged Fellowship Trust, 260

## Mexico

American Friends Service Committee, 4
American Mexican Medical  Foundation, 7
Amigos de las Americas, 9
Breakaway, 25
BUSCA, 28
Casa de los Amigos, 38
Global Volunteers, 102
Interplast, Incorporated, 126
Los Medicos Voladores—The Flying Doctors, 142
Los Niños, 143
Mar de Jade, 147
Mingan Island Cetacean Study, Incorporated, 155
One World Work Force, 183
QUEST, 198
Samaritans, 205
Third World Opportunities, 225

## Middle East

## Pacific

## South America

## United States

Wisconsin Department of Natural Resources, 261
World Horizons International, 262
Wyoming Dinosaur Center, 266
Wyoming Recreation Commission, 267
Zoetic Research, 271

## Worldwide

CEDAM International, 40
Christian Medical/Dental Society—Medical Group Missions, 49
Christian Movement for Peace, 51
Council on International Educational Exchange, 64
Earthwatch, 75
Foundation for International Education, 90
Global Volunteers, 102
International Camp Counselor Program, 119
Interplast, Incorporated, 126
Service Civil International/IVS U.S.A., 208
University Research Expeditions Program, 231
Volunteers for Peace, Incorporated—International Work Camps, 245
Volunteers in Overseas Cooperative Assistance, 248

# Project Season

Project and expedition directors, as well as vacationers, often have their favorite season. Sometimes this is because their project can only be completed during some natural cycle. Other times it is because of seasonal climatic factors. But often projects are scheduled to coincide with the season when the most volunteers are available—summer. The following index lists organizations that offer projects or expeditions in more than one season but not year-round, or that offer the bulk of their projects in one or two seasons. Those organizations that spread their projects fairly evenly throughout the year, however, are only listed in the year-round section.

## Spring

Appalachian Mountain Club, 13
Bala Lake Railway, 21
Belizian Department of Archaeology,
Caribbean Conservation Corporation, 36
Caribbean Volunteer Expeditions, 37

## Summer

**Year-round**

Florida Department of Natural Resources, 86
Florida Trail Association, 87
Focus, Incorporated, 88
Frontiers Foundation—Operation Beaver, 94
Genesis II Cloudforest Preserve, 96
Global Citizens Network, 98
Global Service Corps, 101
Global Volunteers, 102
Greenpeace, U.S.A., 105
Gurukula Botanical Sanctuary, 107
Health Volunteers Overseas, 109
Heritage Trails Fund, 112
Heron Island Research Station, 113
Human Service Alliance, 114
Illinois Department of Conservation, 115
Indiana Division of State Parks, 116
International Center for Gibbon Studies, 121
Involvement Volunteers of Australia, 127
Joint Assistance Centre, 130
Kibbutz Program Center, 133
Koinonia Partners, 134
Little Children of the World, Incorporated, 140
Loch Arthur Community, 141
Los Medicos Voladores—The Flying Doctors, 142
Malta Youth Hostels Association Work Camps, 145
Mar de Jade, 147
The Mendenhall Ministries, 150
Michigan Nature Association, 153
Midwest Medical Mission, Incorporated, 154
Missionaries of Charity, 156
Mobility International U.S.A., 158
Monkey Sanctuary, 159
National Audubon Society, 161
National Park Service, 163
The Nature Conservancy, 168
Nevada Division of State Parks, 173
New York–New Jersey Trail Conference, 174
Nicaragua Solidarity Network, 175
Northern California Community Development Corporation
    (NORCAM), 176

## Project Type

Many of the organizations listed in this guide are involved in a wide variety of activities, while others focus on only one. The following listing is an effort to give readers an idea of which organizations offer expeditions or projects in each area of interest. However, some organizations, such as Earthwatch, offer expeditions that aren't included in any of the types listed. Readers can determine which organizations are most likely to offer unusual projects by seeing how many of the following categories each organization is listed under. Those listed under several categories are more likely to have unusual offerings that don't fit well into any of the following categories.

## Accompaniment and amnesty work

Case de Proyecto Liberad, Incorporated, 39
Committee for the Health Rights in Central America, 57
Nicaragua Solidarity Network, 175
Third World Opportunities, 225

## Agricultural and farm work

American Friends Service Committee, 4
Amigos de las Americas, 9
Centre for Alternative Technology, 42
Farm Hands–City Hands, 82
Frontiers Foundation—Operation Beaver, 94
Global Volunteers, 102
GSM—Youth Activities Service, 106
Heifer Project International, 110
Involvement Volunteers of Australia, 127
Koinonia Partners, 134
Land and Culture Organization, 135
Loch Arthur Community, 141
Mennonite Central Committee Canada, 151
Pax World Service, 193
Plenty U.S.A., 196
Travelers Earth Repair Network, 228
Volunteers for Israel, 243
Volunteers in Overseas Cooperative Assistance, 248
Willing Workers on Organic Farms, 255–257
YEE Office, 268

## Archaeology

Andover Foundation for Archaeological Research, 11
APARE (Association pour la Participation et l'Action Regionale), 12
Association pour la Défense et l'Étude Canton de Levroux, 19
Bardou Restoration Project, 22
Caribbean Volunteer Expeditions, 37
CEDAM International, 40
Chantier de Jeunes, 45

## Community development

## Environmental protection

## Environmental research

## Executive and technical assistance

## Historical restoration

Land and Culture Organization, 135
Old Fort Churchill Archaeological Project, 182
Passport in Time, 192
Rempart, 201
Société Archéologique de Douai, 215

## Marine research

Bermuda Biological Station for Research, Incorporated, 24
Cape Tribulation Tropical Research Station, 33
Caretta Research Project, 55
Caribbean Conservation Corporation, 36
CEDAM International, 40
Earthwatch, 75
Europe Conservation Italy, 81
Heron Island Research Station, 113
Mingan Island Cetacean Study, Incorporated, 155
Oceanic Society Expeditions, 180
One World Work Force, 183
Pacific Whale Foundation, 190
University Research Expeditions Program, 231
U.S. Fish and Wildlife Service, 234
Wildlands Studies, 254
Zoetic Research, 271

## Medical and dental

American Friends Service Committee, 4
American Mexican Medical Foundation, 7
Amigos de las Americas, 9
Association for All Speech Impaired Children, 18
Christian Medical/Dental Society—Medical Group Missions, 49
Committee for the Health Rights in Central America, 57
Dental Health International, 71
Focus, Incorporated, 88
Global Volunteers, 102
Health Volunteers Overseas, 109
Human Service Alliance, 114
Interplast, Incorporated, 126
Los Medicos Voladores—The Flying Doctors, 142
Midwest Medical Mission, Incorporated, 154
Samaritans, 205

## Museums

## Outdoor and recreation

## Public health

## Railroads

## Religious organizations

Habitat for Humanity, 108
Heifer Project International, 110
Jewish National Fund—Canadian and American Active Retirees in
   Israel, 129
Kibbutz Program Center, 133
Koinonia Partners, 134
The Mendenhall Ministries, 150
Mennonite Central Committee Canada, 151
Missionaries of Charity, 156
Northern California Community Development Corporation
   (NORCAM), 176
QUEST, 198
Religious Society of Friends, 200
Samaritans, 205
Sioux YMCAs, 213
Volunteers for Israel, 243
Volunteers for TAU, 247
Winged Fellowship Trust, 260

## Scientific research

Andover Foundation for Archaeological Research, 11
Artimas Cloud Forest Preserve, 16
Belizian Department of Archaeology, 23
Bermuda Biological Station for Research, Incorporated, 24
Cape Tribulation Tropical Research Station, 33
Caretta Research Project, 55
Caribbean Conservation Corporation, 36
CEDAM International, 40
Centre for Alternative Technology, 42
Cerro Golodrinas Cloudforest Conservation Project, 44
Crow Canyon Archaeological Center, 68
Cultural Heritage Council, 69
Earthwatch, 75
Europe Conservation Italy, 81
Four Corners School of Outdoor Education, 91
Genesis II Cloudforest Preserve, 96
Heron Island Research Station, 113
International Center for Gibbon Studies, 121
Mingan Island Cetacean Study, Incorporated, 155
Monkey Sanctuary, 159

## Social action

## State and national parks and forests

## Trail building and management

## Work camps